Our Elders

Our Elders

Six Bay Area Life Stories

Janet Clinger

To order additional copies of this book, contact:
Xlibris Corporation
1-888-795-4274
www.Xlibris.com
Orders@Xlibris.com
27098

CONTENTS

In Memory of Our Elders

Forward

When Ruth Morgan and I talked about this project our initial plan was to honor several San Francisco Bay area elders by giving them an opportunity to talk about their experiences. As long-time emigres to this region we both are aware of the special nature of the San Francisco Bay area—its awesome physical beauty and its attraction for those who, for various reasons, were born to be outsiders in their place of origin. We inadvertently connected with elders who had made the same transition. Beginning in 1988 we spent three years photographing and talking with six unique people. Taking the time to know someone of another generation, to savor their company, their life, and that special connection which allows us to transcend the limited horizon of our own time, is a rewarding experience. For Ruth and I, these elders represent what is still bright and shining about this region.

I felt that in order for each person to draw an in-depth verbal portrait of her/his life, I needed to spend many hours getting to know and talking with each subject about her/his past experiences. My method could be described as the 'open-mike' technique. I have found that it is not a good idea to press people with clouds of questions. On a number of occasions after several hours of conversation one of the subjects would say, "I've been rambling. I'm sure you have some questions you want to ask." But by that time they had answered most of the questions I had jotted down as reference points. Invariably I would find holes and blanks in the story and would then ask for clarification and amplification at a later date. This method takes time and patience but it works best for my purpose, i.e., to provide a space for the proper telling of a life story. This does not mean that I simply left the recorder on and did not edit. Although the stories are presented for the ear as much as for the eye, and I hope the reader will listen to each distinctive voice, I did exercise some control over content and form. All of the participants helped in the editing process. I spent many hours with each person pouring over the story, trying to make it 'jell' as a piece without compromising the integrity of the facts. I encouraged each subject to read each draft scrupulously, to look for errors and to make absolutely certain that everything within the story could be made public. I do not try to explain certain gaps in the stories. For various personal reasons, several subjects removed key components from stories. I respected those decisions, even though I realized the stories were more complete prior to the deletions, our object being to honor, not harass the participants. As a result of wanting the reader to hear each of these elders tell their life story as if they were in the room listening, the chronology occasionally suffers as people rarely talk in a straight line. With the approval of the subjects, I did re-arrange the order and edit for clarity in all cases and at the same time I tried to leave in a sense of spontaneity, of true story-telling. My other interests in the stories were twofold: highlighting the intersection of each life with the main undercurrents of the time and place, for example, Joe Sprinz' personal experience vis a vis the integration of baseball; second, charting their inevitable journey to the San Francisco Bay area and their subsequent contributions to this unique community.

I can only call our method for locating the subjects existential. We did not have a clear plan except to include the most lively, creative, fractious people we could find. Ruth and I both wanted to include a cross-section of the Bay area which in some ways we failed to do. While working on my graduate degree in history, I interviewed C.L. Dellums, for many years organizer and director of the West coast Brotherhood of Sleeping Car Porters. When Ruth and I decided to start this project I wanted to include him. Unfortunately by that time he was too ill to participate. The reader will observe that occasionally I intrude into the story with a question. Questions tend to destroy the storytelling but at some points I found it necessary to leave the question in the manuscript for the purpose of clarity, particularly in the last section of each story where I ask several questions about life in the Bay area. Throughout the stories I asked them how they dealt with change both in their personal and professional lives. I wanted to reveal something about how strong, creative people deal with failure and disappointment during difficult times, as well as success.

We thank the participants who so graciously allowed us into their lives. As this project began to take shape several people read various drafts and gave valuable suggestions. My mentor and friend, Joseph Illick, Professor of History, San Francisco State University and Rochelle Gatlin, who has taught at San Francisco State University and San Francisco City College, encouraged me to continue to refine the project. I owe special thanks to my brother, Robert D. Clinger, our family baseball expert, who read Joe Sprinz' story and offered some positive criticisms from the perspective of a life-long baseball fan. My aunt, Evelyn Hart, read an early draft and made several valuable suggestions. This project would never have been completed without the support of my family, particularly my husband, James McCready, who held the line as well as my hand through the lean times.

Ruth Morgan's extraordinary photographs grace these stories and serve as a fitting tribute to our elders. I feel blessed to have her as a collaborator and friend.

Unfortunately, we were unable to publish before the deaths of our elders. Ruth and I feel honored to have known them, and committed to making sure they are not forgotten.

Janet Clinger, San Francisco, California

Our Elders

For two years I talked with half-a-dozen Bay area residents about their lives, while Ruth Morgan photographed them. We sought and found six older people who exude a certain joie de vivre, who contribute to the well-being of our community, not only by their deeds and works, but by their very presence. The San Francisco Bay area is a magnet attracting spirited and creative people who wish to live out their dreams to the fullest extent, in the process contributing to a human environment which makes that very dream fulfillment possible. All of our subjects immigrated to the Bay area. By living and working here, these people contributed to the history of the region, shaped its collective ambience and character, and reified the spirit of place.

The cast of characters: Dorsey Redland, who grew up on a Wyoming ranch, came to San Francisco after World War II to study law. She became the first woman trial lawyer in San Francisco, doing ground-breaking work in maritime and personal injury law and successfully taking on such giant adversaries as C&H Sugar and the San Francisco Police Department. Ida Jackson, raised in Mississippi, fulfilled her parents' dream by graduating from University of California, Berkeley in 1922. She was the first Afro-American to teach in the Oakland public school system and the first Afro-American woman to own and manage a ranch in Mendocino County. Eleanor Roosevelt invited her to the White House to honor her for her efforts to provide health care for rural black Mississippians in the 1930's. Bill Bailey, who struggled through childhood on the streets of Hell's Kitchen in New York City, escaped to sea when he was fourteen, fought in the Spanish Civil War, and helped to organize the maritime industry on both coasts. After 'retirement' he began a new career as a movie actor. Thelma Kavanagh, experienced rural poverty in Northern Minnesota as a child. Overcoming a physical handicap, she became a teacher who volunteered to teach the "dumb" kids. After retirement she moved to San Francisco's Tenderloin district where she fought for the rights of the elderly and the poor. Joe Sprinz, born in St. Louis with a glove on his hand, spent twenty-four years as a catcher in organized baseball, including several years in the majors. He was number one catcher for the San Francisco Seals from 1938 to 1948 when they won the Minor League World Series. He fought the hardest fight of his career: battling to overcome the debilitating effects of a stroke. Sally Binford, earned a Ph.D. in anthropology at the University of Chicago and did innovative work in Old World prehistory. She was engaged in social concerns, particularly those involving seniors and sexual issues of various kinds. She taught a workshop on sex and aging and naturally refused to become a 'respectable matron'.

The past does not die unless we ignore it. In America we no longer rely on the village elders to guide us. Because our lives are increasingly cut off from the network of family and community, we tend to view life in ahistorical terms. This tendency creates a climate permeated by a quick-fix, bulldozer mentality which destroys our critical sense of responsibility toward both past and future generations. By studying soul geography we, as individuals, can create our own council of elders. By summoning the village elder principle, women and men of character and experience serve as guides and mentors in our struggle both to preserve and progress. Oral history provides us with a method of connecting us to our common past in a visceral way. We intend for those who listen to the life stories of our elders to become involved, as we did, in this living historical drama, allowing multiple generations to communicate across that cold barrier of time. We feel it is critical to seek out exemplary elders to illuminate the hidden process of regional character renewal. We are most interested in the dialectical and synergistic relationship between people and place which unfolds within these life stories. Our need for positive role models in our fragmented society has never been greater. To listen to elders who proved themselves during difficult times and who continue to rise to the occasion is a special blessing. People of character who have paid their dues teach us how to move through the maze. We need elders such as Bill Bailey, who told a San Francisco State University class, "The worst crime is to see an injustice and do nothing about it." He can say that with authority because he spent a lifetime taking a stand against injustice, and fought for the well-being of the community in his daily acts. This work is not in praise of famous men and women, but rather of persons of character and spirit. Elders often are ignored, to the detriment of our community. Ruth and I feel an obligation to allow them to speak to us of their experiences. We take Emerson's position that "men [and women] of character are the conscience of the society to which they belong".

*I*ntroduction

To leave one's birthplace by choice to seek one's fortune is an integral part of the American dream. Explorer blood courses through our collective character. During our brief history as a distinct people, Americans have become inured to rootlessness while engaging in a slash and burn path across the continent. Early we set a pattern favoring the nihilist, the adventurer, the wanderer, reflected in our literature from Cooper to Kerouac.[1] We inherited this tendency from our own ancestors who, for whatever reasons, "changed their sky"[2], left their native lands, and in that journey, partially severed that vital connection with place and past. The immigrant experience is wrenching—displaced persons has a terrible ring to it. In the process so much is lost—connections with the ancestors, with the minute details of the geography, with customs and traditions which depend on the matrix of both of the former. For instance, it's hardly possible to conduct a true harvest festival, which must involve those who participated in the actual event, in a city apartment. We adapt, but we also lose. We lose the connection with the web, involving not only

---

[1]   Jack Kerouac, who turned rootlessness into a hip zen exercise in the late 1950's, also turned a generation of mostly young people toward the road and the California coastline, particularly San Francisco and Big Sur, infamous havens for Bohemians, Hell's Angels, and various other assorted 'fruits and nuts'.

[2]   Ronald Blythe, Akenfield: *Portrait of an English Village* (New York: Pantheon Books, 1969).This is a quote from one of the subjects interviewed by Blythe in his oral history study of an English village. Blythe, by carefully listening to their words, allows his subjects to create the entire community, past and present, for the reader.

the living members of our family but the entire community, and what the naturalists now call the eco-environment—the flora, the fauna, the weather, the smells, the look of the landscape during a particular season. So much is lost. Family connections no longer seem so critical when we find ourselves separated by three thousand miles, no longer dependent on one another for survival through another hard winter. In the past family elders, community elders taught us almost by osmosis, simply by how they lived their daily lives in close proximity with the younger generations. They told us stories about their own past experiences, directly connecting us to our heritage.

Hope and necessity, often in combination, traditionally push and pull people from their place of origin. The immigrant dream of finding a true home and community also appears to be a part of the American quest. Where do we belong? In America—especially urban America—home is not a given; one must find it or sometimes create it.

Americans pay a heavy price for this lack of roots. However, those who make their home in the San Francisco Bay area benefit from the positive side of this wanderlust tendency. Since the frenetic gold rush era, this region has drawn adventurous spirits looking for a change of fortune. The San Francisco Bay area is a dream, at least for those of us who love it so dearly, who crossed the desert to get here, who need to live here to draw on its psychic energy. The six elders whose voices we present followed the trail blazed by other wild horses who ran through the clefts in the mountains to get back to where they belong.[3]

---

[3] According to Richard Feather Anderson: "Our sense of place is an emotional response to our environment. It is an innate sense that has evolved and been developed as we adapted to living on this planet. It probably came originally from noticing which places gave us a feeling of comfort, safety, wonder, or 'being part of '". James A. Swan, *The Power of Place: Sacred Ground in Natural and Human Environments* (Wheaton, Illinois: The Theosophical Publishing House, 1991), p. 193. "As 'slashers and burners' Americans tend

Our elders interviewed below were drawn here by various forces and circumstances. Dorsey Redland, who wanted to study customs and international law, gravitated to this seaport city. Ida Jackson and her family left the South to obtain a quality education and to escape the inequities of a segregated society. As a maritime union organizer, Bill Bailey, finding life on the East coast waterfront too dangerous for his health, joined the struggle on the West coast. After living a nomadic life for many years, Sally Binford was attracted by the tolerant climate of the region. After retirement, Thelma Kavanagh traveled here on a visit, found she was needed and never left.

Ruth Morgan and I chose these particular life histories because they are full of piss and vinegar, trouble, guts, heart, and the essential joie de vivre—no deadbeats, no whiners. Our definition of contributing to the well-being of the community is not limited to philanthropic or social works, as important as these might be, but rather a more subtle force—one of freedom of spirit, involving a certain brand of courage or creative energy. Just by their presence in this particular locale, they help to define and mark it. The stories include what Roland Kirk, saxophonist extraordinaire, called, "bright moments", those little turns on the path when 'something happens', those moments which make it all bearable. The trick, which these six elders managed so well, is to expand the strike zone, and to keep it moving for as long as possible. "What one must never do is stop—until one is stopped, that is."[4]

---

to deny our connection with and our responsibility toward place. Except for Native Americans, most of us have not lived on the land where our ancestors have lived for thousands or even hundreds of years. In spite of our denial many of us do long for our true home. The Greek philosopher, Theophrastus "maintained that every living thing has an oikeios topos or 'favorable place', where all the energies and conditions are suitable to its flourishing." Ibid, p.19.

[4] Ronald Blythe, *The View in Winter: Reflections on Old Age* (New York: Harcourt Brace Jovanovich, 1979), p.242. This is a statement by one of the elders interviewed in Blythe's collective portrait of old age in an English village which manages to be both chilling and heartening.

But not to merely hold on to life for that is pathetic. Our subjects appear to have followed the wisdom of William Saroyan who wrote,

"In the time of your life, live—so that in that good time there shall be no ugliness or death for yourself or for any life your life touches . . . .

> In the time of your life, live—so that in that wondrous time you shall not add to the misery and sorrow of the world, but shall smile to the infinite delight and mystery of it."[5]

Our elders did not choose to sit on the sidelines, but rather "played for their lives", as a jazz musician friend defined it.

Two monumental events, World War II and the Depression, altered our elders' lives in dramatic ways, even if they did not fight in the War or suffer hunger during the 1930's. Twin social struggles, minority and women's civil rights, connected by the old American dream of equality for all, also simmer beneath the surface of their lives. Collectively their stories read like an American history lesson of the major events, movements and currents of the last three quarters of a century. Was it tough for them to grow up in a less affluent society which had no economic safety net for those below the poverty line? In what ways did the struggle for gender and racial equality touch their lives? How did those catastrophic events and social forces shape their outlook and their future?

Why would one want to listen to these old people talk about events and people long past? What can they offer us that we cannot get by reading a social history of 20th Century America? Can their words tell us something about the importance of studying the past, and particularly the past as recounted by those

---

[5]   From the preface of William Saroyan's play, *The Time of Your Life* (New York: Samuel French, Inc., 1939), p.22. The play is set in a waterfront bar in San Francisco in 1938.

who lived it? Memory may occasionally fail and sometimes stories do get better, or at least different with time, but the telling of personal history allows the storyteller to take the reader/listener by the ear into the past; it becomes then a palpable experience, connecting the generations in their common struggle to not just survive but to triumph over Time, including the limitations dictated by one's own narrow time frame. It is easy to overlook that every time, every generation, has its own sensibilities, currents of thought, cultural expressions, social concerns and unique drama which partially expire with its members. Once those individuals or groups slip under the wave, we lose critical information regarding our collective past. To avoid losing our way into the future Ruth and I decided it was important to connect with elders who took root in this particular place.

Until quite recently, San Francisco, with its strong working class base, thrived as a small, liveable city. Being the 'Gateway to the Pacific', a seaport, and the existential End of the Continent, it also emanates an elusive, dream—like quality, like living in a special time zone where the known boundaries shift, where the unexpected may appear when the fog lifts, where one would not really be surprised to see Sam Spade lighting a cigarette under a lamp post on the waterfront. The grim realities of modern life are eroding the old free-wheeling, Wild West, hanging on the edge of the continent persona. San Francisco columnist Herb Caen, decried,

> "Yep, the old town is in the big time now, with our per capita share of crime, disease, poverty and homelessness, not to mention 'the public school situation'. All the terrible problems that we long associated with the ghettos of the Rust Belt are right here in this beautiful setting. When you jump off the bridge, you get a million-dollar view all the way down."[6]

---

[6]   Herb Caen, *San Francisco Chronicle*, October 1, 1989, Sunday Punch, p.1.

The San Francisco Bay area is in real danger of turning into another megalopolis, a faceless, concrete horror, a real estate developer's paradise which means a hell for everyone else. We need all the help we can get to preserve what remains of the character of the region. One of the ways we, as a community—meaning the entire Bay area, the regional eco-system defining the physical boundaries of that community—can re-establish the vital connection with place and its past, including its pre-invasion past, is to honor both the geographic setting and our unique elders who contributed to the well—being of this region. Ruth and I felt the need to study our chosen home by traveling through it to comprehend the lay of the land and by talking with those who chose to live out their dramas on this rugged coastline. Like many other endangered species, the Bay area suffers from mismanagement characterized by short—sightedness and greed. Looking back, through the lives of those who help to define this region, not in anger or nostalgia, but to chart our present position makes sense, provided we are committed to preserving those unique qualities which define our community.

People from all cultures, past and present, have felt some ambivalence toward the elders in their midst. Americans, however, are the consummate hypocrites. Television advertising, particularly at the holiday season, pictures grandma and grandpa welcoming their adoring children and grandchildren home for the feast. The family members appear to treasure their elders above all else. Possibly this is a dream which we would like to believe is at least happening somewhere, even if only in television land.

Ronald Blythe, writing in 1979, states that the current elders are quite different than in the past, partly because there are so many, many more of them.

"The reason why old age was venerated in the past was that it was extraordinary . . . . For all our new caring and planning, to be old today is to be contemptible. Why? Because to be old is to be part of a huge and commonplace problem, a member of a social group so increasingly demanding in its needs as to create another kind of helplessness in the young and middle-aged, causing them to feel guilty and resentful."[7]

A study by the National Institute of Aging concludes that over the next half-century the number of Americans over 85 may grow to 24 million, twice the number projected by the U.S. Census Bureau, and ten times the current level.[8] This increase has definite, serious consequences for the entire society as the population becomes top-heavy with 'non-producing' aged citizens. According to Dr. Barry Brazelton, only 20% of American families are intact. Children and the elderly will continue to be more and more at-risk in this scenario.

This is not a treatise on the problems of the elderly or the family in contemporary society, however, if we are going to understand the role that elders could play in the social regeneration process, then we must recognize the terrible pattern which is unfolding and shift our perspective. If we began to value our elders and their experience, to make use of their time and energy and expertise, if we took time to find out what they know and how they could help with current problems and issues such as childcare and the homeless situation, for example, those in positions of power at the local level might be amazed at what they have overlooked. In San Francisco we do have an entity called the Commission on Aging which serves as an advisory committee to the mayor but this does not begin to tap into this

---

[7]   Blythe, *The View in Winter*, p.8.

[8]   *Longer Lives: Surprise Prediction on Aged Population*, San Francisco Chronicle, October 17, 1988, p.6.

rich 'natural resource', i.e., the brainstorming power of our older citizens.[9]

The original elders of the San Francisco Bay region, whose bones are in this very earth we walk on, were venerated by the younger members of the society. To the Ohlone, "to be old meant that one had attained a good relationship with the spirit world, and thus one was considered to be holy."[10] In our culture, instead of reverence, many elders feel contempt from the younger members of the society. The Ohlone elders were surrounded by their people; our elders often are isolated and neglected. We need to learn not only from our living elders but from those who were here long ago, who lived in this beautiful area generation upon generation, treating it as sacred territory, as indeed it is.

---

[9] One of our elders, Bill Bailey, a long time labor activist on the waterfronts of the world, told me that he had submitted a plan several years ago to City Hall regarding housing for the homeless in San Francisco. Having been homeless himself during the Depression he well understands the problem from a personal point of view and due to his experience as a labor organizer he often has had to improvise in severe circumstances. Many of the warehouses and piers along the waterfront are now empty due to the collapse of the San Francisco Port. Bill suggested that we furnish several of these giant spaces with beds and kitchens to provide temporary housing for the homeless population and at the same time provide the necessary social services on the spot to assist these people in securing training, jobs, health care, etc. Needless to say, he got no reply regarding his suggestions.

[10] Malcolm Margolin, *The Ohlone Way: Indian Life in the San Francisco-Monterey Bay Area* (Berkeley: Heyday Books, 1978), p.94. If one wants to develop a sense of place about this particular region then this book is one of the starting points. To care about a place one should understand its history, geography, and its original inhabitants. From them we may even learn how to save it.

We are not seeking to glorify those who have acquired political or economic power. One won't see our subjects' pictures on the society page. As Paul Newman said in the film, Harper, "There's a lot of good people on the bottom. Only creme and bastards rise to the top." During this time of disintegration and disruption we felt the need to find exemplars who have lived through severe circumstances, who can serve as guides along this unmarked trail.

Many of our younger Bay area citizens have no positive role models to imitate. Ruth and I have worked on programs for prisoners in the San Francisco County Jail; she, in fact, still does. Many young people who end up in the county jail begin moving toward those cells at a very early age. The terrible shattering of family life, coupled with the rapid proliferation of drugs, is producing a larger and larger group of angry, disturbed, and self-destructive young adults who are a part of the growing underclass in America. Fathers, other than in the biological sense, are quite rare in this population. Where are the community elders to provide role models for these young men and women? With the destruction of old neighborhoods—the 'gentrification' of San Francisco, and therefore community stability, one often finds a vacuum. Sense of place—'The Fillmore', for example, which used to be a vital area of San Francisco has been re-redeveloped. I asked a friend, Ann Walls, retired associate ombudsman with the San Francisco Sheriff's Department, about growing up within the black community in the Fillmore in the 1940's, prior to redevelopment, prior to the black middle-class flight to the suburbs. "A child might come from a poor family but she could see people around her who had made it, who had pursued an education and became one of the community doctors or lawyers." Many of the beautiful old Victorians were razed to make way for empty lots full of broken glass and drug dealers. The Fillmore is trying to make a comeback, but it is no longer the thriving community which existed when Ann was growing-up.[11]

To understand the importance of maintaining strong cultural communities within the larger regional framework, we asked one of our elders, Ida Jackson, who persevered through the trying, but fulfilling, experience of being one of the first black students to enter the University of California at Berkeley in 1918, how she accomplished that feat. Her family and the small, but tight-knit black community in Oakland, helped to buoy up her courage and determination. If we want the young members of our community to 'strive for excellence' then we must find ways to nurture those who do not have stable, loving families standing behind them. They deserve exemplary role models. If we fail, for whatever reason, to learn how to live from the example of wise members of previous generations, then it becomes a 'Clockwork Orange' world in a very short time with "No foundation. All the way down the line"[12]

The old webbing of place/family/ community is tattered. We can choose to re-create a new version, possibly in a less rigid form, by selecting our own elders, by learning from their experience, by experimenting with new family arrangements, and by working together diligently to save our precarious home base. In this striving we require exemplars who live within the code of honor, on and off the field, who are creators rather then destroyers, who are givers rather than takers, who are unsung pioneers in such remote and dangerous territories as

---

[11]   In 1966 the San Francisco Redevelopment Agency bulldozed the heart of the Fillmore district which boomed during World War II when thousands of Southern blacks migrated to work in the shipyards. As one long-time community activist said, " . . . [T]he real purpose of urban renewal is to turn nontax-paying slum land into a high tax-paying land base." Marilyn Clark, *The Tragedy of the Fillmore,* The San Francisco Bay Guardian, Vol. 15, No. 29, June 10, 1981, p. 21.

[12]   Saroyan, *The Time of Your Life*, p.65.

The Tenderloin. Our elders lived through hard times and not only lived to tell about it, but learned to thrive on change. As we spin through space, with the odds and circumstances shifting and heaving in the wake of endless celestial storms, we haven't a wing or a prayer if we can't shrug and say, like Don Ameche's elder character, "Things change",[13] and then work like hell to deal with the new situation. We need that roll-with-the-punches attitude to get us through the next leg of our journey. Our elders are precious, not as relics of the past, not even as storytellers who entertain us about the good or bad old days, but as models who show us how to live with and through the inevitable changes.

Can we learn to grow old, if not gracefully, then with some measure of satisfaction? How can we prepare for this eventuality? Can we continue to serve our community when it is part of a society which does not value its older citizens? What can we gain by listening to our elders' life stories? Erik Erikson believes that all old people are involved in a search regarding their 'life's transcendent meaning', whether they know it or not. Humans seem to have the need to define themselves, their raison d'être. Within the borders of that personal definition our elders can give us the courage to continue the fight, whatever it may be. By telling their stories they validate the past, not only for themselves, but for those of us who must continue the struggles they so bravely undertook. That critical generation to generation bond must not be broken if we intend to progress as a species. As Erikson so eloquently states it,

"From the past, from myth and legend, from anthropologists and historians, we learn that the elders of society were the transmitters of tradition, the guardians of ancestral values, and the providers of continuity. They were awarded such titles as sage, patriarch, seer, and venerable counselor and were consulted as advisers and

---

[13] From David Mamet's delightful movie *Things Change* (1988)

sometimes as prophets, since long-range memories make prediction founded on experience, trustworthy. Their life histories provided the warp on which the lively threads of the ongoing community were in the process of being woven. The interconnectedness of the social fabric, which stressed the interdependence of all age groups, tended to establish a harmonious wholeness." [14]

The six life stories below reflect our concern for our history. Those who deny their past, or have it taken from them, are bereft souls, attached to nothing, committed to nothing, except possibly revenge. Within these stories we hope the reader will find new pathways running out of the past which are rooted securely in this place, our chosen home, the San Francisco Bay area. We could have created the same project, with a different cast, in any part of this country, provided we had a stake in the well-being of that community. For those readers who do not live in the Bay area, we suggest you look to your own elders after you enjoy ours. They are waiting to tell you what you need to know.

---

[14]   Erik H. Erikson, Joan M. Erikson, Helen Q. Kivnick, *Vital Involvement in Old Age* (New York: W.W. Norton & Company, Inc., 1986), p. 294.

*D*orsey Redland

"The quality of a man's life is measured by his commitment to excellence, no matter what his field of endeavor." Vincent Lombardi [from Dorsey's office bulletin board]

Dorsey Redland, who grew up on a Wyoming ranch, came to San Francisco after World War II to study law. She became the first woman trial lawyer in the San Francisco Bay area, doing ground-breaking work in maritime and personal injury law and successfully taking on such giant adversaries as C&H Sugar and the San Francisco Police Department.

Years ago I was a witness to an auto/bus accident and as a consequence was requested to appear at a deposition. Dorsey happened to be the lawyer for the two injured parties in the car. Dressed in an argyle sweater and flannel slacks, she strode into the room with a Katherine Hepburn air, immediately capturing my attention. As the opposing lawyer was late in arriving I had a chance to talk with Dorsey. She told me a little bit about growing up on a Wyoming ranch in the 1920's and 30's. Like most kids I would have sold my soul to have lived on a ranch in the true-heart of the West. As Dorsey told me, "I don't know how lucky you can get, but as children we knew we were." I vowed to hear more of her story one day. The young, brash and breezy 'D.A.', who eventually arrived to question the witnesses, obviously had never been up against Dorsey before. She squashed his aggressive 'lead the witness' technique in the first several minutes. The whipper was snapped early on in the game. I had a difficult time keeping a straight face, and so did the D.A., but for different reasons. Good lawyers never register genuine surprise, but he came as close to it as we lay folk will ever see. He canned the cocky routine for a more circumspect approach. It was delightful.

When Ruth and I began to discuss this project Dorsey was one of the first persons to cross my mind. Lawyers are not easy subjects. Most of them would rather ask questions than answer them and Dorsey was no exception. She was a very private person and extremely dedicated to her clients and the practice of law, but eventually she did agree to be interviewed.

I found Dorsey to be brave, feisty, funny and fiercely independent. We always had a good time when I met her at her office for our discussions. She worried about appearing to be "blowing my own horn" by talking about her life. Her personal relationships, particularly with men, was not a subject she wanted to broach. In spite of those limitations we coaxed some good stories from her, with a suggestion of many more bubbling on the back burner, and in the process we get a glimpse of that cowgirl singing,

"Let me gaze at the moon till I lose my senses
Can't look at hobbles and I can't stand fences
Don't fence me in"

If Dorsey takes your case you will get your day in court.

Wyoming childhood

"I was born in Wyoming in 1925 in a three-room homesteader log cabin. My parents were homesteaders. They wanted a large family, and preferably half and half, which is what they ended up with. I'm one of eight children. My father immigrated from Norway. He was very much a citizen, very appreciative of the opportunities of this country and very knowledgeable of history. My mother's maiden name was Harvard. Her great, great, uncle John Harvard, was the founder of Harvard College. Her father was a very literate, tri-lingual, articulate man. He and several of the Harvards came out from Boston to the West to settle. One brother, Uncle Bill, was a lawyer and a doctor. He took care of the thieves—sewed their ears on, represented them in court and was a renegade. Her mother was very literate and very independent. They came to Wyoming, homesteaded and bought additional land. She was one of eleven children.

Some of the Harvards had moved to San Francisco from the East and had holdings here. They were in 'society'. They liked the opera and the symphony—the type of things the West could afford. My grandfather wanted to move the family to California because he felt there was more opportunity. My grandmother felt they were doing entirely well there and didn't want to move from Wyoming. She borrowed money and bought out his half. He moved to California and she stayed and raised the children. They never got a divorce; they still kept in communication up to their deaths. He spent his time during the non-rainy season in Northern California in Del Norte County where he was into goldmining and trapping and fishing interests. Then for the fall and winter, for the opera and all, he came to San Francisco.

My grandmother raised the family and the girls were all pretty liberated. They got their own car, smoked cigarettes and drove to dances themselves. It was against what normal society was. Along the way, my mother elected to marry rather than push on toward a career. She was engaged to someone else when she and Pop took off and eloped. She sent her kid sister back to the other guy with the ring.

We were raised with a lot of individual liberty and great encouragement both from our mother and father. 'Can't' was something we put on ourselves; it was a word that was not at all encouraged. We didn't just have little nursery tales when we were growing up. We had Greek classics read to us. We were exposed to a lot of different stimulating things—a lot of being out in beautiful, pristine, remote country where you really relied on yourself. It's gorgeous country, but hey, if you were hungry, you caught fish. We lived out where there were no telephones or roads. You pretty much grew your own stuff. You made your own bread. You trapped, sewed, hunted. For entertainment you traded books up and down. You might ride or hike ten miles to trade books or periodicals, and think nothing of it. It was a different thing than this force-fed tv. We were utterly encouraged.

We had a working ranch so we were gathering up livestock and checking fences from our earliest moments. I had a sorrel Arab named Rusty. He had been mountain-raised—very sure-footed and spirited, a one person kind of horse. If somebody else tried to ride him he'd just as soon rear and take their pants off for 'em. He loved to chase coyotes and other things in the wide-open badland country. We'd go out and run with the wild horses for the day. You rode from the time you were big enough to sit up by yourself. Walking wasn't the criteria. Otherwise you would ride, but you'd ride with an adult holding you. It gave us mobility. The nearest neighbor was a mile or more away. Still is.

The first time I went to court I was four. My father wanted to see this trial. He said, "You're always talking—since you were eight months old so as long as you promise to be quiet I'll show you where you get paid for talking and arguing." I thought that whole scene was terrific. I just was transfixed. Then he drove me to where you lived if you didn't apply yourself in school and also where, if you got to be a lawyer or doctor or the banker, how nice it was.

Economically, the country I came from got hit before '29, before the stock market crash, just like the farmers and ranchers have been hit in these last years. I was too small to really recall that much. They did really lose everything and had to start over again. During the actual Depression people were moving from other areas, coming through Wyoming on their way. They were really very destitute. We'd often take them in and see that they had food and more food to travel with. They'd lost their jobs, their businesses, their homes. Most of them were heading West, probably for California, to look for work where the climate was more moderate so they could survive living in tents.

On the ranch we did pretty much everything ourselves. We had a lot of made-over clothes and hand-me-downs. We used to sell chickens and grow a lot of things, and barter. Times were hard but because we lived on the land and could grow our own, we weren't as handicapped as others. There wasn't a lot of extra work for people and what little there was didn't pay well. I was aware of that. But I didn't feel the effects of the Depression like someone who lived in the city and lost their job and was in soup lines. We were part of a neighborly community; if anyone was hungry, of course they could come and eat. It was just the thing that was done. Whatever you had you would share. It meant we all ate less, but we were glad to do it.

One of the things I did to make money was to trap—go out with trapping lines for muskrats and skunks. Now it seems barbaric to me. I never have been able to wear a fur coat. When I was just a little kid my dad said, "Here's some traps; I'll show you how to set them. If you catch anything, which I doubt you will, I'll show you how to clean it, skin it, and stretch the hide. Then you can haggle with the hide buyer." When you set traps you've got to watch them, at least two times a day, and preferably more because you don't want to keep the animal caught in the trap that long. You don't want to be inhumane, that's the main thing. Secondly, if one of them got sprung, why then you don't have a chance to catch anything anyhow. So you may need to move it. It took a little while, I finally caught one poor little thing. I had to kill it. I said, "Aren't you going to kill it?" He said, "No, you're going to kill it. You want some money, don't you? Times are tough. We've all got to help out." Heaven help you if you were not responsible about your traps. If you caught 'em, you're going to kill 'em promptly and with dispatch.

Then my schoolmates asked me, "It would be nice if we could get some skunk glands". They wanted the skunk glands to throw in the school furnace. Part of the deal was they had to throw them in the grade school too. It was always good for almost a week off school. They had those steam heaters. It wasn't all that harmful. Today you'd still be in juvenile damn hall. They never could pin who did it. And I don't believe in confessing. Now the statute of limitations has run, who cares.

I always remember the summer when my sister and I contracted to make money hoeing sugar beets. I think that did more for my determination to go on through and not get side-tracked by a lot of parties and dances. Backbreaking, hard work. Ten cents a row, each one was full of weeds. The guy tried to beat us on the number of rows. That was my first experience at threatening with court and going to the courthouse to check on how to do it.

We grew up driving a six-horse team; moving livestock, handling livestock, castrating animals, going on trails, working in the fields. We grew up in that kind of environment—the way of life of the West. It's more mechanized now. You didn't have the four-wheel drive trucks you have now; the early Caterpillar tractors and Jeeps didn't really come out until the military experience in World War II. So there was use of horses and mules, in much of the farming, certainly in the moving of the sheep-wagons or chuck-wagons which were moved up along with the camps, in the handling of livestock.

We didn't have running water; we had to pump. It taught you to be quick. It's 20 below and you have to go to the head. It was rather challenging—running out there in the backyard, see the moon, hear the owls hooting and the river freezing over, maybe some deer coming along—a whole different and beautiful scene once you got out there. Even if you had to go like this [*holds her breath*]. I think maybe we've got too damn many indoor toilets to tell you the truth. Our toilet was placed so it drained where there was a good wide filtering area. That was a very mindful thought. I think you get certain individual courage and character with outdoor 'plumbing' which is not otherwise acquired.

We went to the school at Ten Sleep, Wyoming. The town was named after what the Indians called it. It was ten sleeps from one camp to the Big Horn Mountains where we were. It was right at the foot of the mountains where several rivers merge together. The Indians camped there and grew their corn, then gradually went up into the mountains for a little hunting and fishing during the summer months. Our high school class was one of the largest—fifteen in the class.

In addition to the encouragement of both parents and other supportive relatives, my father's mother and I were very close. She came from Norway right after I was born. She spent quite a bit of time with me. She was homesick. I think I reminded her of Norway. We had a bonding which can best be described by all the other children in the family who said I was her pet. I always enjoyed every minute of it. I was much more Norwegian than the others in taste of foods, in costumes. Now whether it is from genetic or from inclination, I don't really know. There was a lot of feeling of love and support. We had an open rapport. I could tell her anything. Later we smoked pipes and drank whiskey together. She was very Viking. She lived with us in the house when I was really small. As we got larger as a family, the folks built her a small house near their house. When she died my dad couldn't understand why I didn't go back for the funeral. I knew she didn't believe in funerals. She was a Viking. I was here in San Francisco and didn't have a lot of money and I knew how she felt. It hurt my dad because he knew I was her favorite but I couldn't listen to some Lutheran preacher whom she hadn't wanted to hear.

There's more family unity in the type of environment we grew up in. I know in high school, my two sisters and I, we were very competitive, always. We played a lot of ball. They would try to separate us on teams and of course we had worked out ideal teamwork—which infuriated us. We were always very close and very competitive. We would have the best coordinated team. Basketball, football, whatever—we played everything we could. We were very sports-minded.

In the third grade I had an excellent teacher, though you heard me say I was ditching out of school—sometimes I'd just get so bored I'd want to take off. It wasn't that I was flunking out, it was just that there were other things I wanted to go check on. Naturally my parents couldn't set on me that much about it, as long as I was academically superior at school. They felt if I had to go all the time I might get so bored I'd be a severe problem and lose interest. They weren't worried about perfect attendance.

This teacher, Mrs. Ingram, told me that I could get out of school and graduate as quickly as I learned it, and that if I went through all of the third grade then she would help me with the fourth and fifth grade. I could move on at my own pace. She was a marvelous teacher. I'll never forget her. Thank god for her. I immediately had in mind to get the hell out of school, through high school in one year. So I whipped through the third grade, the fourth grade, the fifth grade. I'm done with math, reading, history—sixth grade, and I'm really moving along. Then the damn school year was over. I could have academically gone ahead but there's a little thing about social adjustment. They advanced me one grade. I was physically always small for my age, late maturing both physically and socially. I was really out of place with the other classmates except for two boys who were late developers as boys are.

I caught up with my sister. I don't think it was particularly good for her though we were so close. We got into more difficulty than we would have because we tend to egg each other on. It wasn't necessarily in our best interest. Socially, I can see why they did not want to advance me even though I was champing at the bit to be advanced even further because I'd done the academic work. It's better to have schools with enrichment programs and still keep the children in the same grade, because of the social and maturity aspects.

It really hit me more in my freshman year of college when I was sixteen. Many people go at that age. I was socially and emotionally very immature. They had all these strict rules—be in, sign in, housemothers—which I wasn't used to and didn't care for at all. It became an immediate challenge to break every rule in the place. The first two years I went to the University of Wyoming. I think that the lack of maturity showed there.

I managed to make it through high school. If it hadn't been for the citizenship, I could have had a scholarship. They had some questions on my problems, or questions, with authority. I didn't want the damn scholarship anyway so I told them to shove it where it counted. I probably said it very vernacularly, which didn't help at all either. They were interviewing as to who should get the scholarship. They told me all the different conditions. I had to take the subjects they wanted me to. I knew I wanted to be a lawyer then. I knew these bastards would never go for it. They'd figure you should be a teacher, a librarian—the chosen few—that you were committed until you married Mr. Right. None of them were on my list. So when they were saying that, I'm sure I spoke very directly about it, which did nothing to enhance, or take away, the remarks that were already in my school record. I remember the principal saying," See, I told you."

My mother always encouraged careers. She took us around and showed us by indirection. We got to help Blanche, who thought she was in love and married old Charlie, got knocked up and had this passel of kids. Meanwhile Charlie was at the bar drinking. Blanche hadn't finished her education and there she was stuck with this nogoodnik husband and these kids, one baby after another, no hope in life. Why, if she had her education, (even if she had thought she was in love with Charlie, even if she had married him and he turned out to be the wastrel he was) she would have been able to go on and take care of herself and the kids and not have to put up with him. This is the kind of reinforced example we got.

My father was very supportive. The best way to describe him was that he refused to go to any of his daughters' weddings where socially he would be required to walk down the aisle and give them away. He said, "Whenever I have anything so worthless I have to give it away, it will not be one of my daughters." His idea of a wedding gift to my older sister, when she was married, was to set up a trust fund for her with a family friend she was close to so whenever she wanted to take off from her husband she could have the money and not have to come home and hear, "I told you so." That was his exact feeling about it. We were encouraged to go on, to do, to be whatever we wanted to be.

My parents weren't rich-rich, but they certainly weren't poor. Every year we'd have a family conference. Every fall we were always going to build a new house that had umpteen rooms and bathrooms inside. Each fall my father said, "Well, this year these five more sections of land are available. The price seems right and if we buy this added land, or this business, then it will produce income (or more livestock or a combination of all of them) and we'll have X dollars more of this land. We can always build a house next year." We were off to college when it was built. My older sister was coming back with her three children to live when the new house had just been built.

We'd been trained to raise our chickens, sell them, dress them, trap. They both wanted us to be self-sufficient. No one was raking in money, but we were learning how to cook, sew, be comfortable at a ten place setting. I hated sewing and cooking and all the table settings and crocheting. My mother finally said, "When you learn to do it perfectly, you don't have to do it anymore. I want you comfortable in society, in life, whatever your circumstances lead you to." We learned to eat with all the silver, how to arrange it. I don't know if I remember to this day now. A lot of that was a carryover from the East but some still followed it in Wyoming. There was not the casualness with which I tended to raise my children, though I still had some carryovers—sending my children to

Ms. Prim's dancing school so they'd be comfortable in any strata of society. They grew up with the broad spectrum.

"Don't Fence Me In"[15]

"My sister went to University the same year I did. We had this room on the third floor with a view. It was supposed to be the nicest, most expensive room in this newest dormitory. It wasn't the first or second day there when we asked the gal who was president of the dorm (the bad actors always spot one another, I don't know how it is, but we do), "How come you're staying in the half-basement room?" She said, "Hey, with all these rules, that's the only place you can sneak in and out and not be noticed. You put the bed below the window and leave the window open; you just dive in and hit the bed. And it's a great sale for your folks; it's cheaper." I get right down to the room and see how it's done, There was still a room available, right at the corner where there were two windows—you could go in either side, which even was a better shot, according to this experienced gal. We promptly moved and got a credit for the money.

Academically, I certainly wasn't getting all A's. I was spending most of my time partying. I remember walking out on one final because our bridge game was due to start up. If it hadn't been for my sister, I'm sure I'd have been expelled. She gave a hell of a performance, how I was homesick for my horse, to keep me from getting expelled for having a large cocktail party at the student union for this friend I met from Chicago, who'd been expelled from all the schools. He had a very rich father. He got all the liquor and I arranged this terrific cocktail party. At a federal land grant university they're not supposed to have alcohol anywhere on campus. We had this planter's punch with plenty of hard alcohol.

I was delighted when I got to move off campus. The minute I was off campus, after the first freedom of it, I woke up one

---

[15]   This wonderful Cole Porter 'Western freedom' song aptly so describes Dorsey.

morning and looked at myself. I had a hell of a hangover."
What am I doing? I'll have cirrhosis before I'm eighteen." I
partied out. I really wanted to go into international law—
customs law is what I had in mind. So today I'm going over and
check the records on what the best schools are and prepare to
move there. My grades went from barely B average up to some
serious looking grades in that last half-year. My sister came
down for summer school and took my place and I went back
home and visited for a while.

I didn't want to go to the East Coast. I associated the East
Coast with the Harvard relatives I'd met. I was really more Redland
than Harvard; they seemed very stuffy and phony to me. The
University of Washington had an excellent record so I headed for
Seattle and got myself a job there with the railroad inspecting
damaged freight. I didn't lie, but I certainly misled them. I didn't
tell them I just got off the train. They had a sign up and it sounded
like an interesting job to me so I took what few shekels I had left
down to the used clothes store to buy some stuff to make me look
more mature, and then sauntered in and applied for the job. It
was near the end of World War II and they were short of workers.
He said," Do you know Seattle?" I said, "I sure should." I got the
map and learned. I didn't have any trouble with it. I really enjoyed
that haggling. From haggling with hide buyers over the years when
I trapped, I really learned how to haggle a lot.

The only serious disagreements or problems I ever had were
not so much with my mother, but with my father. He'd come as
an immigrant; he'd worked hard so his children wouldn't have
to do the same thing. Between the two of them they had
accomplished that—to send us to whatever schools we wanted to
go to, and not have us have to work or be short of the wherewithal
to do whatever we needed to do. But they had also raised us to be
self-sufficient and independent. Our beef was that he didn't
want me to work my way through school. I said, "Pop, you have
also raised us to know that we're independent. I know I have to
do it if I'm ever going to do it. Otherwise I'm going to be a swell
party girl looking for my inheritance. I don't want to inherit

anything from you except some common sense." He said, "You should go to the best school. You're capable of the best and it's a good investment for the rest of your life." I really didn't understand so much. What he was saying was right in that sense.

I think you learn a lot by working your way through. Maybe you don't get all the A-pluses, but you certainly learn to hustle. It gets you a lot of different life experiences. I always had the security of knowing, if I needed help, it would always be there. I didn't have the fear that someone else might well have, who didn't have the support and back-up. That type of confidence is a tremendous asset. Whether that made me more confident or made me softer, I don't know, but I think it made me more confident. I think that someone else wouldn't have taken the chances with different types of jobs and such, because they wouldn't want to risk the all-or-nothing. Where really, down deep, it wasn't all-or-nothing for me. My father was deeply disappointed. He said, "Well, if you're worried about the inheritance, I can take care of that for you in a hurry." I said, "Please do, Pop, because when I get done you're going to have to worry about me cutting you off, not you cutting me off." I was very much like his mother.

My mother was encouraging when I told her I had made up my mind to set out and head in my own direction. Instead of "Oh no!", she said, "We have to strike our own paths."

I left for Seattle when Pop wasn't home cause I figured he might talk me out of it. I knew she'd support me. She drove me to the train, my kid sister crying and crying, "Not yet", like I was never coming back. I get to Billings, Montana, where I'm changing trains and damn if I don't run into Pop. "You know, Pop, I'm like you leaving Norway." We had a grand time while we were waiting for the train; I hop on the train and off I go.

I could tell he was a little disappointed. I could sense some pressure. He and his banker friend thought I should work in the bank, go into the banking business, and marry George, Jr. I immediately felt suffocation over the whole maneuver. That's why I decided right then to take off for Seattle and get settled in. It took a bit longer because I decided to work a while and save up some stash and take some science courses at night which I needed before I could graduate. Get some of those dogs out of the way so that when I went back full-time I really could hit the other and forget the labs, like physics, things that you had to take to qualify for your degree. I didn't mind some of the advanced math, but I had a hell of a time with physics. Thank god I was working for the railroad and could pick the brain of this engineer who loved getting a review of physics.

Of my classmates in high school and the classes before me, well over 50 were killed in World War II. Some of my cousins were killed. The deaths were very painful. There was a feeling that this war was right and it was the last war. We all felt the rationing of things. On the other hand, I was working and going to school and there were more jobs. There weren't as many workers around. The railroads hired all men before World War II. I would have never gotten that job if there hadn't been a war on. There was more opportunity for women, me included, to have different types of jobs, that had traditionally, normally, been reserved for men only, which paid better, and not the traditional secretarial or teacher or waitress type of job which was historically the case until World War II. It did a lot to increase women's exposure to other work. They were able to prove themselves and then to refuse to be put back into the old traditional niches. I was part of that, at least I partially was.

The rationing caused me to cultivate the cooks on the navy ships, particularly because they had access to the items we wanted, like fresh meat and butter. I was very patriotic and spent time at the USO—probably to meet the cooks! I loved to dance and wanted a nice place for them to go. It wasn't a bar room, dance hall type of place where often they were ripped off. The USO's were a different environment; it gave them more of their home life. Most of them were green kids out of high school who enlisted before they graduated. It would be the cook I'd invite home. He was usually someone from the inland who was really homesick. I was living with my aunt and these two other teachers from Montana so it wasn't as though they came home to have a wild swing. We didn't have the sexual looseness or the sleeping around that we do now. I'm not saying that one of them is right and one is wrong, it just happens to be the way you were raised. I can't set another person's standards for them. But there was really none of that, certainly not in our household. And there wasn't amongst the young women I knew who were going to the USO in Seattle.

After graduation I came to San Francisco to work in the Foreign Trade Zone[16] and handle the technical part of the free port. I thought it was a particularly good opportunity. I'd been offered scholarships (teaching fellowships) back East, one to Swarthmore and one to Smith, to go on for an advanced degree. They were both excellent schools but I was champing to go on with the law. I was doing some flamenco dancing at the time and planned to go on with more of that. I was afraid if I got into this ivy-blind atmosphere, as I called it, I wouldn't get back to what I really thought I wanted to do in life. I still had this thing about the East Coast. As I look back, I should have gone. It gives you a finish, a breadth just living in different parts of the country. The whole East Coast has a much longer colonial history and it really controls the whole country—that was my feeling, the times I've been there. Just the experience of being there, of going on with the graduate program then

---

[16] "The foreign trade zone is a free port—no duty. I planned to work in the trade zone for a while and go to a customs house brokerage and then a short stint in an international bank and then go to work for Lawrence, Tuttle and Harper who did the bulk of the customs and international law here on this coast. I sidetracked into personal injury law because of the injury to my leg that occurred dancing. They wanted to fuse the knee but I didn't want a stiff leg for the rest of my life. I had the opportunity to meet this doctor who did original research. We worked on it together for about a year and a half and opted for this new procedure of rebuilding my leg. It worked for forty years till I got hit in October." [Dorsey was hit by a car in 1989 and was still in recovery.]

and adding mental development time, would have been an excellent investment. It would only have involved two or three years, which then seemed like a long time, and now, of course, seems like a couple of months, or a couple of weeks.

The University of Washington is a fine academic school. When I was there, if you were caught using a secondary reference rather than the original source, you were strictly in trouble. You could well be out of school.

There's a reason for it: you need to make your own judgments on the creator's work rather than somebody else's version. You miss a lot—like a copy of a painting. Law, as it is taught, not just here in California, but throughout the ABA-accepted schools, is with the casebook method. These casebooks are shortened-down cases of the actual cases, and they just have you reading so damn many of them. It doesn't fit together and you don't get the whole subject in one pattern. Law schools have improved some with more practical courses, but they still follow this esoteric kind of casebook method, which I felt wasn't ever going to prepare me for practice. I see why the young lawyers getting out don't know what the hell to do. They don't have the training.

Apprenticeship

A friend recommended that I study privately with John Bussey.[17] "I know the most brilliant legal mind in the whole state. He does sometimes give a Bar Review. I think it would be a terrific

---

[17] "John Bussey practiced a variety of law, did a lot of counsel work, and ultimately became a Superior Court judge, back in the time when blacks just weren't in. He should have been a Supreme Court judge. He was a brilliant man. He'd worked his way through Harvard, had an all-time high academic rating. It was a wonderful experience working with him." Regarding the apprentice method of study compared to the classroom method:"In *The Book of Five Rings* there is a discussion of apprenticeship and the zen state of mind. In a one on one situation, your teacher or master and you are able to have much better mental communication than in the classroom. In the classroom

experiment to see how you and he would do in private study."
He arranged to drive me down to his office and introduce me.
I get dressed up in my finest finery, makeup all over the place,
and I'm sure overdone. He picks me up and I think we're going
down in the Financial District someplace; he heads out to the
Fillmore[18] and we stop at some nice old Victorian walk-up. He
introduces us and Bussey says, "I thought you were bringing
me a law student, not a showgirl." I jump on him, "You, of all
people, should not be prejudiced! What do you suppose I'm
supposed to be—built like an Amazon and an obvious dyke? Is
that your epitome of women lawyers?" He started laughing and
that's the way we started out.

I think to myself, "Now if I can talk him into it I'll sure
have to call 'the Bank of Norway'—my father. I figure this
tutoring is going to cost me a piece of change, but I'm going
for it. Bussey insists on aptitude tests to make sure I'm serious.
I don't blame him; he's investing his time. Who wants to waste
their time in a one-to-one situation? He thought I would be
incensed about it. "No, I think that's only fair." The test showed
that I was motivated, whatever he was looking for. He said he'd
do it on several conditions and I was not to haggle with him at
all. He could tell I'm ready to fight. He would set the curriculum,
which had the Bar approval, the amount of time and the amount

---

you always have those who speak up to be heard and some who should
be heard who seldom speak up. It's not that same meshing of minds.
Your time is strictly yours and your master's. Like tutoring in any
subject, one to one you're not wasting your time. You have a chance
to learn so much more. First of all, hopefully, you pick the outstanding
scholar, which I did. And a scholar who had practically lived too. He
worked his way through. He was a very humble person. I came away
with a deep feeling about the law."

[18] The Fillmore, named after its principle street, was a vital, primarily
black district of San Francisco, which thrived until the 1960's when
'redevelopment' moved in with bulldozers and razed a significant
portion of the community.

of money. He said I had to rigidly comply with all. "Yes sir, shoot, what is it?" I was to be there a minimum of three times a week for a minimum of two hours each session, and more if he directed. I was to have all the assigned work done, and have some original work to offer each time. He had me doing Bar exams right along through. The charge would be a maximum of $25 a month. At this point I started to say something like, "You know that is ridiculously cheap." "Miss Redland, I set some conditions; I expect you to follow them." "Yes sir." Now much later on when I'd learned a lot more and was doing a lot more applied work, I asked him about it. He said he could tell that I would end up more black than any black and I would be able to do more for the black cause.

Years later, I'm trying a police brutality case, defending a black man. The cops beat the shit out of him, then charged him with a felony assault on the cops to try to beat him off from suing them. It had quite a bit of publicity—the international press was reporting it. A Swedish reporter came up as we were in the hallway during court recess and asks if I would point out this Redland, the lawyer representing this black person charged with this outrage. I said, "I'm Miss Redland." She said, "But I thought you were black." I said, "I am black. Now what are your questions?" It was automatic. What Bussey said came back to me right then—what he had said years before. I did become black in that process, in the sense that—I don't know how else to explain it. It didn't hit me that it really had happened. It was not something I tried for one way or the other. I hopefully am not really aware of color or race or age or size in the sense of day-to-day life. But you have to be from the standpoint of selecting juries and knowing about inbuilt prejudices that normally come from ignorance. Unfortunately by then Bussey had died.

That case changed a lot of the way that blacks have been handled by the police. That was around 1974. It was the first time a black ever did anything against the police department moneywise, and I'm talking about six-figure justice—and to get acquitted to begin with and then stood and fought. We sued the

Police Department and won and there was a very able attorney on the other side. Plus you're taking on City Hall. They threaten you; they'd love to see if they can't get you for jaywalking. Fortunately, fear isn't something I have. I'm too crazy. They called and threatened. I said, "Come on over! Just warn me before you get here; I won't rest until I have you in a position to drink your blood and eat your skin. That's the way I feel about it. All's fair, but don't sneak around and slur and try to scare us; it's not going to work." They made phone calls, threatened the children, told them they were going to be orphans. They're psychopathic, sick people. They seek out police kind of work.

If your going to be out in the mean streets you can get into a bad pattern. I'm not saying every cop is bad; they're not. Unfortunately there are a few sickos who slip by. San Francisco did not then have the necessary psychological screening for applicants. A lot of these characteristics show up classically in psychological profiles and then they could be weeded out. When they'd say to me, "You hate cops", I said, "No, we've got a problem—sick cops, bad cops, and the top cops who won't do anything about it, either to remove them or have some psychological testing to see if they can't be treated and removed from the stressful situation so they can get on with their lives. Now if we've got a psychopath that means that they're not ever going to be safe to the force, and will make it dangerous for the rest of the officers and citizens, then they should be removed and put into some other kind of position or sent to psychological treatment centers. The Police Officers Association really opposes testing. It's a two way street. In some ways it's an invasion of one's liberty. But because of the dangers in the career, it seems to me it's just one of the things that's necessary."

A view of San Francisco in the 1950's

"Things were much freer and there were more artistic places than in Seattle. It was a different feeling, more cosmopolitan. I like to live and let live. Seattle is very nice, but it just didn't have the same Bohemian feeling. San Francisco still has it some, but nothing like it did when I first came here. Maybe it's because I was younger and going around more, or maybe it's because the places don't exist. Now it's more pretense. I don't think you can generalize on it, but I don't think there's the realism and naturalness. You saw people from all over with that natural creativity, like Bill Bailey.[19]

The Black Cat, which served food, wine and the greatest coffee, had every kind of person, with every kind of sexual persuasion, artistic endeavor—writers, painters, Bohemians. It was part of that Montgomery block where now stands our great mound, the Transamerica Pyramid. It was a place where you were free to say and do pretty much anything you wanted. A great place—a terrific elixir and mixture of people. We don't have that now, at least I'm not aware of it. Some of the South of Market places tried to capture some of it, but the people are different—different generations. It was just after the War and people felt good that the War had been won. The country was bouncing back, changing from wartime industry into so-called non-wartime industry. There wasn't as much money around. There wasn't the attitude that you could buy everything—not so materialistic, that's the way I would describe it. There were all different age groups at The Black Cat; it wasn't just those in their twenties or thirties, but also those in their sixties and seventies. Since they served alcohol, they had to be fairly careful because they were frequently raided because we didn't fit into the mainstream. It was a place you really looked forward to going. A great cup of coffee for five cents and all the cups you wanted after that. Now you get some dismal cup of coffee for seventy-five cents and the charge you so much for each refill. Now they're here to get you to drink so many drinks before they serve you and then eat and get out so they can fill the table again. You can feel

---

[19]   *See page 44 for the connection with Bill Bailey. When I was in the process of interviewing the subjects of this book, I discovered that Dorsey and Bill's paths crossed many years before.*

that pressure. We didn't have that feeling then. The Black Cat, The Iron Pot, 12 Adler Place. I never slept very much. For instance, I'd be reviewing my notes and then I'd take a walk down through Chinatown, stop at Portsmouth Square, then walk on down to The Black Cat and drink a cup of coffee, sit around and listen to some good music with friends of all ages, then make a stop in at 12 Adler or another place along the way. I might get a bowl of chili or soup or spaghetti and meatballs at the Iron Pot on the way back, then come on back and study a little more and grab two or three hours of sleep. I've always been blessed with a lot of energy. That was the environment of my choice."

Flamenco dancing—the path not taken

"I studied flamenco dancing in Seattle and San Francisco. It's a mental and physical discipline. I planned to dance professionally for three or four years. I felt it would be a rewarding experience, giving me an opportunity for more travel. I figured I'd be a worn-out dancer by then and then go into the law with some seriousness. The dance company I was involved in was planning to go on tour to New Orleans, Central and South America, and then up to New York. We were booked to go. It never came to fruition. I think this dancing kind of life obviously wasn't meant for me. I knew it at the time of the accident. I caught my heel in a crack in the floor as I was moving very fast into a flamenco dip during a performance. I wasn't able to move my heel and the whole leg fell apart. Goodbye dancing [waves a kiss to an imaginary audience]. All my life I had planned to be a lawyer. It had crossed my mind, would I really get back to the law if I went on and did this. I had come to peace with myself and I knew I would, but it was like a hand from out here says, we'll make sure you do! I knew right then that our lives are more planned than we realize."

Pioneer trails

"The general concept regarding women lawyers when I first began practicing law was that you had to be a big mannish-looking dyke—butch haircut with an Amazon kind of build. I think that occurred because maybe up to then the only women in the trial or litigation field who got through the law school curriculum and had enough courage to go forward, had that physical presence so the men didn't try all the shit on them that they did on somebody else. I did run into that with John Bussey in his preconceived ideas. His remark was, "What did you bring me, a showgirl?" I didn't overdo my makeup THAT much. I did know how to do that. I'd modeled. It was one of the part-time jobs I had. For two reasons: one, I could study while they were doing my hair—I did hair modeling; two, I got paid well for it which helped pay whatever nut I was cracking that month. Remember, we were just coming out of women having any right to own any property! A lot of that has changed in my lifetime and it's still not all it should be.

My background is helpful in explaining the difference—cause it just gave me a different springboard to bounce from. I don't know how lucky you can get, but as children we knew that we were, particularly the women. I think the boys were under the cloud of Richard Redland and Sons. They were the ones who got the prejudice, in the sense that they didn't have the freedom of choice. I tried to encourage it, and there was encouragement within the family, but still there was always the daddy that visualized all this land and ranches, and one of them being in politics. He was a realist, very highly principled, and believed in his civic duty—a devoted citizen. He also was a real caring, touching, high-type guy."

"You think like a man!"

"I took the Bar and was admitted to practice in 1954. I was looking around to see where I'd want to be situated in practice, having initially planned to be in customs and international law, but I got sidetracked because of an injury. I naturally looked for personal injury or tort litigation trial firms. From every office I applied I got an offer. It wasn't going to make me rich, but what I wanted was experience. I went with Lou Ashe and Van Pinney, who had just broken their partnership with Melvin Belli, figuring that, one, they were able trial lawyers; two, they had a volume of cases to try; and three, I would have substantial opportunities to try cases, not only in San Francisco but in the other counties in the state. I did get that opportunity. The senior partners really did not want to travel to some of the smaller counties. I was willing to drive to Oroville or Fairfield or Glen County or Nevada County. Those forums were considered a bit more difficult for the plaintiff and it involved travel out of town.

In the more rural counties, I've had opponents, early on, pull this city-slicker lawyer business. I found dealing with jurors that there was interest because you were different. They had not seen many, if any, women trial lawyers. As a consequence I had a more judgmental, but more attentive audience than the opponent. Everyone was used to male lawyers. The jurors, I think, did have a preconceived notion, probably the same notion that the judges and opponents did— that it was not a field for women, yet they seemed open enough once you started the trial. They were curious. If you were there for a period and able to sell your case, in some ways it was a benefit. When I'd go into court and hadn't been there before, they never thought I was a lawyer. I was somebody's secretary, or wife, or a relative of the litigants. I had to almost wear a name tag and show my license. I was asked a number of sexist questions, by both judges and lawyers, such as my sexual preferences—if I were interested in men. I wasn't saying one way or another. "There is no need to answer because here in the room all I see are boys, and I'm definitely not interested in boys." I did have them ask, what was the difference. I'd look at them very knowingly: "A man lets you know he's available, and a boy makes a run on you."You just hit it head on. I've found it's a lot better. The word got around pretty quickly I was just trying the lawsuit without having to get into personalities. It was part of their ego thing to try to date you. I'm not against dating, but I do not believe in mixing business and pleasure as a rule. If I'm going to try a case, I'm not going to try it in the bedroom. Because I showed no interest in them, they figured I must be a lesbian—a 'dyke', using their term at the time. After the first couple of years of practice it never came up again. They'd pull all kinds of things."I'd do it but she's a woman." I'd say,"Look, shoot your best shot. You can be assured ladies and gentlemen, I'll try to vigorously represent my injured client, who deserves to have a full measure of justice here. We're not dealing in personalities or trying the lawyers; we're trying the case." Usually I would tell my clients,"Please stand up. These are the injured victims; I have the privilege of representing them. One opposing attorney said that he hoped they wouldn't turn the trial into a beauty contest. I got up and said, "I hope to hell you won't either. I've never won one in my life, but I've had the privilege of representing a number of women victims."

"You're not like a woman lawyer" or "You think like a man": this frequently occurs, even today. I've always found this quite offensive. You try a case to win. You want to use all within your legal power, cross examination ability and tactics.

My job is to vigorously defend and I intend to. I do the level best with what I have at hand at the time, but that doesn't mean I'm a man. It's offensive to have someone say,"You really try a case like a man." It should have nothing to do with sex. I don't hear it any more but I've been around so long now I'm more of a fixture than either sex. There are many fine women lawyers out there trying cases now.

People weren't used to the idea of women lawyers. They were used to women lawyers in probate, in divorce work, business law, but not too many trial lawyers. For some reason they expected you to cry or fall apart. I never could figure out where they got these notions. It hadn't been where you'd had five or ten women lawyers come into courts and cry and fall on their faces; they just hadn't gotten the opportunity to get there. I was lucky; I got the job opportunity. I found it interesting that our only U.S. Supreme Court Justice—and I don't mean to put her in a token status, because she's earned her dues in a lot of ways too, though we differ in many personal ideas and beliefs—that with her background and her Stanford scholarship, she had difficulty finding employment in the trial field, from what she writes and talks about. I really can't say I did. As far as men feeling threatened, there's the psychological threat of not wanting to be beat by a woman.

There had been other women lawyers before, but not really day in, day out jury trial lawyers. Agnes O'Brien Smith, who was with the City Attorney's office, came about the same time I did or a little later on. She worked up to be one of the top trial deputy city attorneys, who tried a lot of litigation cases for the City and enjoyed a good reputation and was very able. She didn't have crying spells either. I never could figure out what the story was. That was the misconception, or we wouldn't be able to deal with death or injury, or too delicate—some of the same kind of mentality that permeated when Clara Foltz[20] and some of the early women pioneers in the law had litigated to get to be lawyers to begin with. Talk about women's 'delicate condition'—women always have to do the scut work, take care of the family, run all the errands, do a lot of back-breaking work, mentally plan for the family, make do with brutal or alcoholic husbands, and still withstand and rear the family under very trying circumstances. My god, if they could do that, they certainly could be a lawyer and try lawsuits!

They soon found out I wasn't delicate, whatever that is. There was just more curiosity. In some ways I think the women lawyers coming along now don't have that same receptiveness. I'm not saying it's for the right reasons, but when you're

---

[20] Clara Foltz was California's first practicing lawyer

different, you stick out. As a consequence there's more interest. Now, hey, if you blow it, you're going to get banged down worse. On the other hand, if you prove to be more than their preconceived ideas it tended to be a benefit to the client.

Going into a new forum was definitely interesting. In each place there was a groundbreaking. When I'd start out, they wouldn't say my name or would hardly acknowledge me; the second day they're calling me "Miss Redland". The third or fourth day I could tell how I was doing because the court personnel would warm up. I'd always make a point of learning their names and something about their background. I don't mean doing anything improper, like exchanging gifts, but to recognize their professional abilities and to treat them as professionals. These are people who are putting in their time to make the system of justice work; I think they deserve personal recognition. I've tried to always see that occurred during the trial. I bore in mind that they were serving a very worthwhile purpose in the system of justice, and without them, no matter how much work I'd done with the case, it wouldn't go well or the exhibits wouldn't be kept right or the records wouldn't be kept, or order wouldn't be there. By the third day or so of trial, I'm addressed as "Dorsey", and pretty quick there's just a different environment. This is going to jurisdictions where they'd never had a woman lawyer and didn't like San Francisco lawyers, and were against people suing in general. If it's a back injury it must be a fraud kind of deal, everyone claims back injuries—that kind of mentality, which is preconceived subliminal advertising of the insurance industry.

Many of my initial clients were jurors who had sat on cases and relatives of people I had represented, witnesses or people the court personnel knew that needed a lawyer. So I started to develop a base of practice. A lot of the work I did here in San Francisco, some in Stockton and Sacramento too, was for injured maritime employees. I knew quite a number of them, having come here initially to go into customs and international law, and having worked in the Foreign Trade Zone, where we did a lot of shipping of duty-free merchandise. That base of clients formed the basis of a very interesting maritime litigation practice, primarily in the maritime injury field, both Jones Act and straight maritime injuries.[21]

After working with Lou Ashe and Van Pinney for a little over two years, I was noticing that when I was trying cases, not only in the City but around, there were a number of senior partners from other firms who would come and watch. I'd had two or three offers of a better financial deal, but I didn't feel I should leave the firm within the two-year period when they'd given me the opportunity to try a multitude of cases. I felt some loyalty about it. At the end of the second year my loyalty dwindled some, having received a Christmas bonus of a fur coat instead of cash. I think one of the partners felt I should dress better. Secondly, I'm sure it was cheaper for them. As a

---

[21]   According to Bill Bailey, Dorsey is much beloved by the older members of the longshoremen's union due to her expert handling of maritime cases during the 1950's and 60's. "Bill Bailey appeared as a witness in a case back in the 70's for a longshoreman, Joseph Morris, who is a Native American—Blackfoot and Shoshone. Many of the longshoremen, of the old-timers anyway, like Bailey, are very creative, multi-faceted men. They were true trade unionists. Morris lost a lot with the brain injury but before that he was a very creative, talented writer, painter, musician, heavy equipment operator on the waterfront. He and Bailey had known each other for years. Joe was one of the spear leaders of the Alcatraz Indian movement. Bill was a witness as to how Morris was before and after the accident. (Morris sustained serious brain injuries when he fell off a ladder onto the steel deck of the ship which was being unloaded.) Bill has a fine, original mind. To cross-examine a guy like that you'd better say, "Nice seeing/meeting you. No questions." [The opposing attorney] asked some open-ended questions; the minute you give Bill Bailey an open-ended question he's going to write the story the way he wants it."

consequence I left and accepted a position with Marvin Lewis,[22] again to try cases. At that time my own practice was developing to the point that I really had to carve out time in which to try my own clients' cases. I was there not quite two years. When I left, by then my practice was so big I was actually having to utilize their lawyers. I elected to form my own firm at that time. At the present time I'm solo and intend to stay that way. I've been in partnerships and in professional corporations with others and I feel I'm better off as a loner. There's more flexibility. I plan to change the direction of the practice some. I've always been interested in real estate law. Recently I took the time to update myself in real estate law and also get my real estate broker's license. I plan to do more on the real estate side of the fence, both as an active participant in investing and brokering, and in real estate litigation.

When I first started to practice, I'd try anything that I could find to try, put it that way. The first criminal case I was involved in was a felony embezzlement case. I've tried the gamut of criminal cases—robberies, forgeries, murder, drugs, burglaries. I enjoyed criminal work, but it's very difficult to combine an active civil practice with a criminal practice. It's hard to coordinate the calendars and difficult to keep up on a both sets of the law. (Criminal law, from the standpoint of the accused, is more depressing. The whole Hall of Justice system is so depressing because it's where the haves and have-nots stick out a lot. Most of them never plan whatever they're doing, or they plan the crime and not the after.) I really had trouble coordinating the two but I found it very challenging to try one side to the other."

---

[22]   "Marvin Lewis is ingenious. He is an original mind and a legal pioneer. He was a trial lawyer whose specialty was what we commonly think of as the 'nut cases'. He had a deep understanding and feeling about another person's plight and knew how to make the jurors understand that plight. This was before there was as much acceptance of the psychological injury."

Maritime Law

"The Longshore and Harbor Workers Act came about because we pressed for case law which went up through the U.S. Supreme Court that said that longshoremen and other maritime workers were doing the work traditionally done by seamen. As things became more mechanized and specialized it was still truly in the seamen's category to get in under the Jones Act[23]

---

[23] "Andrew Furuseth was a Norwegian seaman who decided that seamen, because of their long periods of time at sea and because they were under the control of the master, were a group of workers who needed extra protection, both from the inherent dangers of the work on ships and to protect them against themselves. In order to go to sea, the seaman signs foreign articles that commit him to that ship for the duration of the voyage. These long periods of isolation could lead to drinking and an inability to cope with general citizens on the street in an interchange. He pushed for the Jones Act which was the first act to put the burden of proving the fault on the part of the shipowner and to have contributory fault on the part of the injured workman. He has to work as directed. He could be knocked out and chained at sea. The master is the master of the ship and crew. The dangerous working conditions were so great— the food, the medical care, the watches they had to stand—all of this is in the complete control of the shipowner. The Jones Act is one of the best laws we have for the worker. It puts a great burden on the shipowner, the way it should be. Now because sailors used to load and unload the ships, as well as sail, and because of mechanization and specialization, they developed longshoremen who did work which was traditionally done by seaman. The law began to develop substantially during the time I practiced. The Jones Act was extended to longshoremen and other workers, such as ships carpenters, who did work which traditionally had been done by seamen. The shipowners and stevedore companies then tried to change the law by introducing the Bonner Bill. We were fortunate in being able to kill it in Senate committee. The Jones Act is the seaman's law. It spread to other countries in different forms."

seaworthiness causes of action and to gradually extend it to dockside. I worked on that. All the way to the Supreme Court.

I decided to take on the Crocker sugar outfit—C & H. They used wooden conveyors to unload the raw sugar from the ship which were really unsafe. I filed this motion for discovery[24] in federal court. I wanted to inspect as this whole thing was unsafe. Actually I had been up there a number of times surreptitiously. This particular ship was coming in that involved the injuries of these two men. I wanted to get pictures of it. The ship owners (Matson) and C&H had refused so I filed this motion in court to have this formally photographed. I was in court arguing the brief and in the middle of it I began visualizing the whole operation. I said, "Pardon me, your Honor, a compelling message has come to me and I must excuse myself." He said, "I'm right in the middle of things." I said, "So am I."And I walked out. I went to the phone—411—Rick's Helicopters. I remembered the name of this fancy aerial photographer from Sausalito so I call him. "Do you have a helicopter where we can do aerial photography—with safety belts where we can lean out? Can you meet me at the San Francisco airport? I want to get this sugar ship and the conveyors down through. Can you zoom me in and do it in color?" He said, "Be at Rick's Helicopters in a half hour." I threw on my old levis, got my old zoom movie camera, jumped in the car and headed for Rick's Helicopters. It was a beautiful trip. We hover over the damned thing, come down low—they're cussing, screaming. They had bullhorns. I said, "Piss on you!" We're taking all these pictures. I'm looking through my field glasses.

I wanted one of those control boxes and scrapers. I see some of them and they're all stacked in back. I had this Russian galfriend who was game for anything. They got guards all over the gate. We drive up and I'm wearing her wig and falsies. I said, "Is the old

---

[24] Discovery: information which may be helpful in perfecting or defending a law suit which is turned over to the other side pursuant to either statute or motion in court.

man aboard? Look, the *?!!†"*"¡ didn't leave me any money and he's not getting out to sea! He's catching it this time!"We act like we're going toward the ship. We slip around and get the scrapers and the control box and load them in the trunk. On the way out the gate I said,"That *?!!†"*"¡ is hiding!"

Come to trial I show up with the scrapers and the control box. The scrapers were great metal things which cut up people's legs. They were used to scrape the raw sugar out of the inside of the ship and also off the conveyors. The judge and the attorneys were furious afterward. I said, "I realize you can control a lot, but so far, not the air. I have to be grateful to you, Your Honor, and my able opponents here because you caused necessity to be the mother of the creation of these photographs which are far superior. When this case ends up in the U.S. Supreme Court, as it will, it will enable the Court to have a full understanding of the entire operation." It did go to the U.S. Supreme Court and the Court sustained our position, that under the extension of the seaworthiness causes of action, the vessel extended all the way into the sugar factory. Here I wasted all this time with these motions. I could have gone up anytime and taken those helicopter pictures. It just hadn't occurred to me. Necessity is the mother; when you're forced into the corner and you're still not going to give up, somehow, some gene is going to click in.

Rick and the aerial photographer used a lot of these pictures as advertising afterward. The case really hit hard. Shipowners were not going to get down with all these longshore third-party claims for unseaworthiness. It cost them money. They got Mr. Bridges[25] to get respectable. And the East Coast unions, the same way. It's all pricing. They tried to amend the Longshore and Harbor Workers Compensation Act with the Bonner Bill which I tried to prevent from happening. The object was to give the longshoremen a few more dollars in compensation and sell them out on their unseaworthiness claims. Profit is

---

[25]   *See Bill Bailey's story, page 107.*

the bottom line. The bottom line is paying a little more compensation and getting rid of the unseaworthiness cases rather than having to improve the safety conditions which would cost them a lot of money. It's cheaper to pay for two or three death claims than it is to have to modify your whole fleet. With the Bonner Bill, the chairman of the committee happened to be a guy from Wisconsin. The shipowners felt safe—they wouldn't have to worry about votes from these union people out on the coast. Of course, in Wisconsin he would know a hell of a lot about shipping! I figured this isn't so bad. It's a heavy Scandinavian state. I marshalled support from that ethnic community, both on the West coast and in Wisconsin. The rank and file blitzed the committee and the bill was killed before it reached the floor in the mid 1960's. But I knew they were going to come back. I could see that we were going to go down. All the stuff I had fought for since '54 was knocked out when the bill was reintroduced in 1972. After the bill passed, the only way the workers could sue the ship was if some utter catastrophe happened.[26] In 1984 the act was amended again, further reducing benefits.

Law took precedence over my social life. I worked hard and played hard, that's the best way to describe it. A lot of times I was in trial back-to-back. When I was in trial I felt that the client just had that one time to try the case, and unless I was so mentally stove up that I might catch a movie to get a mental rest, I really spent my time on the case. I was dedicated to advocacy. I've never been really super-social. I enjoyed going to dances or movies or out to dinner, but it wasn't a big thing. I think I burned myself out before I was twenty-one on social life.

---

[26] Talking about the union sellouts in present times: "They're all busy thinking about their campers, their EZ payment plans—consumer credit was the worst thing that could ever happen. It was good for the country in building up more industry and running on a credit economy. I suppose it made for more jobs was the idea of it, but then everyone gets hooked into these consumer items."

Single Parent

"I have one natural child, a son, and a foster daughter, who is very much my daughter. I was morally bound to volunteer to take her because my husband and her father had promised each other that they'd try to look after each other's child if something happened to the other one. She was a ward of the state from the time she was born and something happened in the last foster home she was in. The mother was not too reliable, to put it kindly. So I volunteered as a foster parent, actually not giving it a lot of thought, because I understood the rules were that there had to be a mommy and daddy in the house, and preferable mommy was home. It wasn't that I wouldn't do it, but I volunteered really thinking I wouldn't be accepted. I found all of a sudden I was accepted.

She was just ready to turn five. We really had a baptism by fire. They never did get me the medical records for the child. She came with a little small sandwich bag of clothing that didn't fit her, even though they represented she had a full wardrobe. You don't want to deprive the child; you want to see that they're kept in the same circumstances as your own. But more important, she was too young to know whether she was allergic to whatever, what shots and diseases she'd had. It was apparent to me she had rickets. I finally gave up and just took her to my son's pediatrician. The poor child had to go through all the shots and testing. It was a painful experience for both of us to get her health up to normal. I used to sit with her for hours and assure her that, "The reason I'm having you drink milk and eat your vegetables and have some meat is that I love you so much I wouldn't be able to face myself when you get to be an older girl and have all crooked legs and snaggly teeth. You'd ask me why, and I'd have to say I didn't love you enough to see that you did right now." It took about a year until her body craved the things that it had been missing before. We didn't have proper eating problems after that. Years later she came running into my office one day and grabbed me and hugged me and kiss, kiss, kiss. I said, "What's all this?" She says, "I've got to thank you for loving me so much that you saw that I have beautiful teeth and nice straight legs. I got a lot of compliments today."

My son was three, turning four, when she came. He was the youngest in the family. He was delighted to have her. His remark when we picked her up at the juvenile center was, "Mommy, I think we should stop by Sears on our way home and get Sissy some things." I said, "Why Sears?" He said, "That's the only place I know that would have everything she needs." He never was envious in that sense. He was concerned that she have clothing and toys.

Once I volunteered for her, before I knew it, I had her half-brother. There was a big shortage of foster parents. Then the social workers came by with three teenagers from the same family and said they couldn't find any other place. They were from our neighborhood. My son did learn to live in a large family. It worked out. Fortunately all the children have gone on to prove themselves. It was a matter of teaching them a little self-confidence, that they're in charge, and trying to encourage that self-pride and sense of family. I'm proud of them. It's up to them; all you can do is point the direction. I was very persistent about the direction.

We used inner-family discipline—children having their own children's council of judging what proper conduct was. I carried the veto, which I seldom used. I found that they were much stricter on each other than I could ever be. Also they listened to each other better. It had a very salutary effect. You get five other children looking down their noses at you, the other kid shapes up pretty fast.

My son is like I am. He's not in a hurry to marry early. He's going ahead with his own career plans. My family tends not to be early at running into marriages. We take it very seriously. I was in my thirties. Love, when it hits you, it hits you. I was very involved with someone else at the time. I fell for his father, married him on the spur of the moment, really hurt this other very fine man in doing so. I have a delightful son as a result.

It's a lot of give and take, in any relationship. There are pluses and minuses—there were in that relationship."

Talking about using her maiden name, Redland, even after her marriage: "That was my name. Only two classes of people have had their names changed: slaves and women. It's insane. My husband knew it upfront. I think probably socially sometimes he was a little uncomfortable but that's the way it is. After he died I went fairly steady with this man who was more my contemporary; he had some vigorous objections to it. I said, 'Now look, your name is _____; mine is Redland; that's the way it's going to be. If you don't like it, take a hike.'

I didn't have my son until I was in my mid-thirties. It's like career women are doing now. If I had been more liberated I definitely would have had the nursery here in the office and had him with me every moment in and out of court. He may have been better off with the woman who was looking after him. But from a mother/child bonding, I think you miss a lot if you don't have that opportunity. I was head of the household. In a lot of ways I think it's good for kids to see a working household and realize that you've got to get out and hussle. I would have taken off more time had I to do it again because there's a lot of vital early years that you miss out on if you're working all the time. You're not with the child.

It's one thing I agree with the current administration's profession of interest in the importance of the family. The family doesn't mean to me mommy and daddy—it means the nucleus of the family unit which can be two friends, four strangers by blood. It has to do with a unity of purpose and a common desire of support for one another. It's like me trying to supervise and discipline all these children. I realized I was making a flop of it. I said, "We're having a family council meeting. I expect you all to have an agenda of what you feel is important and how you'd like things run." I called it to order and said, "Now we're going to take turns every week. Who wants to be in charge of the meeting tonight—and each of you take turns. It's your family. I want you to all speak out." Once

they got started they really got involved in it. I very seldom said
anything. I did set that up at the start: what affects one of us
affects everyone else. We are all the same household. One bad
name and we all get that image. So what kind of a home is it if
someone's stealing, not holding up their end and standing
proud? They liked the idea of decision-making. It really helped
them with their school stuff too.

I had a wonderful housekeeper. She and her husband
pitched in a lot too. I called her when the social worker came
with the three kids. I said,"My god, the social worker's here
and the children are agreeable to sharing the house. The
younger boys will bunk up here and the oldest, being
seventeen, needs his own room downstairs with his aquariums.
The two girls will share."They said, "We can all share your
bedroom", which we did, very often. It was the best place to
talk with the kids, one to one. It had a fireplace in it. We'd
light a fire and relax, maybe all of us, maybe one-to-one. Several
times a week I tried to see there was a one-to-one with each
child where we could be just private, to really get whatever was
on their mind, or what I was doing. To have that openness is
very enjoyable.

I had wonderful family support. You do need to have some
vacation from them. Thank god my parents were alive in
Wyoming and they loved children. In summer and certain
vacations I'd send the kids off early to enjoy themselves—let
them cut out of school here early and go back and enroll for a
week or two in Ten Sleep,Wyoming to see what the small schools
were like. The kids bonded there, so in case something happened
to me they would have another place to go where they already had
roots. You need to make that kind of planning in case it ever
happens."

We still got so terribly far to go
"When I had just my son and daughter, I was sending them to
Montessori school in Marin County. When the housekeeper
came to work with us I said we'll drive over the first day. I

didn't tell her I also had the Marin Junior College enrollment forms with me. So we dropped them off at school and she says, "Where are we going? I have work at home." I said, "It can wait. I thought we'd drive over to Marin J.C. and let you look around the campus. I want to encourage not only my children, but yours, who are still in high school, with the fact that education doesn't stop. I thought maybe you'd like to enroll in a class or two here in the morning while the children are in school. You could take your classes and then pick them up and come back to the City. A requirement of your job is that you go to school too. We'll pay the expenses. I'm sure you can find some things you're interested in." She was in her fifties. She chose dressmaking, and I suggested some basic English, which she took. (Not that she was illiterate but when you do get ready to go on to something else, you can write better, your grammar is better, because we do get sloppy at it.) Her whole family— her husband was tickled to death. They set out in the morning, all three of them, to go to school.

You see the lifelong learning book is right here [indicating San Francisco State University's catalog on her desk]. One of the requirements of the office here is that everyone attend the equivalent of at least three semester hours a year, which isn't that much. We pay for the expense of a babysitter if they have a child at home. One class a week, with a young child, is more than sufficient. The child comes first. But also that child sees Mommy going to school which is important too. So it's a requirement in order to be employed here to continue your education. It applies to me and everyone else—we do not have separate rules—in our pension fund or anything else. If we're all putting in our effort, then we should all have an opportunity to do it together. We expect to use everyone's mind, it's just that simple. It's good business. Besides, who wants to just be doing other people's work? One of the reasons we have these educational requirements is that it is a step in helping people to not become confined or satisfied within a certain job strata.

Just like with one of my employees who is taking the Bar this week. He started out as a grocery clerk and took a paralegal course. He started here doing everything—cleaning files, dusting, putting things together—working up to being office manager and paralegal, and studying law, which I encouraged. I encouraged; he did it. There's a big difference. He's the one who had to have the stamina to do it—to take the Bar and go on to practice law and hopefully go beyond where law is now. Whether it's a man or woman, in that sense I don't think it should matter. I'm just more acutely aware of women's limitations because of societal limitations. None of us should limit ourselves or feel we have "arrived" or finally reached whatever the epitome of the top is because there is no top. If you can leave a message for others, "Do not be limited. Don't stop. Go risk-take. Go for it!" There's always another mountain. What makes life wonderful is a lot of challenges. If we can just keep on that level and not become discouraged and stop, then society will be a hell of a lot better and so will we.

For women now there's a lot of opportunity, but we still lack some things, primarily in decision-making and building our own nexus of referrals and making more risk-taking business decisions. They have very few women in corporations. We really haven't taken control of politics or economics. We really need to work on that. It's one of the reasons for my decision to go more into the real estate investment. For the most part we really don't have the old boy system and the old-girl system. There's a lot of biting. I know a woman who is exceedingly able, who is being considered for president of one of our largest learning institutions, who is without a doubt the most qualified in all respects. Probably the only person who really talked down about her was a woman whom she's helped a lot. She's a little envious. We still have a lot of that. It's unfortunate. I think it's more social learning—both vying for the same man, but it's very troubling to me. It deeply angers me that it happens.

I did have a refreshing experience in Oregon when I'd been checking to find a lawyer [with whom] to associate. Naturally I preferred to go with a woman lawyer. In checking with my male opponents all of them said there were no woman lawyers who did any kind of work like this, none are able, etc. So I did some checking on my own and found two women listed in this town. I called the first one and spoke with her. She sounded perfectly competent to me. In our very short meeting I found her to be very capable and knowledgeable. She said she changed her schedule because it was another woman who called. I was delighted to hear that. We really need to work on it. That's why we don't have women in office. We don't have positions of control, which we HAVE to have. In law, in judgeships, in administrative work, whether it's in the legal field, the publishing field, the banking field, the political arena, the corporate field, the unions—notorious for being sexist— we really need to work on all of them.

There are more women in offices, more women in day-to-day law practice, in business as well as trial work. Many young women—I say young women, because there are very few older ones around. This change came with legislation, and then requirements that the schools admit more women in the later 70's. Now you're getting about fifty-fifty, women versus men, so I'm told. But bear in mind that there are generally more women than men in the general population, it should be more than fifty-fifty, assuming that there are a greater number of women who want to apply. A lot of that has to do with pre-school, grade school, junior high and high school where the preparation is, what kind of career counseling you've had, and how much competitive advantage you've had. There's still a real fight in sports. That's why I went into detail explaining the background I came from. I came prepared to compete, because I HAD all my life. The average women, certainly my contemporaries, didn't normally have that opportunity.

Years ago I was visited by two prominent editors who suggested that I run for State Assembly. I felt there wasn't enough base for a woman, that I'd be strictly owned by them, or if I didn't do their bidding I would soon be out of office. At that time I was trying to make the family's living. With foster children you'd better be ready to pay for them yourself and not count on the State to come through like they're supposed to, particularly if you want to afford them the same quality of education and social environment that you do for your own child. If you're paying for private school and all that goes with it, why then, you're hustling, at least I was with my limited capacity. Between that and trying to see to family life, I really didn't have a lot of time. I looked coldly at the fact that there wasn't a big women's base that you could count on to be real supportive. Knowing that if they're selling big newspapers they've got to protect their big advertisers and many things that I didn't agree with—I opted out. I just asked them what would happen if I voted for so-and-so. The got a horrified look on their face. I figured this would be a one-term kind of thing, probably they're going to try to impeach me mid-term. That was a long, long time ago.

I think the real control begins at the City and County levels. You really need to start there—City council and Board of Supervisor meetings, that's where your real control starts. The real running begins at home. That goes along with my future plans to become much more active in that regard. What I want to see is a really strong women's nucleus. We really have to work it so that women aren't chopping the other woman's leg off. It's a serious, ever-present problem, unfortunately.

REFLECTIONS
On changes in the legal profession

"There are substantially more women in the profession now. It some ways it's much more competitive. The rules are much more complicated now. It's more of a paper and calculator battle where early on it was more artistic ability. The presenting of the facts was simplified. When I first started trying cases we didn't have all the discovery that we do now. There were no interrogatories and motions to produce. You had depositions from each side and that was about it. Into court you went. You were trying blind. Now we have discovery; with interrogatories you can pretty much know the other side's case. So you're trying a different kind of case, with much more work done on the case in discovery and papers. The files are, god! five to six times as thick as they used to be. It's very expensive."

On changes in the Bay area

"On the personal side in the City, particularly around here [indicating her office which is located on Market Street near City Hall], if you look about we have the so-called homeless. The parks are dirty; the people are dirty. I don't mind them camping but I expect them to be clean and not leave trash about. There's a lessening of self-pride. I would definitely cut off all aid programs without the mandatory school and rehabilitation to the workforce—literally cut them all off unless they were in some type of program. If there's a need for psychological counseling along with it, fine, let's give every opportunity and every mode of treatment and education we have at our disposal to quickly rehabilitate them into the workforce."

On special quality of life in the Bay area

"The Bay area has its problems; I still can't think of any place I'd rather live. I've always been a real all-out San Francisco liver, all the way. I like the geography, of course, the climate, the wealth of educational, artistic, and social facilities and activities. I like the cosmopolitan mix of people with differences in ethnic, age, cultural backgrounds. All of those things really make for a rich, rich life. There's less division in the cultural mix. There's more of a melting-in. In New York you still feel it's black or white. Here it's more blended over, which is what I like. It's nice to keep the culture alive that came from your ancestors, but not to limit you in your own life exposure. In the older places it's more formal. Informality is one of the things I like too, obviously—you see the way I dress. There's more social freedom. On the East Coast it's more classist. From what I've observed here it's more what you've been able to do yourself. We don't have a real class system in that sense. They try to in a way with the Junior League. Some of these well-to-do couples from several generations of money—they seek to be the social leaders of whatever. I hope I never get that disease of trying to be social or respectable, either one is a terrible catastrophe. It's really an insecurity disease of the worse sort, it appears to me. It's something worse than tuberculosis as far as I'm concerned. There's a certain amount of it here but nothing like the East Coast. I hope it never catches on any more than it has. It's a more open society. You are more left to develop on your own."

On aging

"I think older people are not as hung up on things that frustrate younger people. The most important one that I've noticed, whether it's a lack of confidence or a lack of living longer, a lot of younger people are worried about the kind of impression they make. They tend to dress more, do more, not necessarily what they want to do, but because they think that's what they are supposed to do. You have more living experience to draw on; as a consequence you have a greater richness of appreciation. A lot of people look at growing older as the things you can't do, or you've given up, or quitting or near death. Frankly, as the three of us sit here, we don't know who is going on to the next life next. I've had people say, "When are you going to quit?" I said, "Not until after you have." Keep your options open, that's what I say about it. You're not as hung-up about things. You've been through it.

I am concerned that I have a whole list of stuff that I haven't done, and then all these new, exciting things to do—all of the computer—word-processing, access the information, travel.

You go to the movies for next to nothing. I can go to the movie across the street and it will cost me fifty cents to see three movies—the senior rate. It's terrific. Then they've got these deals—I don't know whether they planned for some nut like me or not—where if you're over sixty-two, you can fly anywhere for a few dollars. The beauty is, for someone like me who is a notorious poor planner, you cannot make the reservations more than seven days ahead. I never know what I'm going to do within that week anyway except when I got a trial, so at the very last minute I can call up—"Do you have any space on this flight?" and take off for Puerto Rico. You can get eight tickets for six hundred dollars with a year to use them. I'll take a three dayer and fly to Puerto Rico sometime. I've never been there. I'd like to see it. I want to study up on the economics before I go. My idea of going to a place is ferreting around through the native situation and avoiding as much as I can the tourist slot. The historic part—fine. I want to practice up on my Spanish before I go. Some long rainy weekend I'm just going to get on the damn plane and go."

I da Jackson

"In a virtuous action I properly am; in a virtuous act I add to the world; I plant into deserts conquered from chaos and nothing and see the darkness receding on the limits of the horizon."

Ralph Waldo Emerson, "Compensation", *Emerson's Essays*, p.89

Ida Jackson and her family were early pioneers in the Black exodus out of the South. As a result, Ida fulfilled her parents' dream by graduating from the University of California, Berkeley in 1922. She was the first African-American to teach in the Oakland public school system. She was honored by Eleanor Roosevelt for her efforts to provide health care for rural Black Mississippians in the 1930's.

Ruth first met Ida in 1988 when she was invited to do a series of portraits of East Bay Afro-American community leaders for a show at the Oakland Museum of Art organized by the Northern California Center for Afro-American History and Life. After hearing an encapsulated version of Ida's life story prior to the photography session, Ruth immediately was struck by Ida's diminutive size in contrast to her pioneering deeds. We often do tend to see leaders and pioneers in our mind's eye as larger than ordinary folk.

When I first met her I felt a concentrated energy emanating from her being which must have been formidable when she was a young woman fighting for a place in the sun, not only for herself but "for the race", as she so often recalls. As I got to know her and appreciate her sharp wit, I realized she would make a formidable opponent as well as a steadfast friend. Injustice always seems vulnerable to courage coupled with intelligence. When one adds humor, like the cherry on the sundae, the finale is formidable. As an elder she is not afraid to laugh at herself, particularly for being forgetful. We have commiserated with one another now for several years for our endless capacity for losing keys, phone numbers and important papers of many kinds. Ida has very little problem, however, accurately recalling distant past events with amazing clarity, something which all of the elders in this study seem to be able to do. In spite of our shared absent-minded professor syndrome, I would count on her for the right response in a bad situation. When I spend the afternoon in her charming antique-filled house, built to last in the 1930's by an old family friend, I feel as if we slipped back in time to a more gracious, and in some ways, saner world in which one easily could recognize friend and foe, right and wrong, where all the edges were defined. When she tells me of that historic meeting, I picture her chatting quietly with Eleanor Roosevelt and Mary McLeod Bethune in the East Room of the White House—three powerful, purposeful women on lifelong missions to make the American dream come true for all its citizens.

Ruth and I love going to lunch with her. We always have fun eating Chinese while laughing and talking easily about our personal lives and the events swirling around us. We are so fortunate to have made such an eminent friend.

God Bless the Child Who's Got Her Own

"I was born in Vicksburg, Mississippi in 1902. I grew up with six brothers. We were all different shades, as many blacks are, because my mother's father was a Frenchman and her mother was part Indian and African. The oldest one, my mother's first-born, Joseph, who was very fair-skinned, just disappeared, before I was born when he was nineteen. We never were able to trace him. Mama grieved about him. I don't think he would have left her voluntarily. She felt that if nothing had happened to him, she would have heard from him. She felt that some violence had happened somewhere and he couldn't communicate with her one way or the other. Mama never quite got over it. It is hard for a mother to take when a child just disappears. That was about the time that my father and mother began to talk about moving to California. And yet the area was very agreeable outwardly, to us as a family. The next brother, Alonzo, who was six feet four and had light red hair and freckles, became a brick-mason. He married and then went to St. Louis where Negroes lived a little better. They endured less open hostility from the whites than we had to endure in Mississippi. He never came back to live.

We owned our own home, as far back as I can remember. There were six of us born in the house. My father bought the land out there and built our house when the area was just a wilderness. My father, apparently, knew good spots of property. He was good at judging land values. Some of my older brothers helped him build it. As the family got larger he'd add another room. He was never quite satisfied with the house. He added a wing to it so that the dining room and the kitchen would be together. It became very valuable property because the town moved out in that direction; it became a part of suburbia.

I had contact, from early childhood, with whites. Our neighbors, when I was a little girl, were all white. I was used to white people, not like the people who were isolated. In the South, as prejudiced as they are, in some parts the whites don't mind the blacks living around them as much as they do in some of the Northern states. Also, my mother and father were very well-respected in Vicksburg so I never had any problems. I recognized there was a difference very early [between black and white]. When the adults would talk about something that was happening, I would say, "Why don't Negroes do something about it? They should fight it." It was a long time before I realized what my brothers meant when they said, "How are you going to fight it? You have a rake and a hoe and the white man has the ammunition."

My mother and father both had Indian blood, Choctaw, if I remember right. There were Indians who lived not far from our place in Vicksburg. There were two or three who used to visit, come by the house.

My mother was a staunch member of Wesley Methodist Church and most of my associates, naturally, were youngsters who attended that Sunday School. There was one little girl in our immediate neighborhood with whom Mama would let me play. She played with me only when my brothers were not there. She was older than I was and she thought I was just a dumb kid. She told me everything because I was so dumb. The parents of the other kids in the vicinity were a little rough. There was little of value, as I see it now, that I could learn in contact with them. Their home-life was such that Mama didn't feel it was desirable for my brothers or me to visit them in their homes. I think there are character differences in all races. My mother was very strict about those with whom we associated. Mama didn't discriminate where the children were concerned, unless the children used bad language or something like that. Mama was very strict on our playmates. Both the whites and the blacks would let their children come to our yard and play because they knew that Mama wouldn't permit anything but the best behavior. The kids weren't allowed to come back and play if they didn't behave properly. She'd manage to have something for us to eat. If it came to mealtime and there were other children there, she always stretched the meal enough to include them. She did the same with older people. I did have some friends, but they all lived in another area.

Where we lived was considered in the country so my brothers were supposed to go miles to the County school where they paid teachers two and three dollars a month. Papa and Mama would not send us to them. "We can keep you at home and teach you as much as you could learn there." Not until the Mayor of Vicksburg moved across the street from us did they put our area within the City limits. Eventually all four of us went to this private school. Mrs. Bell, a black woman who had graduated from Oberlin[27]. in Ohio, moved to Vicksburg and started a private school. She was rather prepared and a strict disciplinarian. My mother took my brothers out of the public school. I don't know how my mother dug up the money to pay Mrs. Bell.

My brother Sam was my favorite at that time, because he would take me on his lap and I would say, "I want to read in your book, what you had today." That's what accelerated me when I went to school. I would do the multiplication tables with him and that sort of thing. When I went to Ms. Bell's school she brought out a primer for me. I said, "I read that a long time ago. I'm reading Sam's book." Sam was in the fifth grade. She produced this fifth grade reader and I read it for her. I must have been an awful show-off. I said, "And I know my times tables up to twelve!" She let me start at the fifth grade so that's how I happened to finish so early.

My mother and father were largely self-educated. They loved to read. My father was very good in mathematics. He helped us a great deal with math when I was going to private school.[28]

---

[27] Oberlin, founded in 1833, was the first college to adopt co-education and in 1835 admitted students "without respect to color". Strong anti-slavery sentiments and activities prevailed at Oberlin.

[28] "My father was born in Alabama. My grandmother helped him to escape so as not to be enslaved. (Even when we went down to Mississippi in the 1930's, there were black people living on plantations who didn't know they could move. They never got enough money to go very far from home and the plantation owners kept them in debt. It was a form of enslavement.) When I think back on

Papa had a farm down in Warren County where there
were seven families who worked for him. He owned some of
the land and leased some of the land from a white woman,

---

that, it must have been pretty rough on my grandmother to have to give
up this child. He went to Monroe, Louisiana and I think he went to
New Orleans from there. He met my mother in New Orleans and
they were married. Mama's father, a Frenchman, protected his two
children. When my aunt was born, my grandmother died in childbirth.
I never knew my grandmother. How I happened to know about it, I
resented my aunt calling Mama, her mama. She used to do it to tease
me a great deal. As I grew older I asked her why. She said, "She's the
only mother I ever knew." Later I learned that my grandfather, upon
the death of my grandmother, brought this white woman to the house.
She was examining what he had to offer, I imagine. Mama had one pin
of her mother's that she held onto. This woman came in and was
looking over all of the jewelry, then Mama was sent out of the room.
She did stay long enough to hear this woman say to my
grandfather,"What am I supposed to do about these two brats?" He
said, "I guess we could send them to the Sisters." (Meaning the Catholic
people.) The black woman who worked there told Mama that they
were going to be shipped to an institution. These servants helped hide
Mama and Auntie in the black community. There was a part of New
Orleans that whites never entered. They used to call it South of Rampart
Street. I guess he was relieved. He went on and married. You see
during my generation children didn't question their parents as
children do now. A lot of things we overheard when they were discussing
them and didn't know we were anywhere around. You didn't ask
anything. Mama and Papa always wanted us to feel free. They wanted
to shake the notion of slavery. They didn't teach us to fight but they
always wanted us to feel that there was nobody our superior because of
race. We were taught to feel that if got an education and had self-
respect, that we would gain the respect of other people and we could go
ahead. When I think of my mother and what she must have endured
and when I think of her having the courage to leave the South when she
did and come to California and start all over."

Mrs. Nicholson. These seven families produced the cotton—that's all they had in Mississippi. Papa had a produce farm. We got all of our vegetables from down there. He had a wagon, two or three horses, and one mule, so he traveled back and forth. He was a carpenter so he didn't depend entirely on the results of the plantation, 'cause I guess we would have starved to death. During the early planting season he'd go down to the farm and then the rest of the year he'd do carpentry work, house-building and what-not.

We were well-fed and well-clothed. Mama could concoct a good meal out of very little. I've been experimenting with some vegetable combinations lately, trying to get them to taste like the things Mama fixed. During my early years she sewed for me, and in my teens she had a couple of dressmakers who made my clothing. Naturally my parents favored me as the only girl.

Each of my brothers got jobs after school. My brother Emmett was my bestfriend among the boys. He created a job for himself. We lived in what became suburbia. He got to know all the wealthy white people who lived out there. He sold them the idea by saying, "Wouldn't it be nice if you came in and all you had to do was light the fire in your fireplace?"They had fireplaces in bedrooms and no central heating. For twenty-five cents a week he laid the fire. He had customers up and down, so as soon as school was out he would start building these fires.

When I was ten my father fell from a truck. It was harvest time. He was bringing in the hay for the livestock for the winter. The doctor didn't know whether he had a sunstroke and fell off the wagon load of hay or whether he tripped getting off and fell and injured his head. He never regained consciousness. He was alive and breathing for two weeks. I had been trying to sit up with my brothers at his bedside. We'd take turns sleeping. Finally, just before he passed, he said, "Baby". My brothers blamed me. They said if I would have been there he would have said more. But I got tired—a ten year-old can stand it just so long. I blamed myself for a long time, till it occurred to me that I couldn't endure what they were enduring. Several months passed since his death when he appeared in the doorway. I remember getting up and telling Mama that I had seen Papa. He appeared to me so clearly. I don't recall him saying anything. I suppose it was a dream.

Mama said he worked himself to death just to keep ahead. Negroes got very little from their insurance, but he belonged to the Knights of Pythias, the Masons and the Elks. When Mama collected the little insurance each member is assured, that's what she had, and the little that my brothers earned. My mother must have been an unusual person because when my brothers went to work they brought their money home to her and let her use it as she saw fit. They said they wanted to pay for sister's education so I could go as far as I wanted to go. We owned our own home and my father owned some land. That was possibly how she was able to provide for me.

Mama said he spoiled me, but I was always glad when he came home when I'd been promised a whipping. I knew I wouldn't get the whipping. I'd be hard to find until Papa came, then I'd come in and tell Mama, "I see Papa's wagon coming down the hill." Then I showed up. Saved. (*Laughs*)

"Fertile Imagination"
"Most of the whippings I got as a child were because I had a very fertile imagination. I would embellish things the way I thought they should be. If there was a dog in the yard I was as apt to say it was a bear or whatever I felt would make the greatest impression. Mama saw she had to straighten that out. She didn't realize that some of the things I said were because I read a great deal and I imagined a lot. I guess I was a pain in the neck as a child when I think back on it. I must have been a very opinionated young person. I remember the discussions at home. My brothers would say, "Sister, hush and let somebody talk who knows what they're talking about." Papa

said, "Let her have her say. What did you say, Baby?" So I'd come on with my opinion. Later my brother, William, named me Emma Goldman.[29] She certainly worked for the women's cause.

I thought it over at a very early age. The thing I wanted to do was to be a lawyer. I thought if black lawyers, Negro lawyers then, if they had the backbone, this was my childish thinking, they would fight the white man and if they had to give up their lives, what difference—they were fighting for their rights. I said, "I wouldn't take that kind of foolishness!" My brothers would say, "Sister, you don't know what you're talking about!"

I started teaching, in a way, at a very early age—eight or nine, because many of the elderly people in our neighborhood could neither read nor write. I became the neighborhood letter writer for many of the elderly people. They would bring their sons' letters to me to read to them. I remember one brought a letter for me to answer. She said, "You're the only person I'd ask to read it. I read it to her. She just beamed when he said, "Remember Mother, I love you. She said, "Answer it for me." I said, "Now what do you wish to tell him?" She said, "You just write the letter. Well, give him my love." I said, "What else do you want me to say?" "Well, give him my love again." That was her contribution to the letter. Of course I couldn't laugh at her, but I was just choking with laughter. Mama would have punished me if I had laughed in her face. I asked her, "When your boy left, were you living in

---

[29]   Emma Goldman, who, in the early 1900's, advocated such radical causes as birth control, as well as the entire spectrum of women's rights, international peace, free speech and many other causes, did time in jail for being an anarchist and general disturber of the status quo and eventually was deported to Russia in 1919. For more information on this remarkable feminist, who had enough heart and chutzpa for her entire generation, see Candace Falk's biography, *Love, Anarchy and Emma Goldman.*

Legg's Quarters?"[30] She said,"No, I had a house and my husband was living there, but the rent was more than I could pay so I moved to the Quarters." I went on to tell her son that any help he could send would be greatly appreciated and that sort of thing. I had to compose the letter. There were four or five of them who came to me, each one knowing each other but not letting on that they couldn't write or read.

I'll never forget that. I also taught them the alphabet and how to spell and write their name. I told them they had to learn the ABC's before they could learn to write, so I wrote that out for them, pronounced it, and went over it each time. They were so pleased when they could write their name.

Vicksburg was the one place in Mississippi that blacks had a decent high school, because the Principal of Magnolia Avenue High School had graduated from Alcorn College, which is the oldest land grant college for blacks in Mississippi. We had to go to Cherry Street High School for our senior year which was quite a distance from my home. It was more than a mile and we walked. We dare not be late, from both ends—the school and my parents. It was worse on my parents' end.

The principals of each school were college graduates with the result they made us acquainted with the leading writers. We had to do a Shakespeare play to pass our English class in the junior and senior years. Whether you performed it or not, you had to read Shakespeare. We did *Othello* in my senior year and *As You Like It* in the junior year. I finished Cherry Street High School in June of the year I was thirteen.

When October came I went to boarding school, at Rust College in Holly Springs, Mississippi. Unfortunately, I say now

---

[30] "This is where people of very limited means and education lived. They couldn't afford anything better. The owner of the land was named Leggs. He owned these little "shot-gun" houses and rented them to blacks.This could be described as the rural ghetto. Some quarters are actually the living quarters for the workers on a particular plantation."

when I know better, but I thought it was wonderful then, my mother let me choose the college I wanted. Most of my playmates and kids I knew were going to Rust College. We belonged to Wesley Methodist Episcopal Church (now it's United Methodist Church) at that time. Rust was sold to the Church as a freedmen's school. They had long ago stopped any freedmen's aid to the schools before we got there, but it was one of those. It started the same year the University of California did, 1868.[31]

My father had planned for my youngest brother and me to go North to school, out of the South. I don't know where he was going to send us but that was his plan. If he hadn't died, I wouldn't have gone to Rust, because he was anxious to get us out of Mississippi.[32]

---

[31]   "Rust College was a school for Negroes but predominately white teachers. They were supposed to be missionaries from the Methodist Church but we soon learned that they were people who couldn't get jobs in their locale and decided to come down and 'help' the Negroes. They told us they were doing missionary work, but they looked forward to their salary just as I looked forward to mine when I started to teach. It's quite a facility now. They gave me an honorary doctorate in 1983 when I was commencement speaker."
The Freedman's Bureau, established in 1865 by the U.S. Congress, created a network of 'freedmen's' schools and colleges throughout the South. By the time the educational work of the Bureau was terminated in 1870, 4,329 educational facilities had been founded.

[32]   No wonder Mr. Jackson wanted to leave the South. Before Ida was born, the Jackson's lived in Louisiana where the following event took place: "My father owned some land which he leased to a white man. This land later became part of the downtown area of Monroe, Louisiana. It was not developed. Then the city fathers moved out in that area and it became very valuable land. This man, to whom Papa had leased the land, had a crop on it. When the lease was up he claimed that Papa had sold him the land. Papa took him to court. He used a white lawyer from the North who took the case and won it. They were all white around where Papa owned this land where they were living—he and Mama

Mama and he always talked about California. They decided they were going to California for the opportunities it offered the children.[33]

---

and my three older brothers. After Papa won the case a posse formed. The neighboring farmer was white; his wife put on a bonnet, so they would think she was just one of the blacks, and came through the cornfield to warn Mama that a posse was forming around the courthouse to lynch my father and to get out of town as quickly as they could. She said,'Don't bother about anything. My husband sent me word to get word to you." Mama threw what she could in the wagon and Papa followed on a horse. There was a barge which went from the Louisiana side to the Mississippi side; Mama got there in time to put the wagon on the barge. Just as it was leaving Papa came on the horse. They weren't too far out to see and hear the posse. They held up a rope and told him ten years wouldn't be too long and dared him to come back. So he had to leave this land. He gave the tax papers to a white law firm to hold for him until he was settled. They were called Thames & Thames. In 1925, when I was visiting in Mississippi Mama and I went over to Monroe. I wanted to see this land. There was nothing on it but an old Italian vegetable man with his cart. I asked him why the city had left this vacant lot. He said,"They say this land is owned by an old colored man. They think he's dead, but he may have heirs so they can't give anybody clear title to buy it."We went to the law firm that had the papers so we could claim it, pay whatever back taxes. The lawyer told Mama he had them but they were in the safe and his partner had the key to the safe. She should send me back the next day. Mama said, "We've lived this long without any income from the land so we'll just forget it. I'm not going to jeopardize your life."We caught the first train out of Louisiana back to Vicksburg."

[33]   "They also were planning to come out to California because of the gold. I guess he thought it was still available. He saw an ad in the paper for a divining rod which would locate metal. It was commonly believed that during the time of the Civil War, Southerners had buried their treasures when the attack was made on Vicksburg. So Papa got this divining rod and it went off over these spots so [he and his friend] thought they had gold. I asked Papa why all those big metal cannonballs were piled up on the hill in our backyard." (Laughs)

They read everything they could find about California. A black man has a difficult time in the South. That's why they wanted to get my brothers out of the South as quickly as they could. They wanted them to grow to manhood and be respected as men.

At Rust I was just taking over and over the same things I had in high school, so I became quite a problem child. I had the kind of rearing that wasn't appreciated by the teachers at Rust College. They said I was too immature to let me go into the college department. I resented that. Now they recognize ability in kids who excel. I just think what I may have been had I been allowed to enter the college department. It just did something inside me. I became a problem. I'd ask some crazy question, something that would annoy the teacher. I was a showoff, as I think back on it now. I had nothing to challenge me. I knew what they were teaching the other kids.

I think that's why I get along with young people. There's a period one goes through when one is rebellious of everything. I spent a lot of time in the 'study hall' after school by myself because I talked so much. Also they said I was a leader of mischief. I wasn't trying to cause trouble.

Cedella, a very solemn, lady-like, God-fearing young woman, who did no wrong, always told me funny jokes. She was so pious and well-behaved they didn't think she had a comical side, which I seemed to bring out. I was put to room with her because she would be such a good influence on me. She'd say, "I'll tell you this story if you promise not to laugh. That would make me more amused. I would try to keep from laughing out loud because we were supposed to be asleep at nine o'clock. Trying to suppress the laughter, the rest of your body shakes. When I'd laugh the slats would fall out of the bed. Then all the kids in the dormitory would start laughing—"Ida's bed broke down!" We'd hear the keys rattling as the Dean was on her way. Since the slats had fallen off our bed, she felt I was the instigator of the trouble. I was to report to the study hall tomorrow after school. I spent many days in there. Cedella went to the Dean and said, "Ida isn't responsible for the bed falling. We ought to have a different bed." I guess they had those beds since the year one. I wouldn't tell on Cedella because I enjoyed her stories. You know how loyal kids can be when they make up their minds.

My time wasn't consumed in studying, yet I made good grades. It was due to the high school training I had. I was bored stiff. They sent me from chapel because I would be talking. It was a religious school—a little too religious for me.

Mama and my brothers pooled their resources and sent me a box every month. Everybody looked forward to my box when it came. It would always have a cake in it, some foodstuffs, some clothes. The kids shared the food. When you're in boarding school it seems to me you're always hungry!

I had an abscessed tooth. I wrote Mama a letter, that the dentist said he would have to operate to extract my tooth. He would have to go in from the outside. Oh, I manufactured it! When I told one, it was a big one! Mama spoke to our dentist about it. He said, "Mrs. Jackson, that man must be crazy!" The tooth business got me back home. I knew when I told Mama there would have to be an operation she would let me come home because of what happened to my brother, Alonzo when he came home for a visit. He became ill. Our family doctor said he should be operated on. They would not let him be operated on in the hospital. He had to be operated on at home. I remember all these doctors standing around the bed. It was sure death. There was no negro hospital; they weren't allowed to have operations in the white and only hospital. He died as a result of that operation. I stayed home about two weeks. I was enjoying myself. Mama said, "Baby, when are you going back to school? Your tooth is all right now." I said, "I don't want to go back to Rust College." She said, "What? Get your things ready. You chose it and you're going back there and finish the semester." She ruled the roost, so I started packing.

While I was at home with this tooth they changed the Dean at Rust because all of the kids were dissatisfied with her. They were striking and that sort of thing. She just despised black people.

At the end of that year Mama let me transfer to New Orleans University because she knew she was going to California. I didn't know. I graduated from New Orleans University, now Dillard

University, with a diploma from the normal department and a certificate in foods and clothing.[34] I enjoyed my experience there. It was quite a change. Rust was isolated in this country town and N.O.U. was in New Orleans. It was much superior.

New Orleans was Mama's birthplace. Periodically she went to see my aunt, who was a marvelous cook. She liked French food and she kept a good supply of it. I was always ready to go down to Carnival. We went to Mardi Gras from the time I was a little kid. I was glad of the occasion because it meant getting the train going somewhere. It was a festive occasion among blacks as well as whites. They had their separate activities. Even then I didn't want to live there, but it was a darn sight better than anyplace in Mississippi.

My brother Emmett and my mother are responsible for whatever I have by way of education. They started me out with whatever funds were available. Emmett said,"I think we ought to support sister and Mama."They wouldn't let Mama go out and work. They said they would provide her with enough money so she could stay at home and look after the 'baby'.

Mama sent William, first, to my aunt in New Orleans.[35] She had always told Mama to send some of the children to live

---

[34] The normal department was strictly for people who were preparing to teach. At this particular college it was a two-year course above the high school level. It would be the equivalent of an A.A. degree from a community college today.

[35] "He got a job as a cook at Tranchini's, a famous New Orleans restaurant. My brothers learned to cook from my mother. He was only fifteen or sixteen, but he was tall so they hired him. The mother of the owner, Mama Tranchini, said to William, "You're just a boy; you're no cook. How old are you?" William told her, "I'm a man. I know how to cook. Just give me a chance." She said, "Tell Mama Tranchini the truth. Have you ever had a job cooking?" He said, "No." She said, "At least you're honest. So Mama Tranchini will help you. When he gives the order, you say it out loud. You're supposed to repeat the order. I will hear it and I'll help you fix it or I'll start it for you. I'm dago's mama, now I'm nigger's mama— everybody's mama." So he called her Mama Tranchini."

with her. We didn't have a telephone. Mama got all excited when the neighbor told her there was somebody calling long distance. Mama just knew it was something serious. It was William calling her on Mrs. Johnson's phone. They had a telephone because her husband was a fireman on the railroad when they had coal-burning engines. That was the best job a black man could get—feeding the furnace on the train engines. They were considered prominent because he got a good salary for this laborious task. We received our messages there whenever anyone telephoned. I guess this was about the first call Mama had. She thinks William has gotten into trouble with Auntie. He said, "Don't worry. I'm in California. I called to tell you I'm going to send for you to come to California. Sister can get a better education here, free, than you were paying for her to go to Rust College.

I guess he had getting away in mind before he got to New Orleans. He may not have ever intended to stay long with my aunt. After working at Tranchini's for two weeks, he got a job as a waiter on the Southern Pacific Railroad. He got a run from New Orleans to California. He took advantage of that to get out of the South. Mama would have had a fit if she had known he was leaving on his own, although California was the place she had intended to go so that all of us should have a better chance at an education.

In Vicksburg the Mayor lived across the street from us. He spent time talking to Mama, trying to persuade her not to come to California. He said,"Your daughter has an education and she can get any job she wants teaching in the [black] City school system, from the principal on down." Mama thanked him and said she would think it over, but she came back in and continued to pack. There were no other white children for his three daughters to play with for miles around when I was growing up; consequently his daughters came over in our yard to play. We had no feeling of bias. We didn't come up with the feeling that whites were any different than us. Only as we grew older were we made aware of the intense racial barrier. Mama shipped each brother out of the South because of the fact they had these white children as playmates.[36]

California!

"Mama wrote to me about a week before time to leave New Orleans and told me to get ready, we were moving to California! We moved to California in February of 1918. She told my brothers we had to have our own home and we weren't going to rent rooms from other people. My brothers had high regard for her, as well as for each other. They worked together as a unit with Mama steering them. As I grow older I realize how much courage she must have had and how farsighted she was. After we came out, James got a job with the Santa Fe as a car repairman and William was a waiter on the railroad. They pooled their resources. James, after he married, lived apart from us but all the other brothers lived at home with Mama.

There were two black families from Vicksburg out here then that Mama knew. I went to visit them. I graduated from Cherry Street High School at the same time as one of the daughters. She said, "Now that you're in California, what are you going to do with all of your education?" I said, "I'm going to teach school." She almost went into hysterics. She said, "The day

---

[36] Ida's parents had every reason to fear for the safety of their children. According to statistics gathered by the NAACP, 3,442 blacks were lynched, five out of six occurring in the South, from 1882 to 1962. In the year that Ida and her family moved to California, 58 blacks were lynched! In 1919 the NAACP held a national conference on lynching and for many years attempted to secure federal legislation to prevent lynching which continually was defeated by Southern politicians. As a teenager, growing up in the safety of small-town, white, middle class Ohio in 1955, I remember being shocked by the murder of Emmett Till, another teenager who was visiting relatives in the Mississippi delta. He was lynched for allegedly making eyes at a white woman on the street. Lynching is not merely an aberration of the distant past.

you apply to teach school, the *Oakland Tribune* is going to come out with 'Burly Negress Applies for Position in the Oakland Public Schools'."That made me so mad! She was being sarcastic. She was portraying the way the *Tribune* would present it. The *Tribune* printed some pretty offensive remarks during this period. The owner was very much a racist. They would print anything they'd want to that was unflattering about blacks. I got the trolley and asked the conductor where the Board of Education offices were. When I got there I asked to see the County Superintendent, Mr. Martin, who said,"Sure, you can have an application blank but you're rather young to teach, aren't you?" I said,"Oh no, I have a diploma and a certificate." He said, "You are eminently qualified for the elementary school. I'll give you an application but have you ever thought about [furthering] your education by going to the University of California? You wouldn't have to pay for it. Of course school has been going on for some time now, but you may be able to get in. Why don't you go up there and look it over? Have you ever been to the campus?" I said, "No, we just arrived about ten days ago."While I was talking with him, it seemed that everybody in his office came to look over this black specimen who had the nerve to ask for an application to teach in the Oakland public schools.

When I was leaving the County superintendent's office I looked on the bulletin board and there was an announcement for a Civil Service examination. Prior to that time they weren't hiring women at the Post Office, but now women who passed the examination also would have an opportunity at the job. I took the examination and came out number 13. During that time the Postmaster General of the area decided on whom they would hire. He told me the only opening they had was at night in the San Francisco Post Office. He thought I wouldn't be interested in that because I would have to go to work at 4:30 and work until 11:30 at night. I said, "That's just what I want." At that time I had to be in the house at dark. This night work sounded great to me.

The branch post office where I was working was down on the Embarcadero, a long block from where the ferry docked. I talked to the supervisor about coming to work a little early so that I could leave 15 minutes early. I was willing to come in at 3:00 and give them an hour's work if they would let me off 15 minutes early. He was a nice person. He said, "The 15 minutes is all right." I decided I would come early anyway and put in the 15 minutes. The first few weeks I did not leave as early as I had originally intended. The man who put down the gangplank would stall around, loosen the chain and what-not, delaying it while I'm running up the street. He said, "You barely made it!" It's things like that make you know there are people who care. People are not all alike. One should not lump any race of people together and say, this is the behavior of the race.

I worked at the Ferry Post Office five months and twenty-nine days. If I had worked six months they would have been required to keep me as a clerk. Two other women, both of whom were white, and I worked at night. But they told us they were dismissing all women because the men were returning from the Service at the end of World War I and they had priority for the jobs."

CAL

"I filed an application to teach in the Oakland public schools, then the next day I went up to the University of California campus. A friend of mine whom I had known at N.O.U. was going to the University. He took me over to the campus in his little Model A Ford and showed me around. We went to the registration office—California Hall. The Registrar (whose name I've forgotten now, but I remembered it a long time) said, "It's a little late but I'll let you register anyway, provided you can get signed up for ten units. This is March and I don't think you can make passing grades at this time even if they let you in the courses." My friend, Alvin, said, "Come on, I'll bet old Kroeber will sign you up in anthropology." I'd never heard of anthropology before. Sure enough, he did permit me to register. Alvin said, "Now since you have a diploma from the normal department you should major in Education." I ended up with thirteen units. When I went back to the Registrar he said, "I think it would be unwise for you to try to carry thirteen units, coming in this late, and these are heavy courses. You're not used to the campus so I'd advise you to sign up for ten." As time went on, I discovered he was smarter than I gave him credit for being because it was all I could do to handle that ten units, but I did come out of it with good enough grades to let me go on and take upper division courses. I got my B.A. in two years and then my Master's the next year.

When I went to the University my brothers still said, "Sister, we will support you, as long as you want to study because you've done well and some one of us has to have an education." Mama said, "It's only normal that a girl would want to marry at some time. I hope you will marry. When you get ready to date, then you will have to be on your own because boys and books don't mix. Your brothers and I are willing for you to go to school." I know now she was sacrificing but I didn't pay much attention to where the money came from then.

When I think about it, my mother was a very determined person. She came out to California so I would have a better opportunity for an education. She was very strict, but very loving—not the kind that was demonstrative, but she was always there when you needed her. As long as she lived, and even when my brothers were married, there wasn't a day went by that she didn't see all of her children. They were very loyal to her. One brother worked in Richmond and he arranged to come see Mama every day before he went home. We were a very close-knit family. I stayed with Mama until she passed. Now most parents don't seem to expect anything of their children. I think my mother deserves a lot of credit handling the family.

After a midterm I said, "Mama, I made a C+." She said, "Hmm-mmm. That's pretty good." I said, "Mama, you don't realize what it means to make a C+ in Econ. 1A." She said, "It seems to me you could have made a B- or a B." That kept me trying.

At the time I started at UC there were eight black students—
five men and three women. Then the next semester there were
eight women. Having come from an all-black school, where
there were clubs of many kinds on campus, I suggested that we
form a club. We did form the Alpha Pi Club. Mr. Butler, the
man who built my house, was the head of the NAACP branch
for the Bay area. He thought it was wonderful that so many
were going to the University. One of the great things that
happened to us was to get our picture in *The Crisis*, the magazine
of the NAACP. That was the thing to do then. You had 'arrived'
when *The Crisis* recognized you. I had heard about Alpha Kappa
Alpha sorority, about some of the distinguished women who
belonged to it. We decided to try to organize a chapter. All of
us black women who were on the campus were meeting
continually. It required getting the Dean of Women's signature
on the Alpha Kappa Alpha application. Dean Stebbins didn't
know any black women were on the campus at the time. Part of
the group wanted to apply for affiliation with another sorority.
Dean Stebbins said, "There are so few of you; why don't you all
become members of the same organization?" One of the three
of us said, "All the white girls don't belong to one sorority.
There won't always be just a few of us on the campus; other
colored girls will be attending." She put us on probation for a
semester and said if we made a 'C' average, then she would
possibly sign for us to have a chapter.

Mama had a large home where the group could dance and
have their social affairs. We decided we'd all study together for
our finals. We were scattered all over the dining room and
living room. Mama kept us supplied with coffee and sandwiches.
We came up with a 'B-minus' average and the Dean allowed us
to form a chapter.

At first we were invited, as were all sororities, into the
Women's Council. At that time the student body, the
Associated Students, just about ran the campus. The main
thing was to be a member of the A.S.U.C. (Associated
Students of University of California). When we were

recognized by the campus we were invited to send a representative to the Women's Council. I sat in on that for two semesters. Virginia Stevens, who became the first black woman to pass the California Bar, succeeded me. She didn't care to attend. She said they were too snobbish. I participated in whatever was going on because of curiosity. I wanted to know what was going on. I wanted to know all parts of the University. I was curious about how the other man did things. There was no way to learn if you were outside. Being a part of the Women's Council naturally I learned what the student body was doing.

I don't think we thought of it at that time as segregation. We were content and accustomed to being together. All the fraternities and sororities were listed with pictures in the *Blue and Gold*, the yearbook published by the student government. It cost forty-five dollars a page. That was a great deal of money at that time. My brother, Emmett, lent us the $45 to have our pictures made. We applied and were given a time to go to the photographer. When it was announced that B&G was on sale we rushed over to Stevens Union to get a copy. Imagine our surprise when our picture wasn't in there. They had kept the money and they hadn't told us they were going to refuse our picture. We were quite crestfallen. We went to Dean Stebbins. She said she had nothing to do with it and couldn't help us at all. We went from the Dean to President Barrows. He said, "All I can tell you is you don't represent the students." That was a slap in the face. We never quite forgot that. We kept after them until they finally did return our forty-five dollars the next year. But they never did print our pictures. [37]

---

[37] "Most of my friends now are people who were members of the sorority (Alpha Kappa Alpha)." Ida attended the Alpha Kappa Alpha national convention in Hawaii. She served on the housing committee which is in process raised funds to buy a house for the UC Berkeley chapter.

Something like that does something to a young person. We had come to California believing in the equality of opportunity. We were taught that behavior counted, character counted, that, plus education, would help black people to achieve equality of opportunity. It's always disturbed me. I felt that an educated white person was above petty prejudices. That's been a rude awakening. I learned very early that people are what they are, and education doesn't eliminate prejudice. This is a broad, sweeping statement, but I think the average white feels that just his whiteness is enough to make him superior. I was taught to believe that education was the thing we needed. My folks felt that the racial situation would be solved as more and more people became educated—blacks and even the poor whites. But that isn't true.

At CAL, PE [physical education] was mandatory. I signed up for swimming. We had been refused swimming privileges at the YWCA pool. When the Hearst gymnasium burned on campus the YWCA invited CAL to use their pool. My friend Virginia said, "Maybe they'll let us swim if we come just before they clean the pool." They didn't permit us to do that. Harry Kingman, head of the YMCA in San Francisco (I met him at CAL and he was a very fine person), was very upset that they didn't let us swim. He said, "Why don't you come over and use the pool in San Francisco?" We neither had the money for transportation, and then the distance, but I've always remembered that as a very nice gesture. It made us feel better about the racial situation.[38]

---

[38] "I remember when I was teaching, one of the women on the staff told her class the reason that colored people didn't know how to swim is they had an Achilles heel. I made it a point to ask her, Did the moccasins cause Achilles heels? What you don't know is that colored kids can only swim in the ditches or the gutters or the swamplands and often they had to compete with the moccasins. Maybe that caused the Achilles heels. But it wasn't because they were born with any different heels than you have. I felt better for having told her."

[*As a result of this incident, Ida helped organize a branch of the YWCA for black women in Oakland.*] The national YWCA had one black secretary who traveled for the YWCA. I heard her speak and got in touch with her. I told her we wanted a YWCA.

I was majoring in education and specializing in vocational education. Dr. Brightweiser was in the department of Education and helped me choose the subject on which I would write my Master's thesis. He acted in the capacity of a thesis advisor and was on the committee for my Master's degree. He was somebody with whom I could talk; he encouraged me. He was interested in the racial situation. There was always a group of students waiting to talk to the professors and none of them ever had time for me, other than he and Dr. Lee, the head of the Vocational Education Department. Dr. Brightweiser treated me as he would any other student and that was all I wanted. Dr. Brightweiser left CAL and went to South Dakota, right after I completed my Masters. I have often wondered if there were any connection.

My thesis concerned the development of Negro children in relation to education. What prompted me to write on the subject was at that time the general opinion of educators was that the average mentality of Negroes did not exceed the mental age of fifteen as compared to white children. I resented that. I knew it wasn't true because they didn't give any scientifically prepared data to support it. We didn't have the civil rights movement then. We didn't have the opportunities for an education in America. (I was fortunate. Negroes in Vicksburg had more of an opportunity than blacks anywhere in Mississippi to get an education. This was the exception.) I gave standard intelligence tests to every black child I could reach in the high schools of Oakland and Berkeley. I didn't find that the Negro was any different than the white in comparing test scores. I used the public school records as a comparison.

People had the idea years ago that they were no educated Negroes. I don't think anybody is really educated—that's the finished product. The educational process is a continuing deal.

You learn something new every day if you are alert and will allow yourself.

After I wrote my thesis, they sent it to the head of the Psychology Department to read. He left it on his desk. We had until May 19th—it was the last day your record could be accepted to get a degree that year. I went to the head of the Graduate Department and told them that my Master's thesis had not been read although I had submitted it before the deadline date. I had gone to this professor's office repeatedly and I noticed it had not moved from where we put it the day I left it there. He acknowledged that he did not read it because he didn't think it belonged in the Psychology Department. I was the victim and not responsible for that. I took it there because I was told to do so. The fellow who was heading the graduate students organization contacted me. Three of them were appointed to read my thesis. They read it and approved of it and assured me my degree would be issued and it would bear the year 1923. Although it was too late for me to participate in the graduation exercises, as receiving my Master's degree that year, my diploma would be dated 1923. The fellows who read my thesis were very adamant, very sympathetic. They said, "You have to promise us that you will participate in the graduation exercises next year." I did as they requested. I was curious. I wanted to know everything there was to be known about UC, Berkeley. I wanted to do everything that every other senior did. There were three black fellows graduating and two other black women. They didn't participate in any of the activities because of the racial attitude. I decided that I wanted to know what it was like so I didn't mind being alone. I'd been alone all along in everything I had ever done. I participated because I thought I would be cheating myself if I didn't. I've never regretted it.

I earned twenty-eight points above my Masters at Cal. I needed thirty points to earn a Ph.D. At that time the dissertation was worth two points. But in my case no professor offered to sponsor me as I wrote my dissertation. I had one tell me that they were not ready for a black woman to get a Ph.D.

I thought I would be able to find a sponsor at Columbia University. All of my advanced work had been done at the University of California. I wanted to study at an Eastern college to see what it was like and have the benefit of the experience of working with outstanding scholars. Columbia was the greatest center for teachers. I earned 28 points there, but no one in the department offered to be my sponsor."

"You Have to Be Carefully Taught".[39]
"After I graduated from CAL I registered with the Employment Department for a job.[40] I went to El Centro, first, to teach. The Mexicans and blacks, up to that time, had no children eligible to attend high school. They stopped at the eighth grade.

The Principal there had three or four children who wanted to go on to high school and college. Children from all the small towns in the Imperial Valley came to El Centro to Central Union High School, but they did not admit blacks and Mexicans. They sent over white teachers to teach in Eastside High School. The Mexicans and blacks got together. "If we can't go to the white school, then white teachers can't come over here to teach." They just didn't send the kids to school. Will Wood, who was the State Superintendent, called the University of California and asked if they knew of any colored

---

[39]   A song from Rodgers's and Hammerstein's 1949 musical, *South Pacific* : "You have to be taught before it's too late/Before you are six or seven or eight/To hate all the people your relatives hate/ You have to be carefully taught"

[40]   To insure that Ida was hired as a teacher, Walter Butler, who headed the NAACP in the Oakland area, called Rabbi Coffey, an influential member of the Oakland community, and asked him to contact the Board of Education regarding Ida. Mr. Butler sent a copy of her transcript to Rabbi Coffey, who in turn, told the Board that if Ida was not given a chance to teach, the votes of the black and Jewish communities would tell the story at the ballot box. Ida did not know about this behind the scenes maneuvering at the time.

person, woman preferably, prepared to teach in the high school. Somebody in the office remembered that I had been in and left my transcript. He called and told me there was an opening at Eastside High School where I would be asked to teach English and foods. Then later, they added physical education to it. That's what I get for having a general secondary teaching certificate. I had a credential in foods and clothing which I got in New Orleans and I had majored in English, so I did have the qualifications which enabled me to get this general secondary certificate. I ended up teaching a lot of different subjects.

The teaching assignment at El Centro was quite a challenge. I started out by wanting to know the families and background so I visited them. El Centro was a small town at that time. I got a chance to meet the Mexican and Negro families and see how they were living. This gave me the backing of the fami-lies. They liked the fact that I wanted to meet them. I was doing it for my own benefit, so I would know what I was dealing with, and then it was my first experience—I guess I was curious.

I had a wonderful rapport, both with the families and the students. One or two came to live with me. One Mexican girl attended the University of California for a couple of years. Then her father, as was the custom with some Mexicans, found a husband for her sister, and that man had a brother, so he had Elvira come home so she could marry the brother. That interfered with her education, but she did go on and get her degree from UC after she married. But Josephine, who was by far the more brilliant one, stayed married and had seven or eight children.

Then I taught at Prescott Junior High School in Oakland. Most of the foreign-born who came to Oakland, as well as the blacks, started in West Oakland. The early settlers almost all started in West Oakland. Some of the most palatial homes in the early days were to be found in West Oakland, where the whites had lived. I know the foreign-born, the Yugoslavs, Czechoslavs, the Mexicans, various ones of Spanish and

Portuguese descent, all lived in West Oakland. The children went to school together, played together. It wasn't till students got to be maybe juniors and seniors in high school that the differences were emphasized.

There were no black teachers when I started, and it was thirteen years before they hired another. As I recall, the blacks were as surprised as the whites when I did teach. I took a teacher's place for sixth grade. The Superintendent had not told the Principal that I was black. I had come early as most new teachers do on the job. I went up to the desk and introduced myself to the secretary. I guess she thought I was one of the mothers. She said, "Just have a seat. I'll be with you in a few minutes." Finally the principal, George Mortensen, came out and said, "Will you call the Superintendent's office and let him know that the new teacher they assigned, Ida Jackson, hasn't shown up." I said, "Sir, I'm Ida Jackson. If you show me my classroom I can go. I've been here for more than an hour." There were some teachers signing in and the word soon spread that there was this colored woman saying she was a teacher. A group assembled, one telling another. They forgot the bell had rung for them to go their classes. The Principal was as shocked as the teachers were. He was stammering. He seemed to be at a loss for what to say, what to do. Finally he had someone show me where my classroom was, which was in one of the portables.

I was there to teach. I didn't expect anybody to come out and welcome me with open arms, yet I didn't expect any bad treatment. I just thought that I was a new teacher. I wasn't as conscious of racial animosity at that time as I learned later, because I expected that educators were different. They had a different standard of living and when someone had proved they were their equal educationally, that made a difference. But it never has.

There were two women who spoke to me. The rest were in groups discussing the matter. This group formed a committee to see the Superintendent of Schools. They doubled up classes in order to go down to the Superintendent's office. They wanted to know what he was going to do. Did he realize he'd sent a colored woman down there to teach? I was told that they said they wanted him to do something about it, because the white teachers weren't going to accept it. He asked his secretary to bring my file. He said, "I don't know how many of us have Normal diplomas from a college or university. She entered the University in 1918 and got her Bachelor's degree in 1920 and her Master's degree in 1923 and at the present time is continuing to study toward the Doctorate. I don't know if anyone else in the entire Department, including the Superintendent, has any better qualifications." He pacified them by letting them know that I was a long-term substitute and it would be up to them to take care of the situation, whether I was hired permanently or not. That satisfied them. As a result, the sixth grade class to which I had been assigned was taken away from me and I was given an ungraded class. Every teacher who had a 'problem child' of any age gave them to me.

Some of the pupils weren't actually behavior problems, but they didn't know the language. With one language spoken at home, they were trying to learn to speak English. (I always encouraged my students to accept their mother's tongue. It would be valuable later on. Of course many of them couldn't see it, but some told me in later years how valuable it was. Those who went on to college were glad they knew a second language.) We got along very well. Some of them became my good friends. Not too many years ago some one of them got all the Prescott students together and had a dinner for me. I was so surprised to see some of them, the positions they held. I remember one fellow said,"You were a good teacher, but you were strict—in fact, you were mean." I said, "Just think what you would have been if I hadn't been a mean teacher. [41] He burst into laughter as he left, saying,"Okay, you still win."

---

[41] One of my former students is a millionaire. Several went into the professions. One girl was studying law, but I don't know whether she finished.

When I began teaching, I didn't give the other teachers a chance to snub me. I brought my lunch and took the lunch hour to get myself ready for the afternoon classes. I prepared myself, because I had attended the University, which was 99 and 9/10% white. I was really interested in an education and now I was interested in helping other students realize the value of an education. One afternoon, not long after I started teaching, one of the teachers who taught in the portable classrooms, talked with me. When the teachers were meeting and going to protest, Albertine Smith was the one person who spoke up and said, "Why don't we give her a chance. We don't know what she can do. She has a right to have a chance." Albertine was a very popular, capable teacher and a native Californian. I really had a strong person in my corner. We became lifelong friends. She passed away about four years ago.

I enjoyed keeping the faculty guessing. I would come dressed for the affairs after school. Everybody would be worried all day about my coming to the affair. I never went. Finally, one or two of the teachers became friendly and invited me to go with them to the 'White House' (the administration building downtown). The women didn't invite me to join them at lunch time until after the men. All of the men were friendly. I used to eat regularly with them. I learned more. They talked about different things other than classroom matters. I enjoyed being with them. They were more friendly, especially at McClymonds High School. I told someone on the staff, knowing they would pass the word along, that my interest was in getting a job and dealing with children, but my social life was apart from my work. Teaching was a job and that was what I was there to do.

I had very few blacks in my first classes. Five was the maximum I had for several years. Most of the blacks had moved out of West Oakland. The foreign-born were largely in West Oakland at that time. Then suddenly they moved to the East Oakland areas. A white child could cross the line and go to any school they wanted to, but blacks, at that time, had to go to school in their district.

The trouble wasn't with the student body; by and large, youngsters accept each other for what they are. Prejudice is taught to children. It all depends on what age their parents start teaching them the difference. I enjoyed the students. From the very first day I was made welcome by three little Caucasian youngsters who brought me some flowers at the lunch hour and told me they liked me. That made my day. I never had any child show any resentment to me because of race. That's why I feel certain prejudice is taught. One black parent objected to me and one Portuguese mother objected to her son being in my class because I was black. I taught History, English, Drama, Public Speaking, Math—anything anybody else didn't want to teach. I stayed at Prescott for over twenty years when I was transferred to McClymonds.

I was told by former students that I was the most strict teacher they had. I was a very strict disciplinarian but I did enjoy the respect of all my students. Those who were bad in other classes, they were given to me. I had no trouble with them.

I think in order to succeed, a teacher has to understand that children have to have a certain amount of leeway. I always gave my students, not to their knowledge, a few minutes to cool off and then I would say, "Okay, you've had your say, not let me have mine."

I started out with credentials in administration. I applied for a principalship after I had taught two or three years, because I thought that there needed to be some changes in the school system and it had to come from the top people. I felt that if I got an administrative job, I'd be able to help bring about these changes. Most of the people with whom I worked had no degree at all. But the fact that I had my Bachelor's and Master's and was working for my Doctorate, the whole while I taught I was studying I was never able to get an administrative job. The nearest thing to it was a period they allowed me for counseling. One would have to acknowledge the racism. Especially when they had teachers who had never gone to college who were serving as supervisors. While my supervisor was a very nice person, she had no degree and yet she was supervisor. It was years before a black became a principal of a school.

I thought I would advance in administration and get a job as an administrator, if I were prepared. Although my brother Emmett said, "Sister, you're wasting time. At Oakland public schools, you'll never be anything but a teacher."

Dean of Women, Tuskegee Institute[42]

"I took a sabbatical in 1934. Dr. Frederick Patterson was president then of Tuskegee. He communicated with Dean Kemp at UC, Berkeley, asking him if he could name or recommend a woman graduate of UC who had the training to serve as Dean of Women at Tuskegee.

I got a year's extension on my sabbatical and went to Tuskegee as Dean of Women for a year. There the Dean of Women was ranked next to the President. They had not had a trained person as Dean of Women before my coming. Dr. Patterson realized that the Women's Department was lagging. There weren't too many black women then who went on to higher education. I started in by trying to remodel the Women's Department. I found that the head of the social committee on the staff was the Dean of Men. He was a product of Tuskegee. The social committee just ruled the social life of the campus. I came in making changes. When I visited the campus, I checked on all departments. Among the first things I did was to organize the student body and have the students play a bigger part on the campus. We drew up a constitution and by-laws for student government. The students were thrilled over it. They felt more a part of the institution. No student body government existed prior to this point. I suggested to the women that some of them go out for offices in this student body group. I went after the Women's Department to put women in more conspicuous jobs on the campus.

---

[42] Tuskegee Institute was founded by the Alabama legislature in 1881 under the direction of Booker T. Washington, the apostle of vocational education for Black Americans.

There were horses on the campus but nobody but the police rode them. I introduced horseback riding for the women students. It was a beautiful campus and beautiful horses. They were thrilled. The female students were very cooperative, very enthusiastic about having me as Dean of Women. I was nearer their age. These really elderly women were head of the dormitories. I changed my office and put it in the women's dormitory. I had an area where the students could sit and be at ease. I took two girls on my staff.

I had the satisfaction that I did a job that was needed at the time. Dr. Patterson said, "You're going too fast. These people are not ready for you. You've done ten years work in one year here." He was so upset when I left. I said, "I have tried it out and I don't think I would be very happy here. I like California better than Alabama. Although the people from Tuskegee were very privileged; if you taught at Tuskegee you were not treated as the ordinary Negro. When I told Dr. Patterson that I wasn't returning, he said, "That's why I tried to slow you down."

At that time they had segregation on the trains.[43] They called me the commuting dean. They said I commuted between New York to Tuskegee. Many weekends I found myself in New York.

When my sabbatical was up I had a letter from the Superintendent saying that since I had done such a good job with 'my people' in Tuskegee, he thought I would prefer staying down there where I could make a greater contribution to 'my people' than returning to the Oakland public schools. He included a form for my resignation for me to sign. I replied,"Please let me know what my assignment will be when I return in the fall to my job in Oakland." He sent me my assignment. I didn't take his hint about resigning. My roots

---

43   "When I wanted to travel I would contact Mr. Johnson who worked with the railroad company. He knew who to contact to arrange for blacks not to be segregated.Whenever I was going they set aside a suite for me in the parlor car, but I had to keep the door ajar. I didn't question why. I got the best of attention."

were here and Emmett and I had just bought the ranch in Mendocino."

Depression memory

"My brother Emmett was a chef on the railroad and later owned a restaurant in the 20's and 30's. Since he had a restaurant, he could get supplies that other people could not get. It was difficult to get certain kinds of meat. Supplies were very limited. There was very little work. We, however, didn't suffer. We were able to share things with people who couldn't get them. Many of the things which happened at that time were unpleasant; it's easy to forget unpleasant things."

Summer School for Rural Teachers, MS

"A black woman from Illinois, Arenia Malory, went down to Mississippi and started a school for blacks in Lexington. The schools were segregated. There were no public schools for blacks in Lexington. The best ones were in Jackson which was sixty miles away from Lexington. She lectured all during the summer at different churches to raise money to carry on the school. My brother James heard her speak about the living conditions for the blacks. There were people there who didn't know they were free to leave a plantation and go get a better job. They were afraid to leave the plantation.

I had taken my Easter vacation to go down to Mississippi and investigate conditions that this woman said existed. She told me if I wanted to come down I could live at her home. When I came back I sent out a letter to the entire sorority and asked for volunteers to join this program to teach summer school for the rural teachers for two weeks. I got thirty-eight responses from the national; I could only afford to take eight. I took my niece and Robertha Wells, who was quite a scholar, in my car. We made up the faculty, all college-trained people.

Before we started the summer school, Dr. Malory went to the Governor of Mississippi and told him that a group of Negro women was coming from the Northern states. She wanted his help in notifying the sheriffs and police that they were not to arrest these people. It was dangerous for a black from the North to be traveling and caught after dark in some of these places. That enabled us to travel with a degree of freedom.

We let the children attend school so that the teachers could do practice teaching and we were the teachers' instructors. The teachers then went to school with us for a period after they had taught these kids. My staff were observers in the classrooms. Many of the local teachers were working in service and could hardly get there until after they had done the day's work. Consequently, that delayed us. There were very few of them who could come in the morning.

For eight years I went back to Mississippi in the summer. The first two years I paid the teachers' expenses and mine. At first I felt it was a matter of wider education for the County teachers. They paid some of them thirteen dollars a month! Naturally they had no college education. If they knew somebody—the boss in the political system, then they got appointed to teach in the schools whether they were prepared or not.

I sold the idea to the sorority and they supported it, first, with a thousand dollars (naturally, that didn't cover all of our expenses). Then the people who worked that first year were so sold; when we reported, the sorority became very interested. There were those who thought we looked forward to it as a paid vacation. They didn't know about all the hardships. They had outhouses—no indoor toilets. It wasn't well-built and the worst thing—one woman fell in! When you had to go you always found one or two other people because it was dark at night on the campus. Durant was the nearest town to Lexington so somebody would announce,"Anybody going to Durant?" It's laughable now."

Mississippi Health Project, 1935-42

"Out of this summer school I realized the need for health was as great as the need for educational opportunities. Children who came to the school were so visibly undernourished and the teachers equally so. When I became national president of the sorority, I interested the sorority in starting what became known as the Mississippi Health Project. I felt that we could not afford to just enjoy life and do nothing about the underprivileged. We were a privileged group who were able to get through college.

The first clinic was supposed to be held on the campus of Saints' Industrial School. We found so few people responding, that upon investigation, we found they weren't able to leave their plantations to come to the clinic, however much they needed it. That gave me the idea of taking the clinic to them. I sent out a letter to all of the doctors whose names I could find in the sorority, calling for volunteers.

We turned this into a mobile clinic, taking the doctor, nurses, and medication out to these plantations. We had the clinic in run-down churches or schools or wherever we could set up the equipment. Some of the people had never seen a woman doctor. They had not thought of having a woman doctor in the race. It was a new experience for the people of that locale. News traveled from place to place, church to church. Some just wanted to be there to see these women who had come down there to help them. We gave injections to the youngsters for smallpox, diphtheria and malaria. Malaria was the greatest problem, possibly due to the drinking water there.

Ruth Handy (sister-in-law of W.C. Handy) and I interviewed the plantation owners. We were all Northerners to them. They were afraid we had come to get the blacks from working on their plantations. We knew how to talk to the Southern white man.

Instead of letting cotton grow right up to the doorstep as they did, we tried to get them to take what little space they could to grow green vegetables for themselves and not have to go to the commissary to buy the stuff they had there for them. The people were very enthused over it. Mrs. Roosevelt helped us to get some supplies through the Health Department. We often took a door off the church building and put it on blocks or whatever was available to make a table which we covered with sparkling white sheets. We demonstrated how to use the foods when they planted more vegetables for themselves.

I tried running the school and the health project at the same time for two years and I found we could not do both so I got the sorority interested in the health project. The health was more important. If you are hungry or sick you can't do much learning or studying. We conducted the project for eight years. The sorority gave me a certain amount of money for the project—a very small amount. I was spending my brother Emmett's money. He believed in what I was doing. He was with me all the way.

Claude Barnett started the Associated Negro Press which existed primarily so that the news about Negroes could be spread. (A & P, we called it.) He would get the news about Negroes from all over the world and send it to every black newspaper. I knew him very well. When I started this summer school for rural teachers he said, "Ida, you don't know the value of that—that's newsworthy!" Barnett sent it out and it made headline stories:"Black College Women Led By Ida Jackson Introduce A Free School For Rural Teachers In Lexington, Mississippi"That gave it the publicity we needed. We got volunteers to work in it.

I do take credit for having changed the trend. Formerly, all the sorority did was give scholarships; they had no service program. Since 1934 we've become service motivated.

Mrs. Roosevelt was interested and invited Dr. Farabee and me to the White House to tell her about the Health Project. We met in the East Room. I met her with Mrs. Bethune first.[44] Mrs. Roosevelt became an honorary member of my sorority. At that time the average person at that level didn't pay any attention to the Negro. We weren't exerting any power in the political scene. (Since the Civil Rights Movement we've become more a part of

---

[44]   Mary McLeod Bethune, President of the National Council of Negro Women and Founder/President of Bethune-Cookman College, became director of Negro affairs of the National Youth Administration, one of the New Deal programs. Eleanor Roosevelt was responsible for her appointment.

the American system. We have more representatives in the Senate and the House of Representatives.) She was such a down-to-earth person. She didn't meet you with display or "I'm the President's wife". She came on like another person; one felt quite at home with her. People didn't appreciate her worth. She was sold on helping the underdog. It was a genuine part of her makeup. As a result of that meeting, I was invited to the lighting of the Christmas tree.

Dr. Arenia Malory, who started the school in Lexington, has passed away now. One of the women, who was down there when I started the summer school, bought a home in Lexington. She's instigating a movement to build a museum. She has me classified as an advisor. I told her not to just let it be a museum; let it have some practical use so that the public would give to it more readily. There should be something going on there. The educational facilities are still very limited for people there. I have donated my library to that effort. I'm contacting my friends here in order to get more books to send."

Black History

"Nowhere in the textbooks did you find anything about the contributions of blacks to American civilization. I was anxious that thinking white people should know some of the facts about blacks. I was disturbed because I hadn't found in California too much difference in the treatment and acceptance of the Negro. The newspapers and the media only carried the crimes and the sordid part of Negro life. I thought whites in general needed to know that there are class differences among blacks as well as among whites—that all blacks weren't criminals.

I was working in the community with young people then. I directed a junior choir. I got a group together in 1953. The librarian at the West Oakland library said we could have our presentation there. I narrated the story and told about the background of the Negro in the making of America. At that affair I had a violinist and a pianist who played an entire program of compositions by blacks. I invited Mayor Mott and the City Council to hear. Not having been aware of the Negroes in the community, because we just existed, he was very much moved by the history that I gave of the Negro in America and California. I did this for several years."

[Mayor Mott would remember Ida's performance to her benefit. When the City began planning the new MacArthur Freeway, one of the plans ran the freeway through her property. One of the Mayor's aides visited Ida and as she was leaving said, "Don't give up the ship. You have a friend at court!" They indeed did select another plan.]

Early involvement with NAACP and civil rights "After Dr. W.E.B. DuBois[45] came to Oakland, Walter Butler organized a chapter of the NAACP (National Association for the Advancement of Colored People) in 1913, which included people from Vallejo, San Jose, San Francisco and Oakland/Alameda. In coming together as a group we got more recognition. We were fighting for the rights of black people. We wanted to see to it that they could get better jobs, and where they were qualified to work, that they would have a chance to compete with the other man.

The chapter created a young people's membership department so that I could work with teenagers. I became a member of the board of directors when I was nineteen. Mr.

---

45 Dr.W.E.B. DuBois, writer, educator, and renaissance man, obtained a Ph.D. from Harvard in 1895. He served as editor of the NAACP's magazine, *The Crisis,* and was one of the guiding lights of that organization. He was a strong and intelligent spokesperson for blacks and an advocate for world peace and socialism. His partly autobiographical work, *The Souls of Black Folk* (1903) remains a classic. Ida met Dr. DuBois at Walter Butler's house, which, incidentally, she has owned for many years. "At the time the hotels did not have accommodations for blacks. That's how I met so many dignitaries, such as W.E.B. DuBois, because they knew Walter Butler. They would stay here. DuBois was a worker for the race. The fact that he was a scholar made him respected."

Butler wanted my input. At that time there were very few blacks who went to college. I organized a group of young people in the high school and encouraged them to go on and finish high school, at least. Most of the black children were stopping at the eighth grade. They had the opportunity [to continue] but they didn't take advantage of it.

Before coming to California, my mother and brothers thought there was full freedom for the blacks in California. Of course conditions in general were much better than in the South, but as I've grown older I find there's just as much prejudice in California as there is in the South. In fact, the only difference is it's a little more refined here. Of course now things have changed everywhere since the Civil Rights Movement took over, about 1954. I've always been fighting for equality of opportunity. Churches and ministers called on me to speak. They thought I was very influential with the younger people. I did organize various groups and work with them.

I found that in the school department you never saw a black child on the stage performing with the other group. When they had them in choruses, they would be in back. The tall ones or the short ones, they'd still be in back. We had one black violinist they let play in the school orchestra, because of his ability. I organized a group which met every week on Friday evenings and Saturdays, sometimes. I directed plays and operettas with them. I got black children from all of the high schools. I tried to have them involved in one way or another so they would all feel like they were part of it. This gave the youngsters a chance to be together socially. I wanted to keep them from getting a complex. Toward the end, some of the friends I had made on the faculty used to attend the affairs.

We did the performances largely at what was then University High School because they had a good stage and I lived two blocks from there. (At that time there were very few blacks in that neighborhood. They couldn't deny my niece, who was living with me, attending that high school because we lived in the district.)

'Retirement'

"My brother supported me to go South because I was not paid the same as whites when I taught in Oakland. My check always would be out on the counter. For a long time I did not know the salary the other teachers got at that particular school. There was no point in my fighting because it would have been a losing battle. I would have to have written proof that they paid me less. I had teachers on the staff who said, "This is a shame!" Not long ago, one teacher saw my retirement check and said, "Oh my God, Ida, is this all you get?" I'd have to have proof. I've tried to get the necessary proof, but was told that the files from that far back are unavailable. If my brothers and Mother hadn't provided for me I would not have been able to continue my graduate studies."

[*Ida left teaching in 1955 after teaching in the Oakland public schools for twenty-seven years.*]

"I didn't retire; I resigned. Just suddenly I decided I'd had it. My brother, Emmett, said, "Sister, you will never be anything but a teacher in the Oakland public schools, so why don't you quit and together we'll get ahead a lot faster than you will with your teaching." My brother bought a ranch in Mendocino County. I went up and took over the operation of the ranch. For a long time we only went up there weekends. We had men managing it for us. It was timberland and a sheep ranch. My brother was smart enough to sell the sheep because people were making inroads, just stealing the sheep and putting their marks on them. We had the timber left.

After Emmett passed, I went up there and stayed seventeen years. His parting words to me were, "Kiddo, don't sell the ranch." I was glad I had the ranch to challenge me. I felt his loss more than I did my mother's because I had him to lean on when my mother passed. He and I were inseparable.

I had a job stopping the people from stealing our timber, which was our main income. When we bought the ranch the loggers' contract for pine had been completed, but they continued to cut. I objected. I stopped one of the trucks and checked on the wood. I told them they had no contract to take

off fir. [One of the loggers] said, "That's the same—fir and pine."
I said, "Now you know better than that." I used Spencer's Logging
Guide, a reference book which had all the sizes. I studied it. I
knew how to measure. I required them to give me a bill and a
copy for the lumberyard. Very often they put in an extra log
which they hadn't put on the sheet. I told them, "You people
make folks learn anything!"

They were logging down in the canyon in an area where
they weren't supposed to log at all. The house was at the summit
of Lookout Range. I could hear the timber trucks coming out
of the canyon. I often surprised the drivers by standing there
and checking the load that they had. That helped to stop some
of the loss. I had a Jeep in which I traveled all over the ranch.

I had a difficult time finding people to work for me because
the people in Point Arena would harass them when they went
down there. If I got a black man, he was isolated. The whites
would just come and make a payday because when they went
down to the community to shop and the bar, they were isolated
and ridiculed for working for this 'nigger'. They undermined
whoever I got. I managed alone for awhile.

When I first went up, people were distant. They kept their
distance and I kept mine. There was one man, a native of that
area, who spoke to me when I went into the store. He hadn't
been much further than Mendocino County in his life. He said
he hoped I would like living there. I appreciated that. The man
who sold my brother the ranch left the community. The people
were so disgusted that he had sold to a Negro that he had a hard
time finding a place to rent for himself and his family.

Some of the leading people in the town were the first ones
to be friendly with me. One of the neighbors came up and
found me wearing jeans and work shoes like anyone working
in the country. After that they became friendly. I didn't seek
them out. Their curiosity got the better of them. They wanted
to see how I was living. They were sorry to see me go.

When the timber contract was out, then I decided to be
big-hearted and deeded 320 acres, one half of a section, to the
University of California. I had often thought that the University

of California had done so much for me and blacks don't get
the kind of jobs that if they wanted to contribute they couldn't,
cause they don't have the money. I kept the homesite with seven
acres. We were surrounded by beautiful redwood trees. It was
very delightful living there—the beauty of the place—watching
the sunrise and the sunset, seeing the ocean. I learned about
timber sales and management. I learned more about dealing
with people. I made some lasting friends up there.

I sold the ranch in the '70s. I kept the homesite until
recently. It was difficult for me to find people who were free
to go up there with me and spend any time. There was no
point in holding on to it, so I sold it. It's beautiful country.
For a long time I missed it terribly. Someone told me I wouldn't
know the place now. There are houses dotted all over the area.
I have no desire to go back. I've just thrown it out of my mind.
One can't live in the past."

REFLECTIONS
On accomplishments
"I was very pleased and flattered to receive more recognition
in 1988 and '89 for my work in community service. I worked
in the community for years. It's just in recent years I have
stopped. My folks supported me and usually furnished the
funds. Almost everything requires some money. When I think
back on it now, I don't know how I accomplished as much as I
did. I was involved in everything. I helped organize the YWCA
for black girls. I had a junior choir that I directed at one of the
churches. I did a great deal of public speaking. I felt that black
people had the opportunity here to get an education better
than they could pay for anywhere else in America. It disturbed
me that so few were taking advantage of the opportunities.
When I was teaching I urged students to get as much education
as possible. Their response was, "What's the use? We could
never endure what you have endured as a teacher." I said, "By
the time you get through school, things will have changed."
Some did become teachers and some went into other
professions. I was very happy about that.

My folks helped a great deal. Some of the students who were from out of town lived with us. When I was in Los Angeles recently I saw Ruby Jefferson whom I urged to come to California instead of the family moving to Denver, Colorado from Mississippi. Ruby persuaded her mother to come to California instead of Colorado. When she heard I was going to be in town for the sorority's annual meeting, she attended. She was telling everybody how Mama let her stay at the house for a semester without paying anything. Then when she did pay, she paid $20 a month room and board. I had met her at Rust College. We corresponded and became very close friends. The opportunities were better for blacks in California. Ruby stayed with me until her mother settled in California. Then Mama took in Beth Wilson, who became a teacher. Alvira came up from the Imperial Valley and stayed with me while going to UC, Berkeley. Few of us could afford to pay room and board and attend school.

Blacks were leaving the South then. A great many moved to Chicago, New York, Ohio—anything to get out of Mississippi, Louisiana, Alabama, Georgia, which were the worst states. None of the states were entirely free of prejudice. Those above the Mason-Dixon line showed less, because the courts were more just in dealing with racial matters. Segregation wasn't legal. The classes here were pretty well integrated all the way through when I started. Prior to when I started teaching they had a black woman, who was not part of the unified school district, teach black children in her home.

In the seventies I received the Berkeley Citation from the University of California which is their highest honor. In 1974 I was inducted into Phi Beta Kappa at the University. In 1989 Women of Achievement, Vision and Excellence, a San Francisco group of women, honored five of us who had received recognition late in life.

I guess a certain amount of suffering goes along with pioneering in anything. I've learned that as I've grown older. My folks believed in me, and they expected results. I was more interested in getting an education than in social life. They told me that they wanted me to get an education. They knew it

was natural that I should want to be married at some time, but
when I started seriously 'courting' then they would not make
any sacrifices to keep me in school. I weighed the situation.
Having been brought up with all brothers, being the only girl—
I think that kept me from being overwhelmed by masculinity."

On special quality of life in the Bay area

"I don't know any place I'd rather live than Oakland, even
with all it's defects.

You can't beat the climate anywhere. Although the economic
factor could be improved for blacks, socially it is the most liberal
place I have been. Not that I am a world traveler, but I have
seen parts of Europe and Africa and the Mid-East and no place
compares to Oakland in my estimation. Just as I feel you won't
find a greater institution than the University of California.
Maybe I'm biased because it is my alma mater. There is more
individuality. You are not forced to follow any particular
pattern. Each individual is more free here.

We need to get more people to realize the value of an
education. We need teachers who want to help youngsters to
be better people without just considering the salary. We need
a movement which would inspire black youths to use their time
and realize the potential they have and that education is
necessary to their success. I think that is one of the most serious
problems we have. I don't think black children have enough
role models. There is not enough concern for what is
happening to the masses. It seems we will always be judged by
the few who feel that laws are made to be broken, to put it
roughly. The tendency is to judge all blacks by the worst ones.
We need something to offset this tendency. I don't think you
will find a black person behind the top drug dealers. They don't
have the money or political power to succeed. Consequently,
until the people who are solid citizens combine efforts to fight
and are willing to have their names used, we will not progress.

The black community has changed in many ways since I
first moved to Oakland. There are more blacks here now. In
the early 1920's the black population of Oakland was about

5,000.[46] You find now a lot of black people who have advanced by studying settling here and taking advantage of the opportunities. There is too much complacency. Those who have achieved have a duty to help those farther down. I don't feel that this is being done here to the extent it should be. Everyone is struggling to get ahead. Up to the '60s I could see improvement; now it seems to have gone back, not only in race relations, but in every way America seems to be going backward."

On Aging

"Think of how much you have learned of life! Each day as I awaken I thank God that I'm still alive. I never dreamed I would live to be this old. You recognize changes in behavior as well as customs and traditions. We seem to be living in another era and I am part of that. I'm glad to see the changes which have come about, and though far from perfect, I have witnessed a change in race relations during my generation. Now we seem to be going backwards. I am a little surprised at some of the things that are going on at the University, but yet there is a black woman in the Admissions Department and there are some black teachers on the faculty where there were none when I attended. There are more opportunities for blacks provided they are scholars. There are more scholarships available at the present time than during my generation.

I think aging gives one a different perspective. I am less critical than when I was younger. I realize that there is no such thing as a perfect person. You may have standards by which you live, but you shouldn't expect the world to live by them. I think I have learned to be more patient and understanding after all these years."

---

[46] According to the 1930 census, 78.2% of black families in the U.S. lived in the South. By 1940 only 50.2% of black families remained in rural Southern areas. The 'Great Migration' from rural to urban, from South to North (and in some cases South to West) continues to have major social and economic impact. Ida and her family were early pioneers in this exodus out of the South.

" . . . the heart of a warrior, the soul of a poet."
from the television series, *Startrek*

Bill **Bailey**

Bill Bailey, who survived growing up on the streets of Hell's Kitchen in New York City, escaped to sea when he was fourteen, fought in the Spanish Civil War, and helped to organize the maritime industry on both coasts.

In this time of lost manhood, of absentee fathers and yuppie males on the big make, Bill stands out as an exemplary role model. When I see strong, young males slouched on the sidewalk in my neighborhood begging for money, I wish I could introduce them to Bill. Although he did his share of hoboeing and knocking on back doors for food, he worked hard at the most menial job and stuck by his family and friends through the bleakest of times.

I met Bill through a mutual friend, Jack Webb, a former police inspector/ private investigator who has dedicated his life to aiding the Irish cause of reunification. Jack knew what I was looking for when he suggested I speak with Bill. One does not expect a tough, brave man to also be gentle and sensitive. This is the shock of Bill. We are not used to this combination in an American man. In the context of the Hemingway/Spillane/Mailer images that many of us absorbed over the last fifty years, how do we consider a gentle-man warrior? Initially I felt intimidated by Bill's 'rep' as a waterfront hero and a Lincoln Brigade veteran, but after our first interview a bond began forming between us. I believe Bill has created this effect on many people over the years. He draws people into his circle, partly due to his ability to recreate past adventures without making himself the hero, in spite of the fact that he is. Aware of the historical forces which have shaped our modern world, he rode through the center of most of these storms and survived to tell us about it. When I first met him he still lived in his little earthquake shack, built in 1906 as temporary housing by the Army Corps of Engineers, which stood in the shadow of Coit Tower on Telegraph Hill overlooking the waterfront. It seems fitting for an old seaman warrior to live with a gull's view of the Bay. Unfortunately in our world of grubby real estate developers, he was forced off the Hill into more prosaic senior housing at the bottom. Bill is used to step-dancing through the changes. He never does expect it to get easier, and yet he never gives up. He still believes individual action makes a difference even in a mad world.

He loves to have a good time with his friends. He walks with some of them once a week from the Marina Green to Fort Point, a two mile Bayside stretch near the Golden Gate Bridge. He and his dear friend, Al Richmond, created the Fort Point Gang, in part to keep old friends from losing touch with one another. *All of the regulars were involved in the early days of the labor struggles and many still take an active part in a wide range of causes. Having coffee after the walk with that group is like attending a living history seminar. On one walk I was keeping pace with a man who had fought with Bill in the Spanish Civil War. He said he tried to stay as close to Bill as possible in combat as somehow he felt safe just being near him. It is a fine thing, he agreed, that Bill survived that ghastly war, living to fight other battles.*

Bill looks out after everyone in the Fort Point Gang plus a million more people who live all around the globe. I was touched when he called me the day after the 1990 earthquake to see how I was doing. I realized I had joined the long list of folks whom Bill watches over.

Hell's Kitchen childhood

"I was born in Jersey City in 1910, but raised mostly in New York City, around Hell's Kitchen on 38th Street between 9th and 10th Avenue. My mother had thirteen kids. Seven died in infancy—miscarriages, starvation, living in rat-infested tenements—which was okay with us six because it gave us a chance to live.

We moved away from my father right before the War—1914. He was a very brutal guy when he was drinking. My parents were both Catholic. The rule of thumb about Catholicism is every time you took your pants off, you had a baby. Hell, he couldn't take care of one kid let alone thirteen. He couldn't stomach all the kids begging—"Where's the food? Give me something to eat!" He'd end up in a ginmill and blamed her for everything that went wrong. One day when she started protesting about feeding the kids, he gave her a few belts and split her lip. My mother caught him drunk one day and packed up, took us all by the hand and we moved to another rat-infested part of Jersey City. I used to go visit him and collect $5 a week from him, when he was working. He'd scowl and hand me the $5, but that didn't last long.

Then she married my step-father about three years after the War. He just seemed to be another drunk, one of the them weak son-of-a-bitches that you had to take care of all the time. He was a drinker who blamed everything on the First World War. He had been gassed in the War. The man spent a whole hour shining his shoes to make sure they were letter-perfect. He had to be so respectable. When it came to eating, he got the best of everything. He didn't care about anyone else.

To get to St. Peter's School if I cut through what we called the secret path through Gowanas Canal, I could make it in ten minutes rather than twenty minutes using the streets. Sometimes I'd step in mud and slime up to my knees because I never wore shoes. If I got there too late I didn't have a chance to go down to the boys room and wash off so when I got to the classroom I stunk. If you didn't get into school on time when you did get there they'd stop the class. You'd put your hand out and the nun would pick up a great big rubber sash that she carried, and slap! If you pulled your hand back that meant double. I got there about a minute late. I got my five cracks. Then she said,"You stink!" She denounced me in front of the class—and she denounced the Irish. She said,"You get out of this class immediately and bring your mother up here!"

My mother was working in some little restaurant around the corner. She took me back to school. The nun said,"How dare you send this boy to school without shoes! He's filthy! Don't you ever give him a bath?" My mother took off on that nun. It was just pitiful. She had great respect for religion but these people weren't gods to her. She really put the nun to shame in front of the class. She did everything but call her a whore. "I can't afford to buy him anything to eat and you're talking about shoes!! The good Lord wore a burlap rag around his ass and that was good enough for him and it's good enough for me. If you want him dressed any better you buy him shoes!" I was so embarrassed by this whole thing. The more I think about it now the more proud I am, but at that time I was afraid of what was going to happen. I knew that the longer the argument would go on she'd eventually come up with her salty Irish—like friggin' this and friggin' that. She said,"I know what goes on with you and the priests at night when they get half drunk!" All the kids were bug-eyed. Life at school got a little better after that day.

Another time she sent me around to the Guardian Angel church. I had a job to go to in Hoboken. She said, "You knock on the rector's door and ask Father Duffy to give you fifty cents for carfare to go to Jersey tomorrow and when you get your first paycheck you'll pay him." I knocked at the door and some young priest comes out,"Yeah, what do you want?""I'm looking for Father Duffy. My mother told me to come round and get fifty cents.""Hey, bum! Get the hell away from the door!"When I told my mother that was all she needed. She banged on that door and the same guy came out. "You son of a bitch, you called my son a bum, you rotten, over-stuffed bastard! You never missed a meal in your life!" Again I was embarrassed. She was screaming so loud that it did attract Father Duffy. He came out to see what the hell was going on. He gave me a dollar— a tremendous amount of money, and a lot of nice words and "Bless you my boy" and "Get the job". No doubt about it, my mother was a scrapper.

She was very good in protecting her brood. She worked in a convent at one time. She would bring an empty two quart pot with her. When we'd come out of the school we'd pass the convent. She'd be standing there with the pot filled with soup which she stole from the priests. I'd take it home and feed myself and my sister with it. Then we'd bring the empty can back to her and she'd see if she could steal anything for supper that night. If I developed any anti-religion feelings, it was certainly from her.

Most of us boys spent time in reform school for stealing stuff like milk, bread. In them days they delivered bottled milk to your door. They put all the milk outside the grocery store in bottle cases. Also they had a bread box. The bread man put forty, fifty loaves of bread in the box. We'd follow him around and first chance we'd glom on to a couple of bottles of milk and some bread. We'd try to make all the grocery stores recipients of a fair share of our needs. They put spotters on you and eventually they caught us. I was twelve. The judges gave you more time for stealing bread and milk than you would get for murder today. Reform school was in Bayonne, New Jersey. I got two weeks. That was the worst two weeks of my life because it was the first time I was away from home.

I got through most of the fifth grade when my mother came into school one day and told the teacher she had to take me out to go to work. There was nobody in the family working."He's big enough to go to work. We got to take him out." They made a deal, "We'll let him out, providing you send him to night school". I went to work for a factory making salesman's fiber luggage. I never went to school after that. I ended up going to sea when I was fourteen."

To sea

"We lived pretty close to the waterfront. I was cognizant of ships all around. Every Saturday the twelve o'clock noon whistles blew up and down the New York waterfront because that was the time all the big passenger ships would pull out, for Europe or South America. The air just reverberated with steam whistles blowing. I went from ship to ship, starting at 23rd Street in New York City, West Side, all the way down to Pier One, which is right at the Battery. I went aboard every bloody ship asking for a job; 99% laughed at me. I get down to Pier One to a ship called the *Lake Gaither*. I went aboard, talked to the mate, lied like a son of a bitch. The mate asked me how old I was. "Twenty-one." He said, "How long have you been going to sea?" I said, "At least five years." I'd never been aboard a ship. I'm sure he knew I was a liar from the minute I got aboard. "We do have an ordinary seaman's job open. Be back here at four o'clock to take the gangway watch." I didn't know if somebody was going to steal the gangway or what the hell was really happening. I was back, sure enough, at four o'clock. I remember standing at the gangway half the night. I didn't know what the hell I was standing there for. Actually it was to make sure that nobody who didn't belong on the ship came aboard or stole anything, but nobody told me that. They could have taken the smokestack ashore for all I know.

After we went to sea, the next day, I was seasick, miserable. The food was awful, but plentiful. Within thirty days I had an idea what going to sea was all about. I picked up the jargon, which meant I could go aboard another ship and talk the old sea-going language.

We sailed down to the Gulf. I learned a lot going down there about discrimination, such as seeing faucets saying, "For Colored Only"/"For Whites Only". I thought there must be something different about the water. After I tracked it down, I seen the pipe that went along to the 'white' faucet and about twenty-five feet away the same pipe ran to the 'colored' faucet. I couldn't understand what the hell was going on. In New York a fountain was a fountain. A streetcar was a streetcar. Everybody mingles. This was shocking to me—ride a bus and all the blacks sat in the back and all the whites sat up front.

On that same ship, some guy came aboard in Houston, Texas. He was a Wobbly[47] organizer. He brought *The Industrial Worker* aboard. He called me "class brother". I didn't know what the hell he meant. I looked at the guy, I don't remember this guy from school. He gave me the paper. He never asked me for anything money-wise. I didn't have anything to give him anyway. I put the paper over my bunk and brought it out the second night out at sea, on the way home, 'cause I had nothing else to read. On the front page was the preamble: "The working class and the capitalist class have nothing in common."The capitalist class, the working class—what the hell are they talking about?

Shipping in them days, seamen were the intellectuals of the world. If you corral the experienced ones in a room, these guys are pretty hep cats. They're constantly reading; they've been every place. Of course they'll tell you every whorehouse and ginmill in the world, but they can also tell you the systems— what's the most brutal country to be in for cops, what they've seen happening in their lifetime. I asked, "Anybody know what this is—the capitalist class, the working class?" One guy says, "You, you dummy—you're a member of the working class. The capitalist class: they're the guys who own this son-of-a-bitch." I said, "What's the proletariat?" The guy says, "You, you dumb son-of-a-bitch." What did they expect from a fourteen-year-

---

[47]   The International Workers of the World (IWW) was founded by American socialists and trade unionists in 1905. They recruited non-skilled workers, including immigrants and non-whites. Their goal was to form one big union of exploited workers around the world who would circumnavigate the corrupt political establishments by creating their own revolution. During World War I the "Wobblies" were accused of treason and the leadership was arrested. Although the IWW never recovered from wartime suppression, they still maintain a precarious existence.

old dummy with little schooling? You don't learn that stuff in the street. I began to know where my place was in society. I got paid off after seven weeks on that ship.

I was sixteen or seventeen; it was between ships. Shipping became bad and I couldn't get a ship. Myself and two other guys went into picking up junk, chopping lead pipe out of houses, stripping rooftops that had copper lining—anything to pick up a few bucks. Sometimes we made good money—ten, twenty bucks, which was a hell of a lot of money. You could go to two shows a day, eat hot dogs and have a good time. We broke into a warehouse owned by George M. Cohan[48], where he kept all his theatrical stuff. You couldn't see through the windows, they were so dirty. We would just sit there five or six hours a day with pliers, ripping off all the copper or brass from the chandeliers, roll it up, take it to junk shops. But we overdone it; eventually somebody saw us go in one day and called the cops. We were locked up and remanded for trial. My sister Kate went up to George M. Cohan's office and told him about her brother. Cohan wrote a letter to the judge. I had been in the Tombs [the New York City jail] for almost six weeks. I went before the judge. He said, "I see you went to sea for a living and you've been in lots of jails."[49]

---

[48]   George M. Cohan (1878-1942), the son of vaudevillians, became the father of American musical comedy. Playwright, actor, producer, director, songwriter (responsible for such chestnuts as "Over There" and "It's A Grand Old Flag"), he also must have been a big-hearted fellow.

[49]   "When the probation man came to the cell to see me he said, "Now tell me the truth and we'll see what we can do for you." The lying bastard. He asked if I was ever arrested. I told him maybe one time on vagrancy. I think it was in Mobile, Alabama. Sometimes you went to these towns off a boxcar and they picked you up and threw you in jail but they let you out in the morning. I told him that in traveling on the highway in the South or West, the safest place to be was in jail. If you didn't have any money for a hotel you went to the

You've been in jail too many times, getting away too easy. I got a letter from George M. Cohan, saying I should let you go and he will employ you so you can pay back for the damage that was done in the warehouse. I'm telling this man right now that he should take care of all his tap-dancing up and down Broadway and leave the penalties to where it belongs—me. I'm ignoring his letter and I'm sentencing you to one year in the New York Reform School." Jesus Christ, two weeks was one thing, but a year!

They handcuffed me and put me in a train along with about thirty other young guys. We all went up to the reform school in upstate New York. Fortunately for me, I happened to know a little bit about tools, since we used them on the ship. The first six months I kept my nose out of mischief and got along okay. Then I got promoted from just digging ditches to a plumber's helper, which was good because it was cleaner and more meaningful. I got to learn more and how to use tools. I worked with one plumber who was a halfway decent character. Not that you ate or slept better, but the idea that your time was more useful. I learned more about the trade from him. I got out in ten months and two weeks, with six weeks off for good behavior.

The biggest sentence you could get in that place was thirty months; that was for rape. These kids were talking about how

---

sheriff's office and told him, "I'm passing through; I have no place to sleep.""All right, get in here and get in one of them cells."They'd let you out in the morning.You were never arrested.That was easy on the sheriff because they didn't have to keep an eye on you.You not only got a place to sleep, which was warm and comfortable, but you was no threat to anybody. In case something did happen, they come along and picked you up, you're a vagrant—hell, you could go to jail for twenty years on their say-so. So it worked both ways. But this bastard [the parole officer] put this all down as if I was arrested each time I spent a night in jail. On the record it looked bad."

they used to go into the raping business, by catching some old scrubwoman on her way home late at night and the whole gang of these bastards would push her into some downstairs basement and then rape her. I used to see my poor mother coming home, exhausted and weary from scrubbing floors in the Woolworth building, getting off at three or four in the morning. These were the most hated characters in the reform school. The idea of even being in with them, being near them made me feel filthy. I said, "They'll never get me into this goddamned place anymore." And they never did. They got me in jail but it was always on principles—the picket line, a demonstration.

As soon as I got out of jail, I went up to Boston and got on a ship which was supposed to go to China; instead, we went to New Orleans. The *John Jay* had run on a sand bar during the First World War, 'broke its back', as they call it. It laid there fifteen years and finally a couple of smart characters decided to use it as a grain carrier. The engines were so bad that when you went through a torrid zone, like off the Florida Keys where it's boiling hot, you don't even whip up a breeze. No wind coming in the rooms—very bad. The wages were miserable; the captain was miserable; the food was next to nothing. We were starving to death half the time. When we got to New Orleans everybody got fired. My whole pay from Boston to New Orleans was about eighteen dollars. Here I am on 'the beach' covered with hometown guys. If there are any jobs coming in, they're going to get them. I used up all the money, running up to Baton Rouge, trying to get a job on an oil tanker.

Now it was a question of getting out of town. My roots were back East. When ships came in from the East I walked aboard and told the skipper I want to go back to New York or Boston. They called it a workaway, which meant you worked as much as a sailor. You slept in a spare bunk if there was one. You set down with the guys to eat; if there was no room then you waited until the regular crew got out and you walked in and ate. You worked your passage. We didn't like it because on every ship where you tried to unionize, you always found a half a dozen workaways, going and coming. They got three meals a day and some security and they were working—not getting paid, but maybe one of the sailors might drop dead or quit or get off, and at least you had the next chance to get in. But primarily, if you put up a beef with the engineer or mate about conditions, he'd say,"There's ten workaways out there that will take your job right now. Now shut up!"You didn't talk union no more— you didn't raise any beef. That's what was bad. Two other guys from New York and I took a Morgan Line ship because they were fast. There was a halfway decent mate on the ship. When we got to New York, each crew member gave us fifty cents or whatever. I got off the ship with three or four dollars. I was just a snotty-nosed brat.

Years later we had a MWIU [Marine Workers Industrial Union] convention. In them days you didn't have money to travel so you traveled by boxcar or workaway. Like delegates coming up from Mobile, got on the next ship as workaways to come up to the convention in New York to learn how to go about unionizing people. There wasn't money to send people on buses or trains. It was ironic that on one hand we were trying to organize people, and the other hand, we're succumbing to the method ourselves of workaway, which we hated.

Back on 'the beach' in New York shipping was tough. 'Shipping crimps'[50] controlled much of the hiring. They usually had some other enterprise tied in with their job—either a rooming house, a restaurant, a whorehouse, a clothing store, a loan shark racket, or a speakeasy, or some combination of these. Regular patrons of these establishments got the first crack at available jobs. I was not a regular patron.

---

[50] "Shipping crimps, who were in the employ of the shipowners, were the most despicable characters on the waterfront.They made sure that no union guys got hired."

I accepted the invitation of an older guy to stow away on a passenger ship bound for Jacksonville, Florida, to escape the oncoming cold winter and pursue shipping in the Gulf. We ended up on the chain gang."

He served thirty days in jail working for the county in Jacksonville along with many other 'vagrants' who were roaming the country at that time. Some states used convict labor for construction and road work. While on the chain gang Bill helped clear the area which eventually would be the Jacksonville airport. He hoboed all over the country, riding boxcars and learning the language and survival tactics of the road in the process.

"I came out here [San Francisco] in '29 on a boxcar and stayed for six-eight months, trying to ship. I couldn't because there were no ships, except for the natives. If you're from New York and the shipping master has a chance of shipping someone out, he's going to ship the natives. He gets paid off by them. Surviving was easy. I devised a way. I got on a ferryboat and went over to Oakland and Berkeley. I always went up to nice houses that had lawns and flowers in front, knocked on the door and said,"I'm a young guy looking for odds and ends—little jobs like fix your garden up, do this, do that." Here's a young kid trying to keep himself together. They'd say, "All right, I'll give you two hours work." They'd pay fifty cents an hour and sometimes throw in a few sandwiches or a glass of milk. Sometimes they'd say, "My son is off in college. I've got an old suit here that looks good. Try this on. Here's some shirts." Within three months I had twenty-one dollars in the bank, at least three suits of clothes and a dozen shirts that people were constantly giving me. People were just goodhearted. Something we've lost track of— now it seems to be just the opposite.

One day I thought, I'm getting no place here. I ran into another guy from New York and said,"What do you say we go back East?" I took the money out and we had a big fiesta. We grabbed a boxcar from here to Sacramento and from there on back across the United States. It took about three weeks to get to New York.

I walked back into the house and there was poverty there the same as when I left it. Soup lines were bigger. Things were bad. I was only in New York one week and I got a ship to South America. Here in San Francisco, I had tried for six months to ship and I couldn't get nothing.

It was so great in Rio that I fell in love with the place. I thought next trip I'm going to jump ship. In them days there were no unions. What the human being will do for security, to hold down a job, curry favor! Somebody told the engineer that if we make another trip, Bailey's going to jump ship in Rio de Janeiro. When we hit New York, bang! The first guy he fired was me. The same thing happened on a London trip. I made the mistake of telling some bastard on the ship that next time I was going to jump ship in London. When we got to New York, bang!—fired. From then on I learned to keep my mouth shut."

Stowaway

"The crew discovered a stowaway from India on a trip from New York to London. His mother was dying in India, and being an illegal alien in the U.S., he hoped that if he got to England the British would send him home as they controlled India at the time. But the British government insisted that he be returned to the U.S. on the return voyage.

On the way home he was treated miserably because the Company would probably be fined. The officers showed their hatred of him and even the bos'n threatened to punch him out. I was down on watch in the fire room. It was the most fearsome weather you would ever see. The waves were sixty, seventy feet high—mountainous waves. The engine was slowed down to almost a standstill. They couldn't keep traction because the propeller was up out of the water most of the time. It was like that every single day. Instead of a ten day trip across it now took eighteen days, which meant that many times we were being pushed back. Snow was coming down the ventilator and into the boiler room. I heard a "Whoom! Whoom!"—the whistle going. I started listening to the number of it—four, which means fire and boat drill—man the boats. You could barely stand up in the engine room, let alone on deck. I could hear the ringing of bells in the engine room to slow the engines down further. I was laying up against the side; I felt the ship was going to roll over. When it calmed down a little bit, some guy came running down and said there's a man overboard. It was the Indian stowaway. This poor son-of-a-bitch had the idea that if he dressed himself up in all sorts of warm clothes, a blanket around his neck, tighten his galoshes and put on a life jacket, that if he jumped overboard, he would be able to stay afloat until another ship came and picked him up and took him to India or back to London. His emotions had completely run amuck with him. I found out that previous to this he had asked the captain to please put him in a boat and set him adrift so he could meet another ship going to London. They chased him off the bridge and then he felt that the only thing left to do was to jump overboard. As soon as you hit the ice-cold water, you're dead, almost. When the ship came up out of the water, it would almost sit on top of a wave. You couldn't jump forty feet out; you'd have to jump within two or three feet of the ship. The ship came right down on top of him. They never found him.

Everybody became so demoralized, so disgusted. We lost a human being. That's the thing that helped set off the trigger in me. A simple little thing like making another human being happy, getting him home to his mother, should have been on everybody's mind. They should have done everything possible, but the son-of-a-bitches let a man jump overboard, commit suicide. That started me off. If I could find a way to right this injustice I would do it. A week later I was sitting in a restaurant on the waterfront in New York chewing the rag with some guy next to me. I said, "I'm off the *American Farmer*", that was the name of the ship. I told him about the stowaway. "The newspapers should know about this." He says, "Why don't you write the article and give it to me. I'll put it in the *Marine Workers Voice* which is the union newspaper on the waterfront." I wrote something along the line of what happened. I met him the next day and learned he was an organizer for the Marine Workers' Industrial Union (MWIU), a left-wing union. I eventually ended up joining this Union because at least they printed the article in their paper and were sympathetic.

Six weeks later I joined the Communist Party. It had not taken long to find out that the men who made the MWIU go, who supplied the essential leadership, who displayed the greatest discipline and readiness for sacrifice were Communists. Working with them I gained in self-confidence as a union activist. In the Party I found a special warmth, a mutual concern, a feeling of comradeship. I felt I had found my niche. People shared what little they had. I had a feeling of being a part of something that was true and noble. My comrades were the best people on earth, fighting for the greatest of causes. From then on in my life I've taken a left trend.

We were preaching that the only salvation to seamen's problems was through socialism, taking over ships—lock, stock, and barrel. Our little MWIU membership books had slogans on each page. One said: "Make every ship a bastion of socialism." That shows you how sectarian we were. It never got anyplace. I don't think it was intended to make tremendous waves but it did take in those seamen who had a strong class-conscious nature and it channeled their energy. When you got aboard a ship you could tell almost immediately if you ran across a member of the MWIU 'cause he was constantly out there, always fighting for better conditions, agitating all the time. There was nothing quiet about him, but he was also a dependable shipmate. He was always immaculate when it came to his relations with another working stiff."

Baltimore Soviet

"The Munson Steamship Company operated a large fleet with just about the worst conditions of any line operating out of New York and the East Coast. Wages were the lowest; working and living conditions were utterly terrible.[51] I shipped aboard a Munson freighter, the Mundixie. With the help of another MWIU member I took the lead in persuading the crew to strike at our first port of call, Baltimore.

I started to stir up the crew by tramping up to the bridge with my supper plate to tell the captain that I needed more food. When I had asked for seconds the cook told me that the company allocated twelve cents for each crew member and I had consumed my twelve cents worth. The captain ordered the cook to give me more food. My next step was to make sure that the crew read the union literature I had brought aboard. I did this by tossing over the side every bit of other reading matter aboard ship. Then we had a meeting of the crew where a list of ten demands was drafted and a strike committee of three was elected. In Baltimore the captain rejected our demands. The crew struck but remained aboard ship. The MWIU set up a picket line on the outside. At 3 a.m., with the entire crew asleep, including two men who were supposed to stand lookout, twenty-five Baltimore policemen sneaked aboard ship from a motor launch and within five minutes they had the men handcuffed and marching down the gangway.

[51] "At that time there were no unions. You got the job through a shipping master who 'belonged' to the Munson Line. You got to work only by literally begging. Wages were less than $1.00 a day. As a fireman I was getting $30.00 a month but a wiper only got $25.00. The average on other shipping lines was $57.00 to $62.00 a month. You could be fired anywhere [on the voyage]. Twelve men were in one room. We washed in salt water. There was no refrigeration. A typical meal was stew. Lot of potatoes. Once a week we had chicken and eggs. Miserable conditions."

A scab crew, recruited in Philadelphia, was brought alongside in another motor launch. The strike was over without the MWIU pickets at the dock gates knowing what happened."

Bill felt "defeated, humiliated, outmatched" by his first attempt at leading a strike but he was reassured by his comrades that the men would be taken care of in Baltimore and the fight would continue.

"Baltimore was then the strongest MWIU port. Under the union's leadership seamen had won the right to administer the government-funded relief program. The MWIU also exercised control over a Centralized Shipping Bureau which dispatched some seventy-five percent of the seamen hired in Baltimore. We made all the shipping, at least four or five big lines, go through a hiring hall. It was the first port which had rotary shipping. No discrimination, no hanky-panky, no paying anybody anything. Your card was dated the minute you registered. You got the job before anybody came in back of you. You couldn't beat that. It was real utopia. You knew eventually if you stayed around long enough that it was going to come to your number. It was fair. It was a landmark for the future of what we've got now. Baltimore was quite an eventful thing. We called it our 'soviet'. We had our own food and our hotel—the only port in the United States that had it. This MWIU strength was a key factor in convincing the crew to strike in Baltimore.[52]

The 'Soviet' lasted a couple of years. It was like a beacon to every damned port in the whole United States. The employers decided they had to break it any damned way they could. They couldn't afford this. In every port you have a seamen's mission, maybe two; the 'skypilots' run it and keep you under control. Like the little two-bit Baptist churches did it for the blacks— kept them under control and away from politics. "We'll do the dictating." These missions, where you come in at night and

---

[52]   "The Party guys set up the Baltimore Soviet. There's a big difference between the Party then and the Party now. We were dedicated, strong, hard-fighting, honest. The Party founded the MWIU. When I got off the ship which we struck, the foundation already had been set up."

maybe get a bowl of stew, or if you 'get saved' enough you might get a night's flop, or if you tip your hat to the reverend or say a couple of nice words that put you in good for the rest of the week—you pick up an old suit of clothes or whatever. They were losing out as a result of the Baltimore 'Soviet'. Who the hell was going to go to a mission? They could holler, "Come and be saved!" "What do you want me to be saved for? I got my three meals and a little hotel on the waterfront. To hell with you!" They were losing their political organization too. The Left was radicalizing these guys. As soon as they started cutting down on the food, "Okay, on to Washington!" The next morning you had a hundred and fifty men all ready to march down the highway all the way to the White House and beat on the door, saying, "We want more relief!" The 'skypilots' wouldn't do that.

They ganged up on the 'Soviet'. The government pulled the old Red herring out, "It's all run by Communists, a Communist front outfit." Intimidation by the shipowners. They got some little hotelkeepers to join their side. Some right-wing officials from other conservative unions were opposed to the 'Soviet' because it was making the Communists stronger. Marine workers were saying, "The Commies did this for me—they got me three meals a day. Look at the hotel I'm in—nice little spot, shower bath, hot water, shaving creme, razor blades. Them Commies are all right!" With words like this going around then the big fears set in. The government cut the relief down, from three meals to two, for a starter, then one, then no meals. They cut out the hotels. They made you keep fighting twenty-four hours a day to try to hold on to something. Now if we'd had the same thing in some other ports it would have been very difficult for them to break it down. They knew they had to break it down quickly otherwise we were going to spread this to other ports. Seamen were going to say, "We want the same thing the Baltimore guys got." We probably lined up more Communists from a seaman's point of view in Baltimore than in any other port. You'd say, "The Party got you all this. How about joining?" How could a seaman turn you down?

After our little strike, I remained in Baltimore. Assigned to help with a daily MWIU news bulletin, I learned from a more experienced comrade about the propaganda of the written word. This was in 1934. On May 9th we got the news that the great maritime strike on the Pacific coast had started. The best we could do in the way of solidarity was to persuade the scab crews of several freighters from the West Coast to pile off the ship. We tried to convince the East Coast seamen to make it a national strike, but with no results.

Then the Party shipped me to Norfolk, Virginia to act as the MWIU port secretary. My duties included visiting every ship to talk with the crews and distribute newspapers and leaflets. All the coal colliers came into Newport News and Norfolk to load coal for Eastern ports. I tried to organize these crews. There was something going on all the time, seven days a week. A ship come in on Sunday, I'd be there to meet it. I didn't think of going to the beach or anyplace else. The idea of the class struggle permeated everything.[53] It meant lots of work.

---

[53] Bill, in his newfound fervor and devotion to the principles of Communism, was given a reality lesson by his older and wiser friend, Harry Hynes, a highly respected MWIU organizer who was to die fighting Franco's forces in the Spanish Civil War. While visiting Bill in Norfolk and learning that he was sleeping on the floor at Party headquarters and subsisting on five dollars a week he said,"'If the Party didn't have the money I could understand that. But we have the money, at least enough to see that our full-time professional revolutionaries get a bed to sleep in and decent food to eat. It is a disgrace that you have to work seven days a week and panhandle your meals . . . . When I get into New York you can bet I'm going to raise hell about this starvation plan. The nerve of those bureaucrats.You can bet your last dollar that none of them are sleeping on the floor or bumming their meals . . . You're the guy who's out there in contact with the enemy everyday, while they are snug and safe behind the desk. Don't let no sonofabitch browbeat you when you think you're right. They may have read all the fancy books about class struggle and think they know all the answers, but you're the one out in the weather.'" [from Bill's autobiography]

Anytime anybody decided to join one of the unions, they [the ship owners] put the finger on them in some way. The Marine Worker's Industrial Union was created by the Trade Union Unity League (TUUL) which came out of the Soviet Union. They were forming these unions all over the United States as a counter-reaction to conservative unions. We did an awful lot of good things. At least we had organized enough seamen during them days to bring about the successful 1934 strike.[54] The first batch of seamen to walk off any ship were members of the MWIU, after the longshoremen had walked off.

Some of the seamen wouldn't move. "I've got my job. I get my three meals a day and I don't want to get involved." But the MWIU called all their members off the ships. It wasn't that many but it didn't need many. Sometimes you make an impression where a guys says, "I'm not going to work with scabs" and walks off, another man will follow.

---

[54]   Bruce Nelson calls the 'Big Strike of 1934' "one of the great battles in the history of the American working class" which "transformed labor relations in the Pacific Coast maritime industry and ushered in an era of militant unionism." The strike created a rank-and-file solidarity which overshadowed the traditional factionalism and animosities among the various craft unions. Striking longshoremen and seamen closed down the maritime industry from Seattle to San Diego. As a loosely knit confederation, maritime workers, for the first time, won their a significant victory against their formidable opposition, including the shipowners and other powerful members of the business community, who were quite willing to use local police and national guard to back up the status quo. After several strikers were killed by police on the San Francisco waterfront on "Bloody Thursday", the maritime workers organized a funeral procession up Market Street. This event triggered a general strike. San Francisco, Oakland and Alameda County virtually were shut down for three days. For a visceral view of this critical event, see Rhian Miller's film, *Strikestory* For an in-depth analysis, read Bruce Nelson's *Workers on the Waterfront: Seamen, Longshoremen, and Unionism in the 1930s* (Urbana, Illinois: University of Illinois Press, 1988)

As secretary of the MWIU in Norfolk, Virginia during the 1934 strike, my job was to try to get the East Coast seamen to come out. It was very difficult at that time because that was where Joe Ryan[55] and his strong-arm characters were, plus the fact that the basic leadership of the old ISU, the International Seamen's Union, were also on the East Coast. They controlled the situation through gangsterism and intimidation. The main effort was to keep any militant spirit down. We got a few crews to come out, but nothing to give the '34 strike of the seamen and longshoremen here in San Francisco the support they needed. We slowed things down. They said, "Promise no violence." We said, "We'll even escort you to the railroad train to see that no violence will happen." They were scared. All we wanted was to get them off the ships. We made it costly for the employers, let's say that.

After the '34 strike the maritime workers voted out the MWIU since it had served its purpose. We only needed one union now that we had a chance to clean up the West Coast maritime union and elect some decent leadership. Then I joined the old ISU while I was still on the East Coast, which was led by conservatives and gangsters.

From Norfolk Bill was sent to the National Training School of the Communist Party located at a campsite in New Jersey where he fell madly in love with one of his fellow students, Pele, a stockyard worker from Chicago.

The maritime movement was brutal on women, as well as men. It was common knowledge that all the full-time male

---

[55]   Joe Ryan, who began his long career on the waterfront as a stevedore, eventually became international president of the ILA in 1927. "During his long reign, there were no authorized strikes on the New York waterfront, even though conditions for the majority of dockworkers were abominable. He fortified his regime by courting politicians and hiring criminals." Bruce Nelson, *Workers on the Waterfront*, p. 142.] The labor boss in the film, *On The Waterfront* (1954), was patterned after him, and, if anything, plays down his sociopathic character.

revolutionaries, when they started going with a woman on a steady basis, that is being responsible to her, the maritime leadership would break this up because they didn't want you spending all this time with a woman ashore when you should be out on the ships organizing. When I tried to go to Chicago, to the Great Lakes, to work, they said no. "You don't have time to screw around there with your girlfriend. Get out in the Atlantic where the ships are." Being disciplined I said okay. That meant I was away from her, from the relationship. That was the way the Party worked. They would keep you away from steady relationships with women because they felt women would end up dominating you. The movement was very bad that way.

Many of the women who got into the movement, the leadership would use them to pass out leaflets or take minutes—secretarial work, typing. Many accepted this because they didn't know any better; few women would stand up and tell you, "Hey stupid, take your goddamned typewriter and shove it! I'm not going to type! If you want to use my brain, okay, then let's work on something." Only in the latter years would qualitative things happen. Some women were strong and vocal, there's no doubt about it. Some would say, "Hey flunky, you're looking for someone to jump in the sack with, go to your favorite whorehouse but this I don't need the Party for!"

They accepted many menial tasks in the early days of their Party life. When you think about it now, it was not only demeaning, but look at the great brains we allowed to be wasted, brains galore. Here we were, amidst the most dangerous bunch in New York, along the waterfront, the ILA (International Longshoremen's Association) which was controlled by gangsters. These poor women who joined the Communist Party—good people, schoolteachers, professional people—we had them handing out leaflets to these gorillas on the waterfront. "Hey, you two-bit whore, get out of here! Commie whore, get off the street! We'll bat you one!" What the Party allowed to happen to some of the women was just criminal. They used them—"Hey, these gangsters won't punch a woman around."

It got to me a little bit. That's why I never got involved in long shore work. I was better off on a ship someplace."

A bully lesson

"I was an oiler on a ship in 1935. I was taking up a collection for some particular cause. The deck engineer was one of the most powerful men I ever seen in my life. Here was a man who could just pick you up in one hand and sling you in the air! I used to think, you don't ever want to get in a beef with this man. You'd just have to lay there and get stomped on.

I passed the collection around to the guys down in the engine room. They all said, "Put me in for a dollar—or two bucks."There was an old Spaniard on the ship who didn't speak good English. I come up off watch and he got hold of me, a little shaken up, and said, "Bill, take my name off the list, please. I'll give you the money anyway. The deck engineer said it was all for Communism and he was going to report me to the Immigration. I may get in a lot of trouble."That hit me so much that I lost all reasoning about who could fight who. It now became such a principle beef.

I'm passing the deck engineer's door to call my relief. He was sitting there, smug. I said, "I'm calling the watch now. I'll be back up here at four o'clock. You be ready to come out on deck and fight. What you did to that man—intimidated that man who signed his name on the list! You son-of-a-bitch, you be ready to come out and fight!" I didn't give him a chance to answer. When I went back in the engine room all I thought of was the way I was going to fall. I'm going to try to hit him with my right and I'm going to fall that way. I knew I couldn't last a minute with that man. One blow and I could feel the bones already crushing. But I felt as a matter of principle I had to make a showing. I really steeled myself by the time I reached the deck.

He stepped out—"Bailey! Bill! God almighty, let's not do this." He grabbed me so fast, with his arms around me that had he squeezed a little bit harder he would have broken some ribs. "Shipmates shouldn't fight. If I offended you, I apologize." He completely disarmed me. I was so happy, so relieved. I could just see myself laying there and people coming along saying, "Who's that bloody mess?" A couple of guys saw it and they passed the word around about what happened. We became friends later on. It just happened I ran into a guy who was more loudmouth than doer. He didn't know his own power or maybe he just felt that one punch would have done harm to his looks. It was a lucky break. It made the Spaniard feel good. He said, "You did it! He didn't fight! Put my name back on the list."

I went to Spain on a ship called the *S.S. Exchange* out of New York in 1935. It was my first trip to sea after coming out of the Communist school. It went to six or eight ports in Italy, Marseilles, and all the ports in Spain. From Marseilles we moved down to Barcelona. King Alphonso had taken it on the lam and sailed out of the country and the Republic was being set up. The country was in ferment; you could feel it. People were arm-in-arm, smiling, laughing, talking—some sunshine had come into their lives. I'd already become a left-winger so I had an idea of what the hell was taking place. It felt good seeing people coming into the 20th Century. I didn't understand the language but there's a certain amount you do understand— hand and eye language, waving, shaking hands. In the little towns like Malaga I tell the people I believe in socialism too. They wrap their arms about me, hug me, invite me to come have wine. They didn't even have lights in the little cafe but they gave me a glass of wine and made me feel I was a good human being. Spain stuck in my mind as being not only a beautiful place, but the people had something special about them—their big heart, their generosity. It was a great trip."

S.S. Bremen

"Hitler was making big inroads all over Germany at the time— setting up concentration camps. I got back to New York in '35 after the Mediterranean trip and nobody seemed to be taking an interest in what was going on. They weren't alarmed, outside of the Party people or people of the Left.

I stayed in New York for awhile. A seaman, Lawrence Simpson, from Seattle, sailed on the *Manhattan* which ran out of New York City to Hamburg, Germany. I had never met Simpson but I knew him to be a half-way decent guy. He also had belonged to the old MWIU and the Party. They were giving him packets of literature printed in German to smuggle aboard the Manhattan

Then when he got to Hamburg he would give it to a friendly longshoreman in the underground. Since the Nazis had wiped out all the working-class presses you couldn't get any left-wing or anti-Nazi stuff at all. Simpson made the mistake of being on a ship which also had a lot of Nazis on it. The whole steward's department was German. They reported him to the Gestapo who arrested him going into Hamburg, took him off the ship, and threw him in jail in Hamburg.

The American consulate made a report that he was in Moabit Prison in Berlin, the same prison where Ernest Heilman, who was head of the German Communist Party was being held. We thought they would let Simpson out and send him home but now he was in the big main prison which meant he was going to be there for some time.

The *S.S. Bremen* was coming into New York from Hamburg. She was the flagship of the German merchant marine. She had made all sorts of records crossing the Atlantic and carrying thousands of passengers. She docked uptown on the West side at an open pier. On the bow of the *Bremen* they had a big flag with a swastika. From the bridge of the ship they had two big Hollywood spotlights that would crisscross and shine right on the swastika which meant from half a mile you'd see a glow in the middle of the night. You'd see that rotten goddamned swastika waving.

The Party organized a big demonstration at the foot of the pier. They said to the seamen, "Here's our plan. You guys are to dress up as passengers, go aboard the Bremen on sailing night as if you're going to see some passengers off, work your way to the bow of the ship, take the swastika down. We're all going to stand there and protect you as you walk through the cordon and bring it onto the deck below and hand it to the soap-box speaker who will throw gasoline on it and burn it up."

There were ten or twelve of us seamen who were the vanguard because we understood ships. We were acting like we were drunk and having a good time to get into the pier. Once aboard the ship things started changing around. It seemed like two other seamen, Arthur and Blair, and myself, were the only ones who knew the seriousness of what we were getting into. The big wheels in the C.P. didn't know a damned thing about a ship. What was the crew supposed to do, sit there and watch you lock arms? We thought we might even be beaten to death. What would happen on an American ship? Would the Americans just sit there and let some guys do this? You'd get up and fight. It's a matter of honor. We knew that plan them idiots made in that office was impossible. First, they had the gangway guarded. You couldn't move up to the bow. Second, all the crew lived in the bow of the ship and on sailing days they generally come out and loaf around on the deck. They stand by waiting for orders to let go of the lines. It happened to be a good summer night in July. The big demonstration had come down on the dock. We were standing mid-ship near the bridge and saw twenty-five crew members come out. These were the people we would have to pass to get to the bow. It looked impossible, absolutely. Even if we got to the bow, we knew we could never get back with the flag because some cops were standing around the dock.

We discussed it among ourselves. "The twenty-minute whistle will be blowing in five minutes. Let us send two men down on the starboard side and push their way up toward the bow while the crew is standing there. That will attract all the crew members to see what the beef is and draw their attention away from the rest of us who will go up on the port side and sneak around them to the bow. If we flop, we flop—at least we'll have made an effort." We hear the whistle—"All ashore that's going ashore." Now we have to step out—the moment of truth came. You have to get into it right away, once that adrenaline hits, otherwise you'll never make it. 'Lowlife' McCormick, just a good seagoing guy, said, "Let's go!" and broke toward the bow. We ran into all the officers who were saying, "No! You can't go that way! Get off the gangway!" 'Lowlife' didn't wait, no explanation, just hit this officer and the quartermaster. Another officer grabs McCormick and they start wrestling. We just ran around the two of them and kept on galloping up to the bow. Blair was ahead of me. He ran into a sailor who jumped him. I managed to get around them and head for the bow. The crew didn't know what the hell was going on. They were watching what's going on down there—seeing everybody getting hit, banging and choking one another. The captain is hollering. Most of the officers are on the bridge dressed in their beautiful uniforms to make it look good to the passengers. I gave a fast look up and seen that whole bridge lined with nothing but officers and VIP people.

I just kept on running to the bow. I was even surprised when I came to the bow because from midship you couldn't get a good look at it. There was an extra six and a half feet of other deck that you had to climb up on a very cringy little ladder. Once you were on that little area, one little movement and you could fall over and into the dock or into the water 'cause there was no railing, just a flagpole with the swastika on it. I'm the only one up there. If anybody tries to get me, all I gotta do is turn around and kick them in the head. I grabbed the goddamned swastika, figuring it would be easy—give it a rip and it would come off. The top part of the halyard came off but when I tried to get the bottom part it wouldn't give. I was in an open area, almost like a stage; everybody on the dock is now watching. All eyes are focused on the bow. I'm standing up there like an idiot, pulling. At that moment, I would have gone over the side in disgrace if we didn't get that flag off. I turn around and see a pair of hands reaching up to the top. I was about to step on the hands because now I'm in a state of panic. Somebody called my name out—"Bill, hold the goddamned thing still!!"—meaning the last part of the halyard. It was Adrian Duffy, a little guy who has long since left the scene.

He sneaked up at the right time. I held the thing "zing!"—he cut it with his switchblade knife. I just threw the goddamned flag in the drink. He disappeared quickly. I heard the mob scream. They were going absolutely bananas on the dock. It must have been about twenty-thousand eyes now watching me. I saw my two friends knocked out on the deck—McCormick and Larry Lane, with blood all around them I heard a shot and screaming. When I was ready to jump off the bowsprit onto the main deck I saw ten crew members just standing there waiting to receive me and lay it on me. When I jumped I fell on my knees and felt two guys picking me up. They all started at one time in their zeal to blast me. Somehow the blows lost their momentum and passed me. They would have annihilated me, had all three blows hit. Again, I fell. They must have thought they had done the job so they left me there to work on somebody else on the other side.

I picked myself up and seen a sailor walking toward me. I could swear to this day I could read in his eyes that he wanted to say,"Comrade, well done." I felt he was anti-Nazi. Our side was always believing that the whole world was just waiting for us to do something. If he's one of us and he's trying to tell us we're doing a good job, the bridge is watching what's going on, so I have to make it look good. "Bang!"—I let him have one and he rolled over. Now the bridge knows that he tried to do his stuff. I started running now for the gangway to get off the ship.

All those crew members who had belted me now discovered me heading for the gangway. Then they really did—a belt here, a belt there. When I hit the deck I rolled over toward the gunwale. One guy had a pair of very pointed shoes on and he gave me two kicks. The first caught me right in the solar plexus— hah!—all the air went out. The next kick, right between the eyes. Everything started to appear in technicolor. A few minutes later I felt somebody picking me up; it was two New York cops. When I opened my eyes there was a mob of cops and passengers standing there. They dragged me with my face bleeding through the mob. One woman said, "It must be a bunch of college punks." I felt such a waste—here we took a beating, ripped the flag off, and this was the social significance—"college punks". I would sooner she said they're a bunch of Commies or anti-Fascists. The first second we went through that mob and the cop said, "Open up! Open up!", I thought I had really found the vengeance of a mob scene. If we got lost in that crowd we could have been crushed, stomped, knifed to death.

On these big piers they have little booths they can wheel around to wherever the gangway is. They put the agents in there collecting tickets. They used that booth to corral us in, once they got us off the ship. There was a guy laying out on the dock, a mess of blood all over. I couldn't recognize who he was, but when the cop dragged me up there, he looked down at the guy and says, "Is this him?" The bloodied guy says, "No." There's an old game with cops—get the son-of-a-bitch, no matter who he is, get somebody! This guy who was laying there was a detective. The crew had beat the Christ out of him because they thought he was a lefty, that he was in the Red squad. He heard rumors there was going to be a big demonstration and something happening aboard the ship. He even got aboard the ship before we did and was standing around making himself look like a passenger. Consequently, when the rising took place, he watched the first two guys run up the starboard side. He knew one of the guys was a lefty so he followed him. One of our guys, Ed Drolette, had brass knuckles on his hands. The detective told him to halt. Drolette, who thought the detective was a German seaman, came toward him; he was going to rap him one. The detective shot him in the groin and he fell to the deck. The crew coming down to see what the excitement was saw he had a pistol in his hand so they figured he must be another lefty. They chased him, took the gun, and started punching him around. He took out his badge and hollered, "I'm a policeman!" The crew grabbed the badge and threw it overboard and kept on stomping on him. They gave him a bigger beating than they gave us; blood was all over the deck. The police never did get the character who they thought beat him up because they were crew members.

They arrested six of us. Blair was beat up pretty bad and Drolette was shot so they took them to the hospital. The doctors didn't think I was banged up enough to go to the hospital. The hospital was the place we all wanted to go because that offered some protection. In jail they could beat you up. I was really shaking because I'd really taken a belting in the chest and a couple in the head. I'm trying to light a cigarette. McCormick, next to me, also had a cigarette. They had rapped his ear with a blackjack; he was also a bloody mess. One cop seen the two of us smoking and he hit McCormick in the face, knocking the cigarette out, saying, "There'll be no goddamn smoking here, you rotten bastards!"What made it difficult was that one of their cops got beat up. New York has a rule—anybody beats or shoots a cop—kill the son-of-a-bitch right then and there, if you can. They were all up-tight. They didn't know whether he was going to live or not.

The pier is now empty of visitors after the *Bremen* sailed, except when I turn now I see at least a hundred cops in a circle. I couldn't hear what was going on, but being paranoid, I felt what they were going to do was give us the old business of saying, try to escape, if you can, and then beat our brains out. I told all the other guys, the true test of a lefty is going to be right now. Taking the first blow or two is going to be the toughest; after that you won't remember anything anyway. They're going to put us through the gauntlet. Actually, one of the cops was lecturing the rest, trying to keep the calm. Then a cop said to us, "All right, you guys, stand up on your feet; we're going out."All the cops were lined up in a cordon on both sides—it's all blue, just shoulder to shoulder, all the way from where we was on top of the pier, down to the bottom of the steps. The whole street had been emptied, nothing but police cars were there. The demonstrators had moved—ten thousand people on a march to 54th Street where the police station was. They put us in a patrol wagon with cop cars and motorcycles ahead and in back of us.

When we got to the police station the cop cars had to fight their way through the mass of people. The demonstration had taken over the whole block. We could hear them saying,"Here they come now!" It's close to midnight when they back the wagon up to the door and get us out. The whole neighborhood was hollering and screaming. The cops incited the wrath of all the people in the tenements across the street who were trying to sleep. Our people are out there banging garbage can covers, making as much noise as they can. So the neighbors are throwing hot water, bags of garbage out the windows down onto the demonstrators. We're being taken up into the station. They now have to try to pin something on one of us to make it easier for them. The detective came out and looked at all of us, and of all the guys, he picked one of the strongest in character—McCormick, who wouldn't open his mouth if they took his head off. They take him in the interrogation room, about twenty feet away. "Bang!"—we could hear the door. "Bang!"—something banged up against the wall. We figured that's poor McCormick being walloped all over the place. I tell everybody,"Fellas, bite your lip. It's going to happen to each one of us now. Tell 'em nothing." The door opens and McCormick comes—pow!—flying out. Most of us had prayer beads—no papers, no identification. The guise was that we were Catholics. Hitler was lowering the boom on the Catholics in Germany, telling them, "We'll tell you what to preach on Sunday. Don't tell us about your Pope—we'll tell you." The priest would have to get up and read: "Hitler is good for the nation."We were protesting this as Catholics. We didn't know anything about the Soviet Union. We were just protesting against Catholics and Jews being persecuted. One cop says,"Now there's six people in here and they're all Irish, not a Jew among them. I don't know what the hell is going on here. They've all got prayer beads."

We were charged with rioting—no big federal type of thing. We laid in jail a couple of days and eventually bailed out and then went on the road, speaking to various groups to get up enough money to set up a defense. Marcantonio, who was a congressman from Harlem, came down to one session to defend us in court.

Mayor Fiorella LaGuardia[56] in the beginning said, "Nobody is going to riot in my city and get away with it! I'll see they're taken care of." Then Goebbels[57] put his foot in his mouth. He said, "This could only happen in a city controlled by a mayor who's a half-Dago and a half-Jew." Of course the papers played this up immediately."

On the Waterfront

The real On the Waterfront starred Bill and a handful of other dedicated marine workers who attempted to clean up the old International Seamen's Union on the East Coast after the '34 strike. Later he was sent to Baltimore during the spring strike of '36 to organize the rank and file against the union officials who were affiliated with the gangster element which had ruled the East coast docks for many years.

"We managed to pull one ship out on strike before I received the worst beating of my life—broken nose, broken jaw. The gangsters were behind the beating; they put the finger on me to the cops. So I came out to the West Coast. They said, "We know what happened there. Here's your membership book." I stayed here ever since. I was expelled from the ISU because I "brought the union into ill repute" when I tore the swastika off the *Bremen*. It was an honor to be expelled by the East Coast crooks. I was made editor of *The Black Gang News*, the Marine Firemen's Union paper in San Francisco.

After the '34 strike, while they got a few things battened down, like better conditions, work rules, and wages, a lot of other matters were not resolved—like complete domination of the hiring hall, where every man going to sea had to go through the union hiring hall. The shipping master of the company would pick a few of his

---

56   Fiorella LaGuardia, the "Little Flower", who served as mayor of New York from 1934 to 1945, was known for his honesty and integrity. He spearheaded an unprecedented municipal government reform movement.

57   Joseph Goebbels was the German Nazi minister of propaganda from 1933-45.

favorites. He'd call into the union hall, "Send me two firemen, three oilers."Then, instead of the men going directly aboard the ship, they came down to the shipping master. He checked them out, looked them over. The union didn't have that type of power to say,"You go to hell! This man is being taken whether you like it or not!" A lot of things were left open. We only had a partial control of the hiring hall. The shipowners didn't want to disturb too much of it until it came time to renegotiate the 1934 contract, the award, as they called it. The employers said, "We want to go back to the old ways of doing things. We're not going to give further concessions. We're going back to the way it was on the waterfront. You come to us and we'll give you the jobs." The union said, "No way." We put in our demands. We wanted one hundred percent control of the hiring hall, overtime after eight hours, and numerous other items. It would take the '36 and '37 strikes to confirm that all jobs went through the hiring hall. Then when you wanted an available job, you gave your card to the union dispatcher who gave that job out to the man who was longest 'on the beach', so it was completely fair.

At that time we had a strong Maritime Federation[58]; that was the good part about it. We played ball according to the

---

[58] The Maritime Federation of the Pacific Coast, founded in 1935 as a result of "the extraordinary solidarity that the marine workers had achieved during the Big Strike" of 1934, was an uneasy alliance involving various craft unions, communists, anti-communists, syndicalists and such colorful and dynamic leaders as Harry Bridges and Harry Lundeberg. At its zenith the Maritime Federation had about forty thousand members which was small potatoes compared to the numbers in other industries such as steel and auto. The influence of this small federation of workers went far beyond their numbers. According to Bruce Nelson, " . . . the ferment generated by the Great Depression and the New Deal made other workers and other sections of the population receptive to the militant tactics and even the radical outlook that so often permeated the waterfront in the 1930's." Nelson, *Workers on the Waterfront*, p.219.

Federation—that included the longshoremen. When we went out on strike now we're united. Everybody went out together—walked off the ships, walked off the piers, shut it down! Every union had to supply so many men when picket lines were set up. We organized and set up one of the best soup kitchens in the world. Where the men couldn't get fat on the ship they got fat on the soup line. No problem with food. The donations were plentiful. In the Fireman's Union I was chairman of the publicity committee. Then I was on the Joint Strike Committee 1936-37. Our job was to make sure that every neighborhood knew what the hell the strike was all about. We'd go to the radio stations and be interviewed. It was a propaganda war, definitely. We won that strike hands down after 110 days. We got a tremendous amount of concessions—increased overtime, wages, job security. It really strengthened the unions, no doubt about it.

The best part of any strike when you win it, you have so much compassion for some other union 1000 miles away which is battling for a place in the sun. Immediately, as soon as they send you a letter saying, "Can we get any financial help?" Right away if they need clothes, give them your clothes. When I went to the Hawaiian Islands right after the '36 and '37 strike to help organize with the Hawaiian sugar and pineapple workers, we didn't have any money to put out a newspaper there. Just with the influence I had as a marine fireman in San Francisco, I was able to go aboard all those Matson ships that came to Hawaii and meet guys I knew. I'd say, "We're trying to put out a newspaper here and organize this place." I'd take up a collection, two-bits, fifty cents, anything they'd throw in. I'd walk away with 5-6 dollars. That was a lot of money. Everybody wanted to get the other guy organized because they knew it would be easier for us all in the end."

Bill laid the groundwork for the formation of unions in the sugar and pineapple growing industries in Hawaii. He left when he found out he was going to be arrested for criminal syndicalism. At that time the International Brigades were being organized to help fight against Franco's forces in Spain. Bill joined the Lincoln Brigade[59] and was sent to France in June, 1937 where he crossed the Pyrennes on foot with other members of the Brigade to join the fight against fascism.

Spanish Civil War

"The Spanish monarchy was brought down by a coalition of the working class and Socialists, pitted against the ruling class. The king had fled. They set up a parliamentary form of government. When they started to redistribute the land, Franco started a revolt and took over some of the towns and cities by force of arms, recruiting his own army of Moors and Spanish fascists. Mussolini and Hitler were supplying them with arms, including over a hundred thousand troops from Italy and Germany. Spain was lost as a Republic by a lack of arms and Allied support. The Allies would not act till most of Europe had been overrun by the fascists."

After the Republican Army captured a town, Bill escorts some prisoners back to military headquarters.

"It was our job to take them under escort out of this little town and back to our headquarters. The military big wheels were there. I took up the rear with my loaded rifle. I was stupid. These guys are all crippled up; they've given up, and yet we're positioned that maybe they're going to make a break for it. We may have to shoot them. On the way, I take out a cigarette and light it up. Two of the guys are dragging along the third guy in the center. He had been hit in the leg. One of the three turned around to me and said,"Senor, give me a cigarette, please, por favor?" He said it two or three times. I said, "Speak with Franco or Hitler

---

[59]   According to Bill the Lincoln Brigade was created "when La Passionaria shouted out,'Where are all you anti-fascists now when we need you?' She gave inspiration to 42,000 people from all over the world who found their way to Spain and created the six Brigades. From each country they adopted the names of revolutionaries for their brigade. Most of the volunteers had no military training. Eighty percent died in the struggle."

or Mussolini. Get your cigarettes from them."That thing has been on my conscience all these years. What a cigarette would have meant to these guys—gosh, especially since I was a smoker, too. It was the same as it would have meant to me if I was in their position. It was the cruelest thing. I've regretted that all my life. The prisoner is thinking, when a man wouldn't even give you a cigarette, what's going to happen to us a half mile away? Boy, these Republicans are going to tear us limb from limb. If I had it to do over again I would have lit the cigarette and put it in his mouth. I was so conditioned that these were our enemies, no matter who they are, no matter what they say. Now the same guy is asking you for one of your cigarettes. I could have shown compassion. I always felt very bad about that, very bad. They were recruits; they were dragged into the army by Franco. I may not have committed many 'cruel' things, but one was enough. I was a sergeant. I was there for eighteen months—it was a hell of a long time. You weren't that long in battle; most of the time you spent in preparation for it, like getting ready to recross the Ebro River, the main river which divides Spain. My God, we practiced for two months getting ready to cross, getting into a little boat, going through the gymnastics of rowing across, then charging up some hill and trying to dig a little trench and get into it. Every day you're going through this stuff, in boiling hot weather. The food became less; sometimes you get stuck with potato soup for five days. Other times you have maybe split peas or garbanzos. Whatever came, you got. That's the way it was, day after day until you ran out of that. But never anything fresh. All the fresh stuff, the good stuff, went out of the country, into big trucks and driven into France to buy medicine or something else.

By the end of the war we were breaking out with boils. I had big ones all along the wrist. The frontline doctor put a piece of gauze over them and said, "You know what you need for that? Eggs, fresh milk, green vegetables."Aaaagh! He'd squeeze it and you'd drop to your knees. He'd take a whole handful of pus out of it. These things are an inch and a half, big boils. After you recovered you could look down and see your bone and tendons, that's how bad it was. Then another week later another one would appear. Malnutrition. You're half crippled up. Feet are the same way; we never had proper shoes. Soap was impossible.

We dried some potato leaves in the sun for a day until they really got dry, then chopped them up fine, rolled them up in cigarette papers and smoked them. That was our tobacco. We took bark off trees, and the green moss growing on it, dried and smoked it. We had to have some sort of a fix. Many of us were smokers. We had plenty of cigarette papers but no tobacco.

Before we took a town, we surveyed it. One guy came back and said, "There are a few Fascists in the town. We're going to give them a chance to take off without a fight so we don't have to wreck the town. It has a tobacco shop in it; there's plenty of tobacco." Within an hour's time we all had a pocket full of tobacco. Now we didn't care what happened. We had all the tobacco we[60] wanted. Sad, when you think of it.

For Whom the Bell Tolls

"Everybody knew Hemingway was in Spain. It was one of them cold windy goddamn days. The clothing we had on was not winter clothing; we were just chilled to the bone. It was way the hell up in Aragon country someplace. As we're marching down a road it was demoralizing when we'd see one of our army trucks go by every now and then with nobody sitting in the back. You'd say a dozen or two of us should have been allowed to jump in the truck and ride back, but that is not the way the army is. There's no difference between the Red Army, the Chinese Army, the American Army, the Spanish Army— bureaucrats are bureaucrats. They think the more you march, the more you suffer, the better soldier you make. So these trucks go by; it's cold, windy. We're trying to sing songs; there's no food. We were told that three more hours of marching we could get something to eat. We pull into some piece of flatland

---

[60] Bill, who suffers from asthma, quit smoking ten years ago.

marsh. It's full of bamboo-like tules. They get us off the road, and we (it was a whole battalion of men) get told, "Pull in here. Make yourselves as comfortable as possible." Most of us are makeshift characters; we see opportunity to break off from the wind, so we chop, chop some tules and zip them together to make a windbreaker. Others see us so they start doing it. We get our little place fixed up and some food came up later on. Just then we see a woman. "That's Martha Gellhorn.[61] She's with Hemingway all the time." There was Hemingway walking a few feet from her. For one second I brushed shoulders with Hemingway. He jawed with us, laughed and smiled. He was well-clothed for the weather.

We stayed in that place two days. We finally went back into the interior of Spain. The Fascists came right down on one side of the Ebro right into the ocean and split Spain in half, pushing us on the northern side of the Ebro. Every bridge was blown up along the way. For the next five days our people were scrambling back in the middle of the night, trying to swim the Ebro and escape from being captured. Merman, our commander, and some of the other gold braid, got caught by the Fascists and were shot. Our guys were drifting back, bodies floating down the river."

While Bill was hospitalized for pneumonia, the tattered Republican Army was in full retreat before the well-equipped and supplied fascist forces. Even the soldiers in hospital were encouraged to leave their beds and shore up the disintegrating front. Bill, of course, went back to the front with a small group of fellow patients in a broken-down truck.

"We got just past Rio Ebro. The Fascists had not come all the way down to the Mediterranean as yet, but they had captured all the interior section. When we got out to rejoin the outfit, there was no outfit to join. There was one man here, another

---

[61]   She and Hemingway were married later. Her career as a war correspondent lasted nine years. Her novel, *A Stricken Field*, based on her experiences during the fall of Prague in 1938, remains one of the best, and probably least known, chronicles of that bleak period.

man some other place. We decided we were safe on the Northern side of the Ebro, and if we'd just stay around and keep within a group, we'd eventually pick up all the stragglers. There were about ten of us standing around in sight of the Ebro. There's nothing to eat. We don't know what the hell to do. I see off in the distance dust rising in the air; it's in our position, so it had to be one of ours—friendly. The wave of dust comes closer—it's an open car with a Spanish driver, and in the backseat was Hemingway and Herb Mathews, a reporter from *The New York Times*. They got out, shook hands, and we introduced ourselves. Hemingway says, "Fellas, you guys from the Lincoln?" "Yeah, we're scattered all over the place." First thing we ask, "Do you have a cigarette?" Out came a pack of American cigarettes. I remember taking one out, handing it back. He said, "Go ahead, keep the whole pack." To us it was like keeping a million dollars. That's the cigarette habit. Then he broke out a flask of brandy. "Have a shot fellows—you guys need it." We emptied it around. Even guys who didn't drink, just drank it for the sake of calming down. We talked some more. We spent maybe a half hour with him. He was going further on down the Ebro. That was the only contact I had with him—thanks for the pack of cigarettes and a shot of brandy.

All of us lefties, we don't want to admit something went wrong. We don't want to admit that we committed cruelties. We always like to put ourselves in the best light. If we are the saviors, the other guys are the devils. When *For Whom the Bell Tolls*[62] came out, it had a piece where the heroine is talking about what happened to the mayor of the town—how they whipped him across the road and then threw him over a cliff.

---

[62]   In *For Whom the Bell Tolls* Ernest Hemingway tells the story of one American who fights against the Franco fascists with a band of guerillas in the mountains. Many of the young idealists who fought in the Spanish Civil War in the International Brigades were upset with Hemingway's portrayal of atrocity on both sides as a natural part of any war.

Then, the reverse of that, was that the Loyalists had done the same to somebody else; it was a retaliation. We all said, "That's impossible—we don't commit crimes. We don't commit these type of things." But we did. Not that we threw people over cliffs, but I know we took people out and shot them on the mere pretext that somebody put the finger on them. If you were under suspicion, you were making bad remarks about the Republic, or else you associated with the Fascists, the Servicio Intelligencia Militaire probably took them out and shot them. It happens in wars. I don't know how the hell you could ever solve this question. Anyhow, that happened. We got teed off about it because we don't want to talk about these things. We talked about their atrocities, but never ours.

Even when I went to Spain for Grenada, British television, in 1983, I was reluctant to talk about bad things, because now it becomes public knowledge and it's coming from somebody who was there, which means it's authenticated. The asked me and I said, "No, I don't know. I never heard." "What was your position with the Trotskyites?" "They were enemies." Now they're proving in Spain that they weren't enemies, that Trotskyites died like flies, shot by Franco too.[63]

We can talk about these things openly now, but in them days you couldn't. Only the enemy committed a cruelty, not us—we're incapable of it. And that's not so. We're capable of doing every goddamned thing, and probably better. You have to start with the truth with yourself—that's where it has to begin. Once you're truthful with yourself, then you can start being truthful with others. That's my point of view.

---

[63] "Now we're in a more open period. Like Trotsky now, in the Soviet Union, will probably become a hero. Half the Russian Army generals had been shot and we wouldn't believe it. We said they were enemies, that these guys collaborated with the bourgeoisie to undermine the Soviet Union, because that's what we were told. Now it's proven otherwise—that they just had criticism of Stalin. Stalin had them taken out and shot because he was paranoid."

That will always be the curse—[*that the Allied powers did not support the Republican government in Spain*]. It was bad enough that Roosevelt had this neutrality act, which wouldn't help either side, but to see a so-called Socialist brother on the other side, France, not do anything, sit there and watch people starve to death, that's pitiful."

Heroes' exit

"Many of us had talked about staying in Spain after the war to help put the country back together, whether it was engineering or plumbing or whatever. But we woke up one morning and got told to get ready to leave. They called us the extranharios, which means foreigners. Now there was a couple of reasons it was done. First, we were beaten to a frazzle. Our ranks had been so thinned out; every day we were losing more, losing more. We didn't have the materials to continue to fight. There was a certain amount of hopeless feeling among the guys. We were just not winning. No food, no bullets, no tanks, no nothing. Fight on, but with what? The other was if the Republic got rid of all its foreign troops then this would be a big incentive for all the governments of the world to demand that Franco get rid of all his foreign troops, meaning all the Italians, the Moors, the Germans. If that was done, then what was left of the Republic of Spain would take control of the whole country, because Franco depended on foreign troops to keep his government in power.

We were ushered out to a little town near the French border called Ripoll. We stayed there for two and a half weeks. We scrubbed up. They brought in delousing machines, civilian clothes, our passports. They gave us $25 American money then put us on the train for France. The first railroad station we came to was ten feet across into France from Spain. They're starving to death on the Spanish side, but when we got off the train in this small railroad station to catch another train, we walked into the area where you can buy coffee. There were hams hanging up, sausages, bars of chocolate, tons of food all over the place for sale, but not to Spain. The first thing we'd say, "You callous bastards, how could you do this? How could you let kids and women starve to death on the other side and you with all this food?"

They put us on a special train, pulled all the windows down, locked the doors—we couldn't get out, then set off toward Paris. Every now and then we'd come to a railroad station, where the train would slow down and maybe wait for a moment. There was people in the station with sandwiches, food, bottles of wine, gifts to us, but they wouldn't allow us out, wouldn't open up the doors or windows. People were greeting us. They had heard we were coming through. In all the railroad stations they had Sengelese guards, from North Africa (the same ones that France was fighting in Algiers), so we could not get out of the train. They chased the people away. That was the policy that France was pursuing, to appease Hitler. We get within ten, fifteen miles of Paris. We hear there's twenty thousand people around the railroad station in Paris to greet us. The French government hears this and reroutes: the train. "Don't bring it in by way of Paris. We don't want the excitement to get out of hand." They switch the train on another track; we go all the way down to LeHavre. They bring us right into the pier. We get out of the train and ten feet away is the gangway to the ship. French troops, police, said, "Get aboard." We stay aboard the ship all night and next morning they pull up the gangway and we sail for Nova Scotia, Canada and then New York. That shows you the French government wanted to take that moment of glory away, that the International Brigades could have had, by going into France and being greeted by twenty thousand people, denying the French people the right to salute the International—that's how bad and biased they were then.[64]

---

[64]   The ironic epilogue: "I am telling you when I hear the name Blum [then the president of France] I get sick. Today in Spain, many of the Italian troops, who volunteered or were sent in as volunteers from Mussolini, get pensions from the Spanish government, Also some Germans. They sent out a questionnaire to all the Americans who had been there to sign up for it. There was some elected official who tried to pass this bill, which says all Internationals, it doesn't

I lasted about two days in New York. They gave me a ticket to go back to the point of origin. I got on the bus to San Francisco. I owed the Marine Firemen's Union about eighty bucks in dues, which was a fortune in them days. They said, "Get a ship and pay it when the trip is over. I got on the *President Monroe* which was going around the world. We were coming down the Mediterranean. The war was still going on in Spain. Both sides were talking on the radio. Spain was getting ready to fall. Barcelona had already fallen, but Madrid was still holding out. By the time I got to New York and then back to San Francisco on that trip, the war was over. Then the real agony began—the rounding up of thousands of people, putting then in concentration camps, shooting them left and right. At least a quarter of a million people were taken out and shot, day in and day out.

On the bus back to San Francisco I struck up a conversation while sitting next to a woman passenger. I told her I was over in Spain for a year and a half, fighting to maintain the Republican government. She said, "You must be very rich. As a mercenary, they pay very big. What are you riding the bus for?" I said, "Lady, we got a dollar a day; we turned the money back to buy milk for the kids. We didn't go over there to make a dollar off the war; we went for a principle." She said, "A principle? I don't know what principle is worth fighting over." I felt like strangling her, but this was the attitude of many

---

matter who they are—Americans, etc., should receive a pension. American papers played it up big. I went down to the Spanish consulate and put my application in. I figured if I got a pension it would be $20 a month or something like that. My deal was to turn it over to the widows' and orphans' fund in Spain to buy books for the kids. But in the process of putting applications into the Socialists who are head of Spain now, he turned around and said, 'We pay them nothing! These Internationalists (meaning us) had no business interfering in a family fight.' So the whole pension deal with the American volunteers was shelved."

people I came in contact with. They did not see or understand the urgency. Of course they did six months later. Franco took control of Spain and bang!—the Second World War broke out in Europe. Roosevelt's last words were, "If I had to do it all over again, I'd support Spain." Too late then.

World War II

"I made a few ships after that and went back into organizing. The Burma Road was hot. Japan had moved into Manchuria and other parts of China. The only way to get supplies into China was via the Burma Road and the nearest port was Rangoon on the Irrawaddie River. I was on the *President Johnson* for a week before we sailed out of San Francisco and on the last day, on comes a guy who was the most Red-baiting son-of-a-bitch in my union—the Firemen's Union. This was just before Pearl Harbor when we sailed to Rangoon. Up to this point it was going to be a beautiful trip. With him aboard, I'm going to end up with ulcers and all my energy is going to fight this character. We worked together. He was an oiler and I was a maintenance man. I was also the ship's delegate.[65]

We got to Manila. Our ship was too big to go into the dock because it drew too much water so we laid at anchor and had a motorboat at our disposal. Every day while we were at anchor a certain number of men would be allowed to go ashore. My name was on the same list as his. I had been in Manila before. He said, "Where's a good place to go?" I said, "We'll go up to the Tivoli Gardens—lots of dancing, good food, women." We had to come back the next day which meant you stayed ashore that night. I could see that since he didn't know Manila, he would be easily taken. I knew some of the streets and streetwise things. I said, "No, don't drink anymore". You're getting a little stupid now. The gals are looking at you and trying to force drinks on you. A couple more and you'll end up with no

---

[65]   The ship's delegate was the union representative elected by the ship's crew to arbitrate between the crew and the officers.

wallet, no nothing. Lay off right now, otherwise I'm going to walk out on you." I could see that the women were constantly conferring with shady characters at the bar—the pimps and hustlers. Now I felt I had to protect him because we were together. We ended up in the Seamen's Church Institute in a big airy room. It was beautiful. He slept off the alcohol and we woke up and had a good bacon and egg breakfast. We were in good shape. He started to feel pride in himself that he wasn't coming back to the ship with any social disease or a busted lip or he hadn't been rolled.

The guy responsible for all this was the guy he'd been attacking all these years—a so-called Communist. It just blew his mind. He got hold of me to the side later and said, "Look, Bailey, every time you ran for office in the union hall, I always opposed you. You run for any job you want in this union from now on and I'm going to be your biggest supporter." This was coming from an outstanding Red-baiter. It was a big ship with a tremendous engine-room staff. It came time to pay the crew off in San Francisco. I'm collecting for *The People's World*, for the King-Ramsey fund[66], and maybe one other thing. I set up a table in the main dining room where the money was being handed out to all the crew. After they'd get paid off, they'd come to my table and say,"What are you collecting for?" I'd get a dollar here, two dollars. Or sometimes the guy says, "Hell, nothing!"and walks out. I thought he'd walk right out but he came over and gave me two bucks here, two bucks there. "Put my name down too." I'm watching him in amazement.

---

[66]   "The King-Ramsey-Connor Fund was established to pay for the defense of these three marine workers charged with conspiracy to murder a chief engineer, an anti-union character. All three were convicted by the then Alameda District Attorney, Earl Warren. As a result they were sent to San Quentin. During World War II, Warren, who was by then Governor of California, pardoned Ramsey."

If I was one of those lefties who got drunk and sloppy and didn't care what I was doing—you're no example to nothing. You're just the regular riff-raff that you meet anyplace. You have to be exemplary. This is the type of system I'm fighting for, where we're all concerned with each other. He was one of those who appreciated that, more than anything else. It didn't take no punching or blackjacking or choking him to death—just plain talk and just being a halfway decent guy convinced him. It didn't make him join the Communist Party, but he had a different viewpoint from there on in—that all lefties weren't devils. I felt very good about that.

When I got back to San Francisco, about four months later, I had to go to New York. There was a union election coming up. We had a branch of the union in New York City. There was always forty, fifty crew members hanging around the port waiting for ships. I did some campaigning—talked to the crews about voting for me. I was elected business agent of the Firemen's Union. My job was to represent our members and see that our contracts were lived up to.

I'm sitting in the Paramount theater in New York City—bang!—the screen went black and a voice came on: "All members of the Armed Forces who are in this theater, you are to leave immediately and rejoin your group. Pearl Harbor has just been attacked by the Japanese. The American fleet has been destroyed." You could feel the tension in the air. I got out in the street—newspaper extras were screaming with headlines about the sneak attack, people were dashing around, looking bewildered.

By the time I got installed as port agent in the union office, ships were now being pulled out of service and sent into shipyards quickly to have guns and extra armor put on them. In that interim there was a few days when ships were loaded up and they couldn't wait for them to get in a shipyard. Those were the ships that went out to sea without any guns on them, without any special equipment, and many got torpedoed. My job was to supply all these ships with men, to keep discipline among the guys. I kept that job for eight or nine months, until the next election. Meantime, kids coming out of school, the military or merchant marine academies where they got thirty-day training, would come down to the Hall. I'd talk to them, get them aboard the ship, inspire them.[67]

They'd never seen ships before. I'm working six o'clock in the morning till midnight, groggy half the time, visiting ships, flying to Washington, talking to Congressmen, before special boards, discussing how to improve the safety on the ships, the welfare of the men, how to make it safer for them. I'm taking up all the union beefs that took place—skippers that thought they now had all the rights in the world to be a Simon Legree. "There's no more union, no more nothing! You take your orders from me! Forget overtime. Take your agreement and shove it!"This was the attitude I had to deal with."

Racism within the maritime industry

"In the Firemen's Union there might have been a few minorities; they came under the guise of Puerto Ricans. There was an unwritten law: you didn't bring blacks in. It was a so-called white man's union. This was also true of the Sailors' Union of the Pacific. Now the longshoremen were different. Harry Bridges[68] had a strong code of racial equality. But still there were very few. There were maybe four or five gangs after the '34 strike. Now

---

[67]   Bill did more than inspire these young men. Some of them came into port "all shook up" after experiencing a bombing raid in the North Atlantic. He would take their pay and put it in the Seamen's Savings Bank so they wouldn't spend it all in one night or he would find them a place to stay outside the City to recuperate for a few days—"anything to get them away from the goddamned waterfront where the leeches were waiting for them".Years later, guys came up to Bill and thanked him for looking out for them.

[68]   Harry Bridges, founder and first president of the International Longshoreman and Warehouseman's Union, led the strike of 1934 in San Francisco. Hated and hounded by the shipping industry and conservative politicians, he was beloved by the rank-and-file

it's predominately black. The longshore and warehousing is about half and half. The Firemen's Union, no; maybe two or three blacks in it. Sailors, one or two, if that much. They know how to circumvent the laws to keep them out.

The CP wanted to break it down entirely. But you're beating your head up against the bulkhead door. There's no sense putting out a leaflet on it every day, exhorting the men to bring blacks in. They'd laugh at you. You only isolated yourself, so you didn't do it. During the War while I was agent in New York, I was in charge of the whole port. A young black guy came out of the Maritime Training School in Sheepshead Bay. He wanted a job in the engine room. This was wartime now. He wanted to go to San Francisco. I said, "When you get there see Walter Stack. Walter is a Lefty and a great fighter for Union principles." I gave him a note which said, "Dear Walter, See that he gets a ship."[69]

---

from which he emerged. In 1970 he was named to the San Francisco Port Commission and finally retired from the waterfront in 1977. When he died in 1990 at the age of 88, James Herman, who succeeded Bridges as president of the ILWU, said, "For half a century, Harry Bridges was the heart and soul of the West Coast labor movement. He was a towering figure of our time, one of those rare individuals whose life gives shape and meaning to an era." Carl Nolte, "S.F. Labor Leader Harry Bridges Dies", *San Francisco Chronicle*, March 31, 1990, p.A1.

[69] Walter Stack is a legendary San Francisco character. As an octogenarian long-distance runner and swimmer he is probably in a class by himself. Hounded off the waterfront, along with his fellow union member, Bill Bailey, for being a Communist during the McCarthy era, Walt became a hod carrier and began swimming in the local pools to build stamina. He joined the Dolphin Club (whose members actually choose to swim in the Bay year round) and then founded the Dolphin South End Running Club. He is famous for running across the Golden Gate Bridge to Sausalito, stopping in Sausalito for a beer, and then running back to the Dolphin Club, located at the foot of Hyde Street on the San Francisco waterfront, for a swim.

A month later there was a big beef in the Firemen's Union in San Francisco. They were going to lynch Stack on Market Street. As a Union official Stack was put in charge of the shipping for the weekend. He had to stay there by the phone because ships were departing in convoys; somebody had to be able to get the men to the ships right away if needed, otherwise they'd sail short-handed. The weekend he was on, all sorts of jobs started coming in. He used this opportunity to ship this black guy out as a wiper. The guy came aboard late in the evening, lays down in the bunk in a six-man room. Some drunk comes in about three o'clock in the morning and sees this black guy in the bunk. "We don't take any blacks on this ship. You belong in the steward department." He shows him his card signed by Stack. The ship didn't sail for about four days. It was just long enough for the right-wing officials to go up and down the waterfront and whip up all the anti-black sentiment they could. "Stack is packing the ships with blacks!" That got everybody into a state of shock. "Every other man on the ship is going to be a Negro! What are we coming to?" Stack fought it but they took the guy off the ship. They found a way to get rid of him. I think they transferred him to the steward's department. It was near election time. They used this to oust Stack in the election. They posed the question in open leaflets about what the waterfront and shipping was going to be like with Stack as a union official. In New York I read about all of this from the San Francisco minutes. I made my feelings known by insisting that, "If you vote Walter Stack out of office because he's putting Negroes on the ship, you vote against me too because I believe in the same thing. This is wartime. This is the right thing to do, the human thing to do. The torpedo doesn't discriminate against the black on a ship—it just kills everyone." A month later when the ballots were counted and the election was over, I'm reelected and Stack was out. Of course the next year Stack was back in because they found out he was very valuable, because he's a fighting son-of-a-bitch for his members.

The government wasn't pressing enough. They didn't have these agencies that they have now. The government didn't want to take on the unions fighting over a few blacks. They weren't about to go overboard on this issue.

One young kid came in from a Murmansk run. It was the worst place in the world, a Russian port, way up in the North. If you got torpedoed and had to go overboard, you would die from the cold water unless you got picked up quickly. He had been on this run, and about sixteen ships out of thirty-five were sunk. He was one of the lucky ones; he got out on a raft with four other guys. They were cold, miserable for about five days on the raft before a Russian airplane spotted them and radioed for the gunboats to pick them up. He was in a Russian hospital for a month. He lost two fingers, several toes, part of his ear from frostbite. I told him as far as I was concerned he didn't have to go to sea anymore. He said, "I want another ship out of here. This is a war; we have to fight to win it." Here he is, agitating the agitator. I thought how can I, a revolutionary, sit here in a safe, comfortable spot, home every night, steam heat, halfway decent food, and send this guy out on a ship after he got torpedoed and spent four days in the frozen Arctic? I'm going to go back to sea. Anybody can do what I'm doing. I resigned in two weeks. I hopped in a car and drove to San Francisco. I enrolled in an engineering school and three weeks later got my engineering ticket and sailed during most of the War, just to satisfy myself. That's where the action was—not sitting at a desk. I felt better for it.[70]

---

[70] Throughout the War the merchant marine transported supplies to all the theatres of war at great risk to the crews. 6,900 merchant seaman died aboard 731 cargo ships which were sunk during the War. 5,300 were injured and 581 were taken prisoner by the Japanese and Germans, according to an article in *The San Francisco Marine Fireman*, June 14, 1991, p. 2.

I was in on an invasion of the Aleutians and went down to New Guinea, Okinawa, the Solomons,Australia, the Phillipines, delivering supplies. I had the great good fortune to go into the Battle of Manila." [*Bill wangled his way aboard a PT boat to participate in a harrowing night raid inside Manila Bay.*] "Everybody wanted to be a PT boat man, same as everybody wanted to be an aviator or a cowboy. It was quite an experience."

"That funny thing called love"

"When I came back from Spain, I get a call from a friend of mine. She says,"Jack Eggan's girlfriend would like to see you." [*He had been killed in Spain and was a friend of Bill's.*] I take her to dinner. (In them days thirty-five cents was a seven course dinner.) She was an attractive woman, very smart. She was a copywriter for newspapers. I told her all about her boyfriend, Jack, how he died. I spend a couple of hours with her and make arrangements to have dinner again next week, and then one thing led to another. Jack Eggan petered out of the picture. Meantime, she's very active in the Spanish Civil War refugee relief. We really got interested in each other. I went out to sea and made a trip around the world, writing letters every port, getting mail. When I came back from the trip my insecurity insisted that we had to get married right away. She said,"That's crazy, why get married?" I think I forced the issue.

She became a radical herself at the old University of Washington. It was the most progressive college in our country at that time. Almost everybody was a radical of some kind. Her family ended up millionaires, but she was such a character that they cut her out of everything. They liked me, by the way; they thought I was a great influence on their daughter because I used to tell her to cut down on the drinking. She was a great jazz fan. She worked for one of the bands at the time, doing publicity work for them. I ended up going to jazz concerts with her, going here, going there. I'm working up in Richmond on a fish reduction ship, twelve hour shifts, exhausted all the time, trying to organize other ships around there, trying to race down here to San Francisco to spend time with her. Our marriage lasted five years.

Being a seaman, where you had to pay for everything—you go out with a woman, you put the money on the line. When you start off that way you think that's the only thing there is, until one day you get it for nothing, and a whole new world opens up to you. You get it for nothing and all you want of it. You didn't think anything like that existed. So consequently, this whole new world blossomed out. You become jealous of everything. You're suspicious of everything that happens. Somebody moving in on you. You're so insecure yourself, as most seamen are.

I'd never had girlfriends as a kid at school. I never went to school long enough to have girlfriends, so I had none of that preliminary type of stuff—that petting and caressing and touching up department—none of that business. I went right into the mainstream and it proved rough. As far as sophistication was concerned, she could walk all over me.

She decided to go to sea. Through The Marine Cooks and Stewards Union she got herself a job as a telephone operator. She got on one of the big ships running to Australia, the *Mariposa*, I think. Her ship was practically caught in Sydney when Pearl Harbor took place. She came to New York and we lived there until we decided to come back to the West Coast. She was still working for the newspapers and had a couple of jobs going at the time. She loved to drink, loved to be at a night club. All the money I was getting out of my job in the union was going for nightclub entertaining, which I needed like a hole in the head. She thought it was great. I had to go to work in the morning and I'd be beat to death. It was becoming impossible, and the more this went on, the more irritable life became. I could see that nothing was working because everything with me was the whole war effort and it meant being there in the union hall at six in the morning to seven or eight at night. I didn't have time for all this goddamn boozing up. Consequently, one of the ways out was I got the hell out of there, went back to San Francisco, became an engineer, and went to sea, which, as I said before, I wanted to do. I could have sat the whole war out in New York but that wasn't my bucket of bolts.

The first ship I got on was headed for New Guinea. I could see the arguments becoming more persistent. All the romance was going up in smoke. We had two different cultures, almost, working against each other. I'm off in the South Pacific someplace and I got one of them Dear John letters. I had made an allotment out to her while I was away which immediately I told the captain to cut off. I wasn't going to finance somebody else's romance with my hard-earned money.

At the end of the War came Ruthie, who's the mother of my kid. That lasted just about five years too. She moved to Los Angeles and stayed about six months. I made several trips down to spend a little time with my son, a day or a weekend and drove back, because I was also trying to fight to make a living. She eventually got married and moved to New York. That was very difficult period because it's not like Los Angeles, a couple of hours in the car. I made maybe two trips back there while they were in New York and saw him as much as I could. But I didn't get that good feeling of enjoyment, of watching him grow inch by inch. When he was still here in San Francisco, after we broke up, I'd take him on most weekends. We'd go to the beach or the zoo or have a meal. It was a lot of fun, a good feeling to be with him. But after she took him away, it made my life very sad. Back in New York he continued to grow and develop, but without my help or influence. They came back to L.A. after four or five years and I saw him a couple of times there but he had grown away from that little cuddling stage. Eventually they moved back up here and at least I could go see the kid and pick up a telephone and call him but there was so much of his life that was taken away from me. It was very sad and very painful. Now when he comes into town he'll call me up. We'll spend time. He's a great kid. I write to him at every opportunity." [*His son is now an Able Bodied seaman, a veteran sailor in the merchant marine, for the last seventeen years.*]

Bill has lived in a 1906 'earthquake shack' near Coit Tower[71] for some thirty years. These shacks were erected by the army engineers as temporary housing after the quake. His back window overlooks the City. If you lean out, you can see the Bay bridge and a good part of the old waterfront. At present, real estate developers are showing the property which means Bill's days there are numbered. That is his turf—his beloved Siamese cat friend, Mrs. Fagin, is buried in the front garden, but when millions are to be made on those slopes by real estate barons, there is certainly no room for sentimentality or place-right.

Fagin and Mrs. Fagin

"His name was Ting Loy when I got him, a cross-eyed chocolate Siamese. Can you imagine me standing out in the street yelling, "Ting Loy! Where are you?" So I named him Mr. Fagin. I got him first and then I thought, well, you got to have a woman with you, so I hustled her up. She was a real class cat, a blue point Siamese. You'd put something on the deck and she would try to tell you, "You want me to eat that on the floor? You put a plate underneath it!" While Mr. Fagin would lick your ear and seek favors, she'd stand aloof. When she had kittens I'd be right there helping her with the kittens. He'd stand there like an idiot—occasionally he'd lick one of them.

Mrs. Fagin became so thin after seventeen years. I used to take creamed chicken and put it on her lips just to keep her going. I'd pick her up and carry her to the pan. One day I come home from work and she's laying in the bathroom, stretched out, thin as a rail. I felt very bad about it. I picked her up and put her in a shoebox. I'm out there [*indicating the front yard*] digging a little hole to bury her. Right next door lived an extremely rich woman who had recently become a widow. She says, "What are you doing, Bill?" I said, "My poor cat

---

[71]   Coit Tower, one of San Francisco's most charming landmarks, was built by Lillie Hitchcock Coit in 1933 in honor of the City's firemen with whom she liked to play poker. Both the exterior and the historic murals depicting life in San Francisco in the 1930's recently have been restored.

died. I'm trying to dig out a little burial place for her." She said, "I think you ought to come up and have a drink. Anybody who's had a beautiful cat like that die, must feel very sad." I put Mrs. Fagin in the icebox. I went up to her house. The next thing I know the martinis are coming out in quart jars! I had about two of them and I don't remember nothing until two days later. I forgot what happened to Mrs. Fagin because I was absolutely bombed out of my mind. I open up the icebox and there's poor Mrs. Fagin lying there stiff as a board. She's buried out there in the front yard."

McCarthy

"I was an electrician on the President Wilson in 1950. When we got to Formosa we heard about the Korean War breaking out. By the time we got home the right wing leadership of the union had made a deal with the Coast Guard and some reactionary congressman, named Magnusen, where they were going to start getting rid of all the Left-wingers on the waterfront. We took it lightly—that it can't be done. We had confidence that the rank and file had confidence in us. But it was happening. The erosion had already taken place. The groundwork had been laid and a plan had been worked out unbeknownst to us.

What was taking place in the maritime unions and industry was on a little scale of what was taking place all over the United States. There were some bad scenes where Lefties were almost dragged out of their homes and lynched, especially in the automobile industry where a Left-winger couldn't walk down the street. We'd try to work out strategy and combat the union wrecking policies but somehow it seemed like somebody was ahead of you, laying your strategy out to be exposed to the Right wingers before you even got it off the ground—as if somebody was working with you. That's what was happening. The FBI had infiltrated our ranks. By the time we got to the next meeting all the wheels knew ahead of time about this. We had so many goddamned stool pigeons within the Party; the old saying used to be that if the FBI agents don't show up to make a quorum, we couldn't have a meeting! It was a joke but it turned out in many cases to be true.

I came in on a ship and a Party functionary handed me what was called a "control questionnaire". Every now and then the Party would have a "control" to double-check the membership to see that there's no skullduggery within the Party ranks. One of the questions was, "Have you ever slept with any woman who was also in the Party?" If you answered yes, they would ask, "Who? When? How often? Where? When was the last time you was with her? Is she married?" You're putting this down on a piece of paper making it possible for some son of a bitch to latch onto it and blackmail everyone named, including the poor woman you were with. I told them to "shove it". Of course they wouldn't dare throw me out but some poor schlob who just got into the Party, they'd intimidate him. We found out later that members in the high echelon of the CP were influenced by the FBI and fell into this type of trap. You had to be on your toes all the goddamned time. You didn't know who the hell the enemy was.

If you were a biologist or a doctor or whatever and working at state-owned places, you had to swear you never was a Red and never will be. My girlfriend was a biologist at Stanford. She was part of a group that fought it, told them to take the Levering Act (the 'loyalty' act) and shove it.

We were having dinner at her house on Grant Avenue and a knock came on the door. She opened the door and there's two guys there. "We are the FBI and we came to do a little investigation. Can we talk to Bill Bailey?" The word FBI thrown out at you is enough to send a little ice up your spine. I continued eating, and I hear her hemming and hawing—"Maybe Mr. Bailey doesn't want to talk to you." The guy says, "We'd appreciate it if he said it." They could see part of me sitting at the table with my back turned. I felt sorry for her. I said, "Hold it, buddy—what is it you guys want?" They wanted to know if I wanted to sit down and have a little talk with them. I said,

"Why don't you consult with my lawyer?" Bang! I slammed the door. This was a big shock to her, because she came from that petite bourgeois background that you don't slam the door in anybody's face, and especially the FBI. But after it happened she felt very good about it.

They came around in twos, banging on the door, pushing their way in to intimidate you. When I think of all the good people they done that to, the shock, the aftermath of what they done, it was just horrible, horrible.

There was one FBI guy whose route and assignment was the waterfront. I'd come out of the pier for a cup of coffee in one of them little restaurants. I'd be walking along back to the Pier and all of a sudden, "Hi, Bill. Why don't you just sit down and talk to us? It's my job to get you to talk a little bit." It'd be the FBI guy walking alongside. "Get the hell out of here—I ain't got nothing to talk to you about—so jump in the drink!" Four, five days later on some other pier the same thing would happen. "Hey, Bill, how are you feeling? I heard your cat died."They knew things that happened which shows they were in the Party, because the only ones I would tell these things to would be Party people—that my cat died. I quit the Party on a Wednesday morning—on Thursday the FBI guy came to my door. "Hey, Bill, I want to congratulate you on quitting the Communist Party." Boom, I slammed the door. The only people I had told it to was people within the Party. That made me furious. One day I come in the house and on the recorder: "Hi, Bill, this is so-and-so. I'm retired from the FBI now. I read that story in the Chronicle about you going into the movies. Keep it up, Bill. I wish you well. I always did like you— you're a good guy." I got the feeling that all the time he's on the waterfront saying,"Come on Bill, why don't you talk?", he didn't really believe in what he was doing. He didn't really like what he was doing, because how could he make that type of message? I kept the tape and now and then I'd play it. Two years ago the documentary, *The Good Fight*, was showing in England. I hear a knock on the door and open it up. He's standing there. "Bill, I was in London. They're showing *The Good Fight*. I think it was great." He shows me some clippings that he cut out of the paper. "I want you to have them. I'll tell you, I'm proud of you. Hang in there." I was flabbergasted. I figured because he was retired no more harm could be done. That's the irony of it.

In the meantime the unions had gone to the dogs due to McCarthyism. They had enough laws passed in the unions to keep out any Left-winger. Just to be caught reading *The People's World* on the street or even make an approving remark about it, that was enough. You had to play ball with the government and the government was supposed to scratch your back. It was supposed to put you in good with the big shipowners and you didn't have to put up a big struggle. Like Harry Lundeberg[72] used to say, when he'd negotiate with the shipowners,"If you don't give me them demands so I can satisfy my membership I'm just going to allow the goddamn Commies to take over this union and you're going to have a headache!" "Okay, Harry, what do you need?" Right away they were ready to concede because they could play ball with him, but they figured they couldn't with the Communists if they took over. That's why the SUP [Sailors' Union of the Pacific] ended up with some of the greatest concessions for the sailors—not because they were militant but because the shipowners were afraid that the unions would go left.

V.J. Malone, who was a real arch-conservative, (but at least if there's such a thing as an honest arch-conservative, he was one of them) said, "Bill, I don't want to take your dues because I'm just taking money off of you for nothin', because you're not going to be recognized as a union member anymore because of all the different laws. I'm just telling you how it is."With him as president of the union and the other officials working now with the FBI and the Coast Guard, it was pretty

---

[72]   Lundeberg, a virulent anti-communist, headed the Sailors Union of the Pacific (SUP) for twenty years, until the mid-1950's.

obvious the handwriting was on the wall. The membership agreed to accept screening because they thought they had nothing to lose. They weren't members of the Communist Party. The rank and file said, "I got to make a living. I got a family to support." They shut up. Any time they did open their mouth and even ask a question, somebody would say, "Hey, you're sounding like one of them." They pulled their horns back in.

Maybe there was a lot of mistakes made during that period, strategy-wise. There was a time in the Firemen's Union, nationally, when the Party position was that it was time for all Communists within the maritime unions to get up and declare themselves Communists, even if the rank and file don't know you was a Communist. You were supposed to say, "I want everybody here to know I'm an active Communist. I'm proud of it." Now that's on the record. I felt very bad. I didn't understand why we were doing this. We were taking young members of the CP who couldn't talk and having them get up and say, "I'm a Communist too." Then they'd write his name down. When it came time to be screened out all they did was look at the minutes and screen all them guys out. It was done by government agents who took over the leadership of the Communist Party. We should have taken some of the Party people we had in the unions and say, "Shut up! Just be the eyes and ears of the membership and keep an eye open for what is going on." We didn't do that so when we got thrown out everybody got thrown out. They hammered away at the integrity of the Communist Party. Prior to that the Communist Party was held in high regard as people with strong scruples, honest, you can depend on them, they would never turn you in. They were good workers, dedicated people. But after these things happened, some guys popped up in court, "Yeah, I was a Communist for twenty years. That guy is one." The were coming out of the woodwork. It was horrible. Every time the Dies Committee met, you didn't know who the hell was going to appear on the stand against you. That's how deep the ranks had been penetrated. You couldn't even believe what the hell was taking place in your own little ten man group.

Screening accomplished what they couldn't do before; it got the Left out of the unions. And where are the maritime unions today? There's nothing left. Their ranks in numbers are down to nothing. They spent their energies fighting the Left while the shipowners were planning their complete demise and sending their money to invest in foreign countries where the labor was cheap."

House Unamerican Activities Committee

"Some great names in the American democratic movement had taken on the Committee. The deck had been stacked against the good people that no matter what they said, they could not win with the Unamerican Committee. It was a witch hunt. They were allowed to break in any time they wanted and hit you in the underbelly. Sometimes the best way is to just get the hell out of their way and say, "Go to hell!" whenever they dragged you before their Committee."

Bill was summoned to appear before HUAC in 1953. The following is quoted from a radio broadcast of HUAC hearings in December, 1953.

"What is your name, please sir?"

"William J. Bailey. I think I could save the Committee a lot of time if you'd allow me to read a statement off that I have laboriously put down on paper. If you'll allow me to read it I'll . . ." (interrupted)

"Did you write it or did somebody else write it for you?"

"I'm quite capable of writing my own statements, Mr. Congressman. Why do you make that kind of inference? Do I look like an idiot or a dummy here? I wrote the statement."

"Are you a member of the Communist Party?"

"Well, frankly, Mr. Chairman, I don't think that's any of your business. I will give the same answer I've given the FBI, the Red Squad, the police department and everybody else, that it's just NONE OF YOUR BUSINESS!"

"Let the record reflect that the witness raised his voice in contempt of a committee of Congress."

I expected to be held in contempt which meant you went to jail. I was all set. Let the bastards feed me, I'm not eating now. I could handle prison food any time they wanted; anything they could do to me I could handle. They just said,"Get rid of the son-of-a-bitch; he's more of a nuisance than anything else. Forget him. We'll go after the bigger fish." And that's what happened. All the CP leadership in New York were rounded up and tried. Then *The People's World* gang, Al Richmond, were arrested and eventually tried in L.A.[73]

It was sad. The fact that it kept a lot of people from working was the small part of it. Several people killed themselves on account of it. One shot himself. It's hard to figure the tragedies that took place because of the fear. I didn't go through all these type of things—I had nothing to lose."

Bill and Harry

Bill was determined to stay close to the waterfront even though he was blacklisted and his seamen's papers were taken from him. He was hounded from job to job by the FBI and eventually joined the ILWU [International Longshoremen's and Warehousemen's Union], headed by the intrepid Harry Bridges, who refused to be intimidated by HUAC. Bill remained a working member of the ILWU until he 'retired', serving as Vice President of Local 10 several times during the 1960's.

"When Harry was attacked he met it head-on. For instance, when they'd say,"Harry, you're a Commie." Instead of him saying,"I'm not a Red. I'm not a member of the Party", he'd

---

[73]   Al Richmond's *Long View from the Left* (Boston: Houghton-Mifflin Company, 1973), contains a vivid account of the arrest and trial of the West Coast CP leadership. Anyone interested in the McCarthy era should take a look at this honest, intelligent memoir.

say, "Okay, Long live the Red Army!" He would come out with this type of thing. They're baffled; they can't attack him. The more you egged him on, the more radical he got, which was great. In court when they tried to discredit him for supporting the Reds, he said, "Who do you think was supplying us food in our soup kitchen? The Party people were going out hustling food for our men to eat. The Democrats or the Republicans could have done it, but they didn't. The Communists did it. Now you want me to condemn them?" He was very, very clever. He made his place in history.

Harry was way out in front. His mind was working all the time. We had some good days together—some good little plots. Organizing the Committee for Maritime Unity in 1948 might have been the greatest thing. It was Harry's brainchild and I helped him plan it. When he threatened the American government that the maritime workers were going to have a national strike, Truman made a statement about sending troops to load the ships. "We'll take care of you." Harry contacted the members of the international union in Italy and Marseilles and a few other places. The ILWU was a member of the World Federation of Trade Unions. They came out with a big declaration. The French, the Italians, the Belgians, etcetera, will not work any American ship that has been loaded by American soldiers. Truman pulled his horns in immediately, right off the bat. We originally had the Maritime Federation during the 1930's but that broke up. We needed something to corral all the seamen and longshoremen. The Committee would speak for everybody and all crafts. Guys like Joe Curran and V.J. Malone in the Firemen's Union helped to sabotage it. They made little backdoor deals. The shipowners were out there in front telling anybody who wanted it,"We'll make a bargain with you. You want a ten dollar increase, we'll give you eleven, but you'll have to do it on our terms. You stab that s.o.b. in the back and we'll take care of you."That's what was happening. Joe Curran said, what the hell, I don't owe Harry anything and

I'll come out on top with my membership. V.J. Malone said the same thing, although he used a different argument—Commie dominated.[74]

The Committee lasted less than a year. It did its work at that particular moment: corraling everybody for wage increases. It was the first big wage increase since the War."

The CP under siege

"The Party wasn't going anyplace in numbers. They were turning on themselves, eating each other up. Very little Party activity, nobody talking, nobody running out with petitions. If you did, few would sign them. You knew something was wrong and it was the whole Party structure. Some of the leaders were living nicely. I couldn't leave while we were under attack, but it was in the back of my head all the time. I finally left the Party right after the Hungarian Revolt—1956.[75]

---

[74] "I always used to get up in the Firemen's Union and preach the old Left-wing ideology. The shipowners came to the conclusion, "We took these guys on in 1934 and tried to whip them and we couldn't do it. We spent millions on it, and we took them on in 1936 and 37 and tried to whip 'em again. We can't fight them in the fight they know best, hand-to-hand on the picket line. No matter what we do to the workers—we lay on tear gas, club 'em, beat 'em, throw 'em in jail. So we're going to have to set our sights on the next twenty years. We're going to have to bust the son-of-a-bitch in the next twenty years—by intrigues, buying all the labor leaders, wining and dining this group against that group." That's what slowly they've been doing. So now almost every union they've got some little ten-cent beef and it's all split apart. The egg has been laid there, steaming away, being hatched and the hatching is one of intrigue and pitting one group against the other within the unions."

[75] The Hungarian Revolt, against the Communist regime, initiated by students, was ruthlessly suppressed by the Soviet Union. Many American Communists, including Bill, left the Party at that point.

When the Party mushroomed and was no longer forced to be underground, I was free. I could breathe some fresh air for a change. It was a hell of a decision to make. I left because the whole Party was bankrupt. No matter what happened, revolts all over the world, they wouldn't admit that something was wrong. You can see what is happening in Poland today. It's hard for a Communist to even get elected. My beef was people go into the streets to demonstrate for a purpose. When the Hungarian people got into big demonstrations they should have been listened to. You can't come out with some Party line that these people are bandits or CIA agents or stupid petit bourgeois. Those answers don't hold. That's an easy way of not addressing the question. And neither does armed force solve the problems of the peoples' protest.

I believe in the principles of socialism. There's got to be a better world someday. We can't keep floundering the way we are. China will probably turn out to be one of the biggest capitalist societies at the rate they're going. Things are so wrong—they've taken Marxism and screwed it up so goddamned much, that the guy no longer even wants to roll around in his grave. He's had it!

The Party had a very cruel system. If they decided someone was an enemy of the Party, they'd put him on a non-association clause list. After a person's name appeared on that list it meant you could not communicate with him in any way. He became a non-entity. Many of my friends, who had left or were kicked out of the Party, I used to meet on the side. I'd call them up, chew the rag with them, but to be seen publicly with them, I couldn't do it. Now once out of the Party, I could see anybody I wanted. I was seeing people who had been put on the list and when I got to know them better, they turned out to be great humanitarians—members of the ACLU who donated money all the time, but they were not Communist. They were on that list because they had criticized the Party at one time. Some little bureaucrat said, "Put them on the list!" I thought about it later on, all this inner knowledge I lost because of this stupid policy.

I could learn from these people because that's what the process is—learning by association. All that was kept from me because of a stupid policy of fear and personal intimidation. When the Party came from underground and found that the FBI wasn't chasing them anymore, they had reduced themselves so significantly that they were no longer a threat to anything."

Bill does not retire

Shortly after Bill retired from active duty on the waterfront, he participated in two documentary films, The Good Fight, *a collection of interviews highlighting those who fought in the Spanish Civil War as members of the Lincoln Brigade, and* Seeing Red, *a chronicle of the flowering of the American Communist Party in the 1930's.*

"When *The Good Fight* came out, I allowed myself to go on the road to promote it. I got a free trip to Holland with the picture. They met me at the airport and drove me to a good hotel where they drowned me with food, big tanks of scrambled eggs, ham and sausage. I just ate myself crazy. In the film festival they ran the picture five times in two and a half days. I presented myself to the audience and talked about the picture. I had to go back to Boston. I had a couple of engagements at MIT and some other college up there. Every time they showed *The Good Fight*, no matter where the hell it was, I was always on call. I went to Houston, Minnesota, New York, Seattle. I would often go for nothing, just the fare and back.

Then I got a call from British TV. How would I like to come to Spain. They're making a picture. I only had one question. Was it going to be anti-Republican government? They said, "No, but we're going to show proper balance. "They sent the ticket and met me in Madrid. They took good care of me. We went to the best hotels that money could possibly buy. I got the best of food, traveling to this front, that front. I spent ten days there.

I brought the tapes to someone I knew at Channel Nine. She was highly elated with them and did all the negotiating. They're showing the series now on every major educational network in the United States. I only have a very small part, two little pieces of it, for ten days work. All that money they spent on me and all I got to say was a couple of words. I could have done that by telephone here. It was nice getting over there and the people were just great.

A couple more documentaries have come up since that time—one on the '34 strike, one on the waterfront and another on the Depression."

Bill's earlier theatrical experiences would serve him well after retiring from the waterfront.

"When I was ten years old I was in a play, *King Arthur's Court* and that was the end of that until we put on a play to raise money for rent for our union hall in Baltimore in 1934. We improvised a play. Some radicals had disrupted the shipping office, got up and made soap box speeches and were arrested. I played the part of the judge. None of us knew anything about acting. I doused my hair with all this powder in order to play the judge. I was sitting up on the bench as the judge. The prisoner was screaming his head off about equal rights and justice. I said,'I've had enough of this!', batting my head for emphasis. I couldn't understand why everybody was laughing. Powder was flying. Enough of that till the McCarthy days when we put on a play called *Longitude 49* at the labor theater on Van Ness Avenue. Sidney Poitier got his start in this play in New York. I played the part of Blackie, an ex-fighter who took too many in the head but he was a good union man."

Bill was contacted by producer/director, Rob Nilsson to play Bruce Dern's irascible, 'Lefty' father in On the Edge.

"Nilsson said Bruce Dern was coming to Marin and wanted to have lunch with me. I said, why not, I could use lunch. So I meet these characters. The guy who impressed me most was John Marley, a character actor who played Bruce Dern's trainer in *On the Edge*. Marley was a great guy. I'd drop a name and he'd pick up on it right away; he'd drop a name and I'd pick up on that. We were letting each other know who we were, where we were coming from. He was coming from the old Left-wing theater back in New York when they were just forming unions. He was a member of the right 'church' so we got along great.

The director just gave us a general idea of what the story is all about. They brought cameras in; there's three of us fighting while sitting around a table. We're carrying on this beef. I'm calling Bruce Dern, "Ya jackass, what's the matter with you? Your poor mother's laying in her grave." They tape it and show it. When it's all over Bruce Dern says, "Let's get him; he's okay." Now they got me so highly blown up, how could I say no.

I had to reassure them that I might screw up. From now on it was hectic, trying to learn lines. I was shaking. How could I let these people down—they have confidence in me. Oh my God, why did I do this? But when it came time for the actual filming, it was not bad, because I had lost all my shyness with the cameras being on me, from doing *Seeing Red*. I knew a few of the tricks. I kept on repeating to myself, "You're doing this for a cause"— talking about unions. It didn't turn out bad at all. The cameraman, Lighthill, an old Lefty, was the guy who did *Seeing Red* and *The Good Fight*. I knew I had a friend behind the camera.

I had a short piece in *Heat and Sunlight*, another film by Nilsson. Acting ain't going to make me rich—a hundred dollars here and there.

The movie world is a corrupted sort of existence. You become corrupted so easy with the treatment they give you. Everybody around you is all bowing down, "Oh, he was super!" You know why they're doing it, because their job depends on being nice to you. It seemed so superficial."

Bill played a small part in Guilty by Suspicion, *a film regarding the impact of McCarthyism within the movie industry in the 1950's, starring Robert De Niro.*

"I can't even find time to do any work on my own piece of work." *He has completed a rough draft of his autobiography. He's written numerous articles and stories, some of which have been published in* The Hawespipe. *Bill was invited by the editors of* The Harvard Review *to write about his experiences in Spain. Bill was thrilled to have his story appear in* The Harvard Review, "plus I got one hundred dollars for it. I never expected a penny."

Marine Workers Historical Association

"About eight years ago a bunch of old Lefties were chewing the rag over coffee in New York. It got onto where is this guy, what was he doing, did you ever see that guy? We concluded it would be nice if a group of fellows got together once in a while. Somebody suggested that we put out a little bulletin. I got a letter from back East asking if I would care to be on the executive board. We had a meeting where we talked about one of the functions should be to record the histories of these people who partook in the organizing of unions, for the young people coming into the industry who don't know from nothing, so they don't get the idea that all that stuff was handed to them on a silver platter or that it came from heaven. Some poor bastard had to get worked over, getting it for them. They'd have more appreciation. That's how it developed. *The Hawespipe*[76] keeps us abreast about people and events and maybe every now and then a little story about our history."

Bill served as president of the executive board of the MWHA.

Ft. Point Gang

"I try to walk as much as I possibly can. One day after I retired in '75 Al Richmond and I were talking and discovered we were both walking in the Marina every day. We decided to get together and if anyone walks with us he would let me know ahead of time and I would do the same with him. At that time we were pretty hostile against some of the old Lefties. If we didn't like him we'd veto it. Finally we had a group, but we

---

[76]   Bill was concerned that those who were responsible for fighting the good fight on the waterfronts and aboard ships would not get an opportunity to tell their stories. *The Hawespipe*, the newsletter of the Marine Workers' Historical Association, is dedicated to preserving the heritage and history of those working men and women who struggled to insure that those who labored in the maritime industries were justly compensated. Bill understands the importance of keeping the record straight by letting those who were there tell their stories.

continued the same deal, by invitation only. It keeps us together and sensitive to each other. If somebody gets sick we call them up:What can we do? How are you making out? Need some help shopping for groceries?" It's keeping some of the old crowd together. We've had people walk with us from all over the world. They go back and carry the story about this walking group. It's a good crowd—some great people.

Every Thursday the 'Gang' meets in the Marina next to the San Francisco Yacht Club to walk about two miles to Fort Point. Against the wall of the old fort they have installed benches dedicated to Al Richmond, Lou Goldblatt, and Jack Olson, deceased members of the All-Star radical labor movement team. After a brief chat and rest the group treks back to the starting point, winding up at Eppeler's Bakery on Chestnut Street for coffee and talk.

I belong to the ILWU pension club. I attend the meetings there, but I'm not overly active in the sense of trying to grab off committee jobs. I don't want to be tied down to it; I'm more comfortable being a free agent."

REFLECTIONS
On changing the past
"Maybe I would have got more schooling. Maybe I'd own a house so I wouldn't have to worry about a landlord's whims, whether you can stay here today or they're throwing you out. But in them days when it was time to buy a house, I thought, "I'm not going to live to forty. The cops are going to wipe me out or I'm going to get in a beef with some union gangsters." A house was petite bourgeois stuff. I can't really put my finger on it—whether to change the love life or change this economic base."

On accomplishments
"I guess these two basic things: Spain and the *Bremen*. Loyalty to your friends, the things you've done with them. You didn't leave them hang out to dry, even if they were wrong; they could depend on you. That you never expect anything from anybody. That if you couldn't make it on your own, you didn't go crimping and crawling and prostituting yourself."

On changes in the marine industry

"There will be no merchant marine in the next ten years in America. It's on the way out because of the type of ships that they're using. The membership in the Marine Firemen's Union in San Francisco, my old union, for example, has dropped from around 1,500 to 400 members, according to the secretary of the union. In conventional ships you hand-stowed the cargo. Now you put fifty ton of cargo in one van and push it on. Let's say the van came from Reno, Nevada and it's loaded by gamblers; it's full of slot machines. Nobody sees what's in it. It goes right aboard the ship with a big crane. That individual socialized thing you had with cargo, where piece by piece, you handed it to the next guy, and the next guy stowed it away—all that is gone. I'm handing [another worker] a piece of cargo—"Jesus Christ, this is heavy!" "Yeah, there's the rotten son-of-a-bitch on the deck making us do all this hard extra work." We'd begin to socialize and raise questions of the class struggle among ourselves. We're blasting the bosses, "Look at that, they're sending slot machines to Ethiopia! They should be sending ham or a sack of wheat." So that consciousness was developed. Now you never see the cargo; you see a big piece of steel picked up by a machine and go right aboard the ship. You don't even get your hands dirty.

Now they don't need that many people. The ship is in and out, quick, with twenty times the amount of cargo it took you ten days to put aboard with two hundred men. Now it's done by six men in eight hours. Before, a ship 500 hundred feet long was considered a big ship—now they're talking about ships a thousand feet long and engine rooms that work by themselves. The negative side is there's no merchant marine today—just half a dozen ships doing all the work.

Instead of some poor working stiff, never went to school, couldn't find a job anyplace else, (all he could find was a shovel in his hand to shovel coal—it didn't take any genius for that) now you have men go down to the engine room, but first they go aboard the ship with a Gladstone suitcase, cufflinks, bicycles. When they get to a port they go bicycling all around. They play golf. Their hands are clean all the time and they're educated. They went to college or at least high school. You don't find no ignorant son-of-a-bitches like there was in my day.

When I was with the Firemen's Union in the early days, we used to get letters from San Quentin and Folsom. "Dear Brothers, I can get out five years earlier if you fellows will promise me a job on the ship. I'll be a good union man." We'd help the guy get out of jail. Maybe one out of ten would be a bum, but the other nine would be good human beings—and appreciated what they got, stuck by you. Now the idea of somebody coming out of jail going on a ship—they're insulted. Now they're all refined characters. Things change.

When mechanization came in the shipowners got together with the unions. Van containers are coming in, no more dirty cargo, no more penalty cargo—like loose asbestos or loose ore, stinking all over the place, lead getting into your system. Everything is going to be enclosed. A new type of ship is being built. We want to make arrangements, to accommodate. The shipowners convinced the unions that this is what's happening. Since we had two longshoremen's unions, one on the East Coast and one on the West Coast, which were diametrically apart— on the East Coast it was controlled by gangsters, and the one here in San Francisco was controlled by progressives like Harry Bridges. Two different ways of thinking. They could easily deal with the gangsters, which they did by paying some gangsters off. The next thing you know, your ships coming into New York and the whole Atlantic seaboard, all vans. Rank and file are looking to see what the hell the unions are going to do. The gangs are going to come down and you say one word, you long-nosed son-of-a-bitch, you're going to wind up in a bathtub of cement. They paid these gangsters off and started bringing in this new type of cargo.

We were left here with the old conventional way, but we can't do it that way. Otherwise the shipowners will say, "We'll take all our ships and bring them all to the East Coast. We'll keep everybody working there seven days a week and starve you son-of-a-bitches out if that's what you want." They said,

"We'll give you an extra bonus for the first year and change your working conditions." I think the bonus would be $900 if you worked the full year. That was for us voting to change the contract. The leaders convinced us that, yes, we needed to make these changes. Why work like a dog if you don't have to? Their fingers are broke from cargo being tossed around. They're old before their time. When they do reach retirement age, they're beat; they can't enjoy their life. Harry [Bridges] and everyone else ran a good moral argument. So we voted for this. Yes, get rid of the work rules.[77]

Now you walk out with a college guy and he just stands in the hold: "All right, men, just hook it on and pick it up." They hook it on with four hooks and out comes the van.

As bulk cargo disappeared you didn't need the old type of piers for the thousands of little cases and drums of this and that. Now you need large areas where with a big boom you bring a forty-foot van out and lay it on the dock. You can't do it with these piers. They couldn't work out a deal to make some of these piers a big area for these vans because the real estate barons came around, "No, we don't want that. We've got in mind to put in big condominiums and hotels." An awful lot of people love living on the waterfront. The big shipping went to Oakland. They could have made some preparation along this waterfront to handle vans. They decided it would be more lucrative to go into real estate. They're already doing it down here. These houses—what do they call it now—affordable renting? It's a filthy, rotten, obscene word—affordable for who? Unless the working stiff's got his whole family out selling pencils and delivering newspapers and sending the wife out to do tricks on the side, they can't accumulate the money to live there. That's what happened to the Port of San Francisco, and it's sad, sad. We'll never see it again."[78]

---

[77] See Dorsey Redland's story, pages 43-49 for ramifications of these contract changes.

[78] See "Bill Bailey Reports Remarks at the MWHA Meeting, October 1, 1988, New York", *TheHawespipe*, Vol. 7, 1988 for further comments on changes in the marine industry.

On special quality of life in the Bay area

"I came here in 1929 off a boxcar. It was like an oasis. There's an old song, "A little bit of heaven fell out of the sky one day"—about Ireland. This is the way San Francisco seemed to me when I got off a boxcar in Oakland and came across on a ferryboat. I'd always heard about San Francisco, the Gateway to the Orient, to Alaska, to the South Seas—the Gateway to Everything. There was no big, tall buildings. You could see everything, both from the ferryboat and from the tops of the hills. No matter what street you were on you could look around and there would be San Francisco Bay. If God ever created anything of beauty, this is what He created more than anything else. The people were different. In New York, you stop somebody on the street, "Mister, could you spare a nickel for a cup of coffee?" "Aw, get the hell out of here!" But in San Francisco—"Well, let me see, I think I can find a nickel somewhere." Never belligerent, never nasty. There was a new way of life here.

Little hotels here along Commercial Street, Clay Street, running all the way up to Kearny Street, with glass fronts. You sat in chairs there and read papers, relaxed. In New York, they didn't have nothing but crummy flophouses, where you wouldn't be sitting around reading papers. Everything seemed different. A slow pace, trusting, no locks on doors. That struck me right away. It was a different spirit, a different mood. The weather too was a big thing. In New York I always remember as a kid, freezing, windy and cold, wet streets. Here we had fog. You could hear the ring of winches, hear the longshoremen hollering out to each other all through the night. When it got foggy no matter where you were you could hear [imitates foghorn exactly] foghorns, bells ringing. It made you feel you was in a place that was alive.

Now you feel like you're living in a reform school or a jail. You can tell how people think by what's happening outside. You walk down the street and you see bars on the doors, steel doors, four locks to get in—absolutely impossible.

The waterfront's changed. There's no more shipping. There's a big struggle now to take over the piers and make big condominiums of everything down on the waterfront, waiting for the right politicians to get in so they can do it. Occasionally they burn one down every now and then to get rid of the piers. Now you can't walk on the street and look down and see San Francisco Bay. It's like painting Mickey Mouse over a Rembrandt or Van Gogh, that's what they've done to San Francisco with those tall goddamn structures. The Bay only belongs to those with the highest buildings. We let them do it."

Bill actively campaigns against the proposed building of hotels on the waterfront. He is responsible for hundreds of signatures on petitions and numerous letters protesting the gentrification of the waterfront.

"The people are changing too. From the early '30s, it was a powerful union place. Nobody would cross picket lines; you put a picket line down on Market Street and people would shy away from it. Now, they just fight their way to get over the picket line. A tremendous amount of aliens have come into the country who've never had any schooling as to the class struggle, what unions are all about. Their lives depend, of course on a job of some sort. The unions fall down on the job many a time; they don't do enough to educate people. They lost a good deal of their community base. I remember in the '36 and '37 strike, the strength of our base was in the communities. We wouldn't put out a leaflet, to support the longshoremen, the seamen, here on the waterfront unless everybody else got it, out in the neighborhoods. Now we just go on strike and nobody knows what the hell is going on. People run across a picket line. We're a lot to blame for it ourselves."

On Aging

"The odds of enjoying something is less and less and less because more maladies are now creeping in. I could see the positive things if you have a bunch of positive things working for you. If you were out in the country and had a nice home with a garden around it where you smelled beautiful flowers, where you could sit out in the sun, where you woke up and didn't have to worry about rent money, this money, that money, somebody around you all the time—"How you doing?", cooking a meal for you. If you have all them things working for you, you'd have a certain amount of peace of mind. If you haven't got those things and you're worrying about an old clunker of a car—will it make it on the bridge, are the tires going to hold up. If you have all these things working against you, it diminishes the exotic way of life we should be enjoying once you pass fifty."

After he reflected on the negative side for a few moments, he finally talked about a recent speaking engagement to a writing class at San Francisco State University.

"What we're supposed to get from age is a certain amount of wisdom. What do you do with the wisdom? I thought I was wasting my time. The students looked at me skeptically, but when it was all over and they asked a lot of questions, I thought it was absolutely enjoyable. The professor called me back a week later and said,"The kids were assigned to write what they got from you." She made copies and they are my prized possessions. The kids kept repeating, "This Bailey, all he talks about is 'to witness an injustice and do nothing, that is the bigger crime'. Apparently it got to them. Just when you think, the hell with it, nothing can be done, you do move people. Somebody does take cognizance of what you're saying. At least if you only accomplish one thing—to make people think a little bit."

Postscript: Re-instatement—35 years later

On the fifty-fifth anniversary of 'Bloody Thursday', when two marine workers were shot down on the street by the police during the 1934 strike, Bill Bailey and Walter Stack officially were reinstated in the Marine Firemen's Union. They were presented with honorary memberships in the Union and their seamen's papers were returned in a brief ceremony at the Longshoremen's Hall. Several months prior to this, Bill asked to meet with the current secretary of the Union. Bill said to him, "All I want to talk to you about is the fact that we took a bum rap. This is supposed to be a working-class organization that recognizes there are working class on one side and capitalists on the other side; our preamble tells us that. All the things that the Left-wingers, including myself, done in this union was for the betterment of the union and for the rank and file. We were abused by the FBI and by the right-wingers in this union to further their own aims. Now the best thing that can happen is that the union recognize. 'We made a mistake thirty years ago. We became victims ourselves of the McCarthy period by allowing some people in this union to put the finger on others, therefore we owe them an apology. Now let us admit this and hand them back membership books as a token of full, honorable standing in the union.' The union is our union. All we want is a clean slate, that a mistake was made. We want to hear, 'We veered from our consciousness and went after you guys with the aid of the FBI.' I know it's a big move but we're not going to be around long. It would be nice to be vindicated. We're not looking for pensions even. We just want the feeling that we are members of this union. We contributed to its growth and we don't want to be labeled vicious bastards, union wreckers."

The secretary indeed did make a public apology to Bill and Walt. The membership voted out those clauses placed in their constitution during the mid-50's which called for the exclusion of any member who was a 'Red' or a 'Lefty'. Unfortunately, at least from one perspective, all of the old Red baiters in the official union ranks have 'crossed the bar', according to Bill, therefore they were not present to witness the reinstatement.

Sally Binford

"Nothing is at last sacred but the integrity of our own mind." Ralph Waldo Emerson, *Self-Reliance*[79]

---
[79] Ralph Waldo Emerson, *Self-Reliance*, Emerson's Essays (Thomas Y. Crowell Company, 1926), p. 35.

Sally Binford earned a Ph.D. in anthropology at the University of Chicago and did innovative work in Old World prehistory. She challenged the old boys' network which had been so successful in keeping women out of such fields as anthropology. She has fought a protracted, on-going battle regarding sexual expression and freedom.

I met Sally through a friend who thought I would appreciate her rebellious spirit and fine intellect. When I called her for an interview she invited me to her place for lunch which turned out to be splendid—shrimp salad, French bread and white wine, accompanied by good conversation. I remember wishing that all interviews could begin so well. On subsequent visits we ventured into her neighborhood streets of North Beach/Chinatown to sample some of the best cuisines in the Bay area. Not only do we have a love of 'la boheme' and prehistory in common, but good food and wine as well. I highly recommend her as a dinner guest or hostess. She has associated with an eclectic mix of interesting people in the arts, academia, and politics. Sally is never boring or bored. She appears to be equally at ease participating in a 'dig' in the Middle East and lecturing on sex and aging.

I am always amazed when someone is honest about their romantic failures; most people would rather glide over that part of their lives. Sally talked about her relationships and in so doing one can witness her growth as an autonomous being who has learned the hard way about the dangers of female dependency. I was so pleased to connect with someone of her generation who could talk openly about their personal involvements.

Sally gives voice to an issue which usually is not discussed in relation to elders, i.e., sex. She refuses to let people off the hook by declaring in word and deed that sex is not the exclusive prerogative of the young. She fought hard for her own sexual liberation and continues to be vocal about sexual issues, particularly those facing women, gays and elders.

This is not your typical grandmother figure. I discerned that Sally is determined to remain true to self and not become a caricature of what society feels is appropriate for an elder. In some ways she is the most controversial subject in this study precisely because she will not fit the stereotype of the sexless L.O.L. (Little Old Lady). Talking with her made me think about the nature of the aging process. Does it mean closing down our sensual capacities? Does it mean be no more excitement or romance? Sally thinks not.

"Not a Jewish princess"

"I was born in Brooklyn in 1924. My parents became upwardly mobile and moved to Long Island when I was nine. I was supposed to be a Jewish princess, but something went wrong. It never quite worked out that way. I went to a very small private school from fourth grade through high school.[80] Played a fair amount of field hockey, studied a lot of French and Latin.

When I was in the second grade in public school in Brooklyn, this little boy and I had a real crush on each other. We were caught passing notes back and forth. When the teacher came to dinner at our house, I remember hearing her and my parents laughing, their being so amused and snotty about it, because this little boy, whom I had a crush on, was Chinese. I was just furious. What was wrong with his being Chinese? It's

---

[80]   "I attended our twenty-fifth high school reunion in 1967. When I graduated from High School there were sixteen of us in the graduating class—ten boys and six girls. Four of us women have stayed in touch over the years, not real close, but we exchange Christmas cards and such. When I am on the East Coast I see them or when they come out here they visit. Of all of them I'm the only one whose life has diverged so much. Most of them are living essentially the life their parents led. They really look upon me as sort of some kind of nut. She's alright, but why does Sally do all these weird things. In 1992 my class is going to have its fiftieth reunion and that will be amazing. Our twenty-fifth was funny enough and turned out to be a totally bizarre experience. All of us had known each other since we were nine years old. We found ourselves at this reunion within a half an hour all playing exactly the same roles, using each other as we had when we were in high school. The guy who had been class president, pounded the table and said if I ever caught my kid smoking marijuana I would call the cops. I said don't be such an asshole. It's a perfectly harmless drug. He said do you smoke marijuana. Of course I smoke marijuana, everybody smokes marijuana. Well, wouldn't you know it, if anyone were to smoke marijuana it would be Sally, the class troublemaker."

one of my first recognitions of my parents' racism. My sister told me that Chinese are dirty and steal and carry knives and murder kids—all kinds of nonsense.

In my family, my sister, who was two years older, was always the good child and I was the bad one. It was made crystal clear. I had "funny" ideas. I was not quite what my parents hoped for.

During the thirties, when I was a kid, my parents were enraged about racism in Germany and then they would sit around and talk about "schwartzes". When I was a teenager, thirteen or fourteen, I said, "Don't you see any inconsistency there?"They said, "What do you mean? We're the chosen people and we're talking about schwartzes." It made no sense to me. My sister is close to my age and was exposed to exactly the same thing and yet we are just as different as day and night. I have no idea why we got different genes, but I am glad I got mine. I have a very low tolerance for bullshit and lies.

I had a big fight with my parents about the incarceration of the Japanese in 1941. I was seventeen when that happened. I got kicked out of the USO when I was eighteen. I was a junior hostess at the local USO and I danced with a black sailor. I was expelled because "we don't dance with black sailors". I said, "Why not?" She said, "Because we don't!" I said, "That's not a very good reason."

One of my father's business friends, who was with Brown Brothers Harriman, a big banking concern, came over for dinner. It must have been my senior year in high school. My father and I had several discussions on race before this. He said, (I'm sure to irritate me because of this) "Atlantic City is a great place to have a convention. You can be sure to get some nigger there to push you in a chair along the boardwalk." I said, "Oh, a nigger pushing a kike, how fascinating." There was this deadly silence at the table. Everybody was so embarrassed, mortified. They just looked at the ceiling or the floor—one of those awful times when nobody made eye contact. My father didn't talk to me for about two months after that. He was just enraged. My mother said that it was a terrible thing to have done. I said he asked for it. He knows my feelings about racial epithets and if he can use them, I can use them.

I went from a small private school to Vassar because my sister's grades weren't good enough to get her into a private, first-rate Ivy League school and my mother had tremendous social ambitions. By having a daughter at Vassar life could be turned around in many ways. So it was either Smith, Vassar, or Wellesley. I got into Vassar and I hated it. It was 1942 and the War had just started. I knew I did not want to be [at Vassar], that was clear to me. The school I had gone to was really, really good academically. I don't know what my expectations of college were, but Vassar did not meet them. The classes were disappointing and the women were extremely snobbish. I was very unhappy there."

"Every thing good is on the highway."[81]

"I came home on spring vacation and announced to my parents that I was not going back. Of course they were just absolutely shattered. I heard all about the sacrifices they had made, what an ungrateful child I was, and how could I do this to them. I just said I'm not going back. They said we're not going to support you and I said fine. I cashed in the war bonds I had, took a course in typing and shorthand and got myself a job. It was a fascinating job. I worked from 1943 to 1945 writing up case histories in the psychiatric treatment clinic of the Children's Court of New York. For an overprotected Jewish princess it was quite an eye opener. Reading about kids from ghettos and slums who came in there after being raped by their brothers and selling their bodies when they were fourteen—just horrible, horrible stuff.

Hung out in New York, slept around a lot, dated a lot of people in the black jazz world. Smoked my first marijuana in 1944; didn't know what I was smoking except I was in an after hours joint and they were passing around 'reefers', that's what they were called then.

---

[81]   Ralph Waldo Emerson, "Experience", *Emerson's Essays*, p. 305.

Took courses here and there and decided it really was time to go back to school. Started hearing strange and fabulous things about the undergraduate program at Chicago which Robert Hutchins[82] had set up there. Wrote them and they said come on out and take the entrance test, which I did. I got in and then asked my father for financial help. I think he was so happy to have me out of the bars and the Village that he said sure. He didn't know what I was going to do there, but whatever it was it was better than hanging out with black guys in jazz joints in New York.

In 1945 when I moved to Chicago to the University of Chicago neighborhood on the South Side, my father would visit and say "How can you stand to live surrounded by communists, faggots, and niggers?" I would say, "But I like communists, faggots, and niggers." He would walk away wondering where he had gone wrong.

I found the Chicago undergraduate program extremely stimulating, loved it, and did very well. The undergraduate program in those days had no options. When you entered the college there was a standard program that all students went through. It was a balanced program in physical sciences, biological sciences, humanities and social sciences. Class attendance was not required. If you could pass an exam without ever going to class that was fine. You were graded on a six hour exam at the end of each course, and how you did on that exam set your grade. In the fall of '45 lots of returning vets were coming back from the War, coming back to school. So being an overage undergraduate, ripe old lady of 21, was not much of a social hardship as it would have been later or pre-War, because the whole age of the student body was older. It was a fine program.

It was really a great time and Chicago was in ferment then, just a neat place to be. I guess from the time I was about 19 on

---

[82] "Hutchins was made president of the University of Chicago at the age of 29. He was the one who started classical education in the undergraduate program there in the 30's."

I really wanted a baby. I met a guy in Chicago who was a grad student and we started dating, and finally moved in with him and married in 1947. He is the father of my child. I was a Roosevelt liberal and he was too. During the time we were married I went sharply to the left and he went sharply to the right and became a devotee' of Milton Friedman[83] and that whole crew in Chicago. Loved being pregnant. Felt great being pregnant. The better I felt the sicker he got. It was just awful. His ulcers got worse and worse. We separated and then came back together a few times. Toward the terminal stages of the marriage he said to me, "You didn't want a husband, you just wanted the egg fertilized." I became totally outraged and thought what a son-of-a-bitch to say that. Then I thought about it for a while and said, "You are totally right. I really didn't want a husband, I just wanted a baby."

I went home and told my parents I was getting a divorce. My mother became hysterical and my father was furious and told me no one in our family had ever gotten a divorce. I said it was probably about time they did. My mother said what could she tell her friends at the golf club. How could I do this to them? It was just insane. My father assumed that I was going to move to New York. I said I was staying in Chicago, that was where my life was, that was where my friends were. He said he wouldn't send a penny of support. I lived on $2700 per annum child support and alimony. It's true that went a lot further in 1950 than it does now, but it wasn't very far for it to go.

I was full-time mom—learned how to sew, learned how to do a lot of things I had never done before. The first year I was separated was the most maturing year of my life. I was 26 and had never been totally on my own. I had always had my parental support and then my husband's. There I was on my own with a baby, being a single parent, which was a shock. I was absolutely horrified by how my married women friends treated me. They

---

[83] Milton Friedman won the Nobel Prize in economic science in 1976. Sally describes him as a "free enterprise fundamentalist".

didn't want me around their husbands. It was awful. I spent a very, very lonely year trying to figure out what I wanted to be if I grew up and how I was to handle all this. It was not easy.

A whole bunch of people who got married post-War, came to the Hyde Park area of Chicago. A lot of us got divorced and then in the early fifties there was a tremendous amount of reshuffling. Everybody was dating everybody's ex-husband and ex-wife. It was very incestuous and very funny. The joke at the lab school[84] where my daughter went was two kids meeting in the hall and one kid says to the other "My father can beat up your father!", and the other kid says, "Don't be stupid, my father is your father." It was really wild. I dated a lot.

I met a guy who was a lawyer and a great cook; he pushed all the right buttons there. I married him. Shortly after we married I realized it was a total disaster. I wanted more kids and he didn't want kids. We bought a falling down house in the same neighborhood. It had been one of the original farm houses in the neighborhood and the city had grown up around it. I got some power tools and remodeled the house. Most of my male friends were so offended by that. I learned by doing, how to do plumbing and such. It was great fun. I had a great garden there.

Old boys' club develops a crack
"When the second marriage started to fall apart I said obviously marriage is not my thing. I'm going to have to get a career of some kind because I don't want to be dependent upon a husband for support. I leaned in the direction of social science, thinking about political science. A friend was talking about the anthropology department. I signed up for a couple of courses. Susan was in school full-time in third grade. I went back to school at the age of thirty-two. I started as a graduate student in 1956. The chairman was a misogynistic little son-of-a-bitch. At the opening tea for new grad students he said, "This is a

---

[84] "The laboratory school was run by the University of Chicago. It was considered a very good school for faculty kids."

professional department and we always get a few dilettante housewives and types like that in here." His wife leaned across the table and said, "Don't you listen to a word he says honey, you stick with it." If ever my feminist conscience was forged it was during the experience of being a grad student in the Anthro Department at the University of Chicago.

My interest turned rapidly to prehistory. The guy who was in charge of Old World archaeology was a famous but not very bright man. He was the kind who came on like gangbusters and implied that my Ph.D. was safe only if I hung around his office and made coffee for his distinguished guests and perhaps put out a little on the side. Anthropology is a strange field because its most famous practitioner at that time was a woman[85], but Chicago's department had an all male faculty at that time and still has. The anthropology graduate faculty at Chicago has never hired a woman. It's just a scandal. I was not taken seriously because I was overage as well as female.

I split with my husband after the first year. He was convinced I was in school just to have affairs on the side. I was working so hard there was no way I would ever have had time to even carry on that way. It became crystal-clear to me while watching what went on: one thing a grad student should never do was fuck faculty. I got it on with a lot of my fellow students, but never with faculty. I chose as my faculty advisor the only guy who did not put out sexual vibes. He was very dedicated and serious. When I told him I wanted to work under him and get my Ph.D. he told me to come into his office and close the door. I thought, oh no, here it comes! He said, "You're very bright, your work is good, and I'll back you as long as you turn out the work, but I want you to know that there is a lot of feeling against you in the department because of your social life and the way you dress." I said, "What do you mean the way I dress?" He said, "You wear tight sweaters and makeup." I thought give me a break, this is just ridiculous. His suggestion was that I look more like a vestal virgin; I said,

---

[85]   Margaret Mead

"It's not my style." He said, "I don't think you'll get a Ph.D. out of this department, but if you do good work I'll back you." I continued to do good work, did some field work, did my thesis and got my Ph.D., much to the surprise of everyone there except perhaps my advisor and me.

The first big hurdle was the prelims. The Chicago department at that point, had a policy of taking in large numbers of grad students. In my entering class there were 44, and perhaps 3 or 4 of us would receive a Ph.D.; it was that difficult. The big filtering thing was the prelims—two days of written exams over physical and cultural anthropology, archaeology, linguistics. When I took the exams the students were identified by number and not by name on them so I passed. The departmental secretary was a black woman who liked me. That summer I stopped by the office and she asked if I had gotten a Ph.D. pass and I said yes. She said Dr. Tax sent in the wrong grade for you. She showed me he had sent into the registrar's office that I had gotten a terminal masters which meant I couldn't go on for the Ph.D. She told me I could get to the very end of my career and it would be my word versus his. I went to the registrar's office and to the various faculty members who knew I had creamed the exam and got the grade changed. It was pretty awful. For me to have to rectify this error was awful. Definitely it was an intentional error.

I went to France to do field work in the summer of 1960 with a crew from Harvard, run by a militaristic man, who didn't like women, didn't like Jews and didn't believe in divorce. I had three strikes against me right there. He wanted me to leave the site at 10 a.m. every morning to help his wife with the shopping and cook lunch for the crew. I told him, "I didn't travel to France to be a cook. I like to cook and I cook at home, but that wasn't what I came for." He said, "I'm the director of this expedition and you'll do as I say." I said, "I'm sorry, I'm not here to cook. I'm here to dig." From that point on, he did not address another word to me all summer. He'd tell the foreman, "Tell that woman so-and-so." He would never directly address me after that. He had his prefixed notions of what he would find on the site. When somebody found something that blew his pet theory, he would call them incompetent. That not only happened to me, but to other people too. He was a very rigid, bigoted man.

I had an ally in François Bordes whom I continued to work with for many years. Bordes was the big name in French prehistory at that time. He was at the University of Bordeaux, near the area in Southwest France where all the famous caves are. Every night when the dig would shut down I would get in my car and drive over to the Bordes' house. They would feed me brandy, pat my hand and tell me everything would be all right and that I just had to stick it out.

My daughter stayed with her father the first month that summer and then she flew over to join me. She just hung around the dig and got to know the local kids. She was about eleven at the time. I was horrified that her French was better than mine after about a month. I came back and wrote my thesis and got my Ph.D. in 1962. My research focused on the middle Pleistocene of the Western and Central Sahara. It was a library thesis. The topic was picked by my advisor. Essentially my thesis was to demonstrate the geological and geographic history of the Sahara. Going over the geology, the stone tools, the animals bones that were found there, showing that the place had been used by human populations and that the formation of desert was very, very recent, probably the end of the Pleistocene. Before then there had been a series of lakes and savannah where human population could and did live.

There was a lot of nonsense written about the great antiquity of the human races, how the black race had been separated from the white race for a long time and the Sahara had been a barrier for gene flow because it was a desert and prehistoric populations couldn't live there and therefore blacks were very, very different from Europeans. It was essentially a racist kind of argument. One of its chief proponents was Louis Leakey, a colonial raised in Africa, a very smart man, but very racist. His son is much worse than he is. Richard has never had any formal training in anthropology and when it was suggested that he go to Cambridge or Chicago and get some training, he said he didn't need it because he was Louis Leakey's son. Apparently he thought he got it genetically.

"Real Work"

My main focus was stones and bones, particularly the transition period from Neanderthal to modern populations which seems to have taken place around the eastern Mediterranean basin, which is why I dug in France and Israel.

One of the major problems in Europe was that prehistoric archaeology and physical anthropology were very distinct fields. The relationship between extinct human groups and the artifacts they left was not systematically analyzed. French prehistorians come up through geology, paleontology; they've had no background in general anthropology, cultural anthropology or ethnology, whereas American students do. When it comes to actually interpreting what these artifacts mean, the French tend to just spin stories about what it was like. One of the main contributions that those of us who went into Old World archaeology from this American anthropology background was to be able to bring some knowledge of how ethnographically known hunters and gatherers lived and what similarities and differences between sites meant. The remains from every site contain different proportions of kinds of tools, of bones. Probably these differences are a difference of function. That is, they were doing different things at different locations. French prehistorians had this bizarre mindset: different artifacts reflect different ethnic groups.

One of the things I was principally concerned with was trying to explain the kind of variability that occurred between sites of about the same period. You can make up a lot of stories about what inter-site variability means, but unless you have formulated hypotheses which can be tested, it's just science fiction. Functional hypotheses, that is differences in what people were doing and how they were extracting energy from their environment, can be tested against independent data, but interpretation about their ideology or their spiritual life or their ethnic loyalties—we don't find this stuff in sites. That's all sci-fi. Paleopsychology is a dangerous field.

Also I wanted to document some kind of change in adaptation from Neanderthal to modern groups that would explain the tremendous population growth in modern groups. Neanderthal groups were essentially opportunistic hunters. They would get a single deer and bring it back and butcher it. They probably lived in a fairly restricted geographical area. When you get to modern population sites, the most striking thing is the overwhelming proportion of a single species of large herd animals. In the Near East it was wild cattle; in Eastern and Central Europe it was mammoth; in Western Europe it was reindeer. These are migratory herd animals that have regular migration routes. Large numbers of cooperating groups harvested the animals as they came through narrow valleys. This is a very different proposition than leaving a hunting camp and wandering out to find food. These guys knew that food was coming through twice a year. They could smoke it. If it was at the height of the Ice Age in France, they could freeze it. They got tremendous time utility out of this resource. When you start getting large groups of people, assembled for a semi-annual protein harvest, they develop rules about reciprocal rights between groups which are most often defined by mating patterns. This increases gene flow between groups which accelerates biological change. It also means a tremendous amount of cooperation is necessary between groups.

If you want to draw lessons from prehistory, it is fascinating to find out the thing that made us fully human wasn't competition but cooperative effort. One of the things I find fascinating too, was there is no evidence for intergroup violence or warfare before about 4000 b.c., and human existence was around a long time before that. It wasn't until people started settling down, building cities, creating a class structure, having investment in corporate capital, corporately owned resources, that warfare started.

I think these are very important lessons to draw from prehistory. Besides, digging is fun—getting away from the library, 'facking fuckulty meetings' and academic politics and sitting in cool caves and then coming out and eating French food three times a day and getting paid for it.

Lascaux adventure

Lascaux was still open to the public in 1960 when I was in France working with the crew from Harvard. It was closed in 1963. The Abbé Glory, who was in charge of Lascaux at the time, said the crew could go after hours when the cave was closed to the public. We went in about 6 p.m. and were due back at the hotel for dinner at 9 p.m. My daughter and I heard that in the unlighted part of the cave there was a gallery with cat engravings. We took a flashlight and tried to find them. When we came back the lights in the main chamber were out and the crew had gone back to the hotel. Lascaux was set up with three systems of doors you had to go through. We found the last door locked. (Lascaux had nothing near it then. Now it has souvenir and soft drink stands.) We are pounding on the door and yelling. Our flashlight batteries got dim and it was black, no light at all and cold. Susan was terrified."Mother, what are we going to do?" I said we may be the first people in 12,000 years to spend the night here, look at it that way. Meanwhile the crew got back to the hotel and were having dinner when halfway through someone said,"Where are Sally and Susan?" They had to get the keys and come back to get us. We were in there about three hours. It was pitch black, freezing cold and just terrifying.[86]

---

[86] "When Susan went back to school she had to do a little essay on what happened on her summer vacation. She wrote this story and the teacher called her up after class and said,"My dear, it's nice to have a lively imagination, but you know this is too much.You simply can't make up these stories." I had to go to school and tell the teacher that it really did happen and that she shouldn't have accused the kid of lying without knowing the facts. Susan was absolutely furious."

When you walk into the main chamber at Lascaux there are polychrome animals, some of them absolutely huge, in full motion galloping, all around on these white calcite walls. It is a psychedelic experience, a very powerful experience. You walk in and you know this place was something special; it really was. I don't know if they did prehunting rites or male initiation rites, but the place has a very, very important feeling. This is not just your John Doe, your average hunter artist. This system was supporting specialists who could produce this level of art. It is that skillful, that beautiful. The art work from the late Upper Paleolithic is exquisite. You are amazed by the level of artistry and the degree of anatomical knowledge they had. There were tremendous techniques developed by master artists that were lost and not rediscovered until the Renaissance.[37]

I worked near there at different sites about a third of my time between 1960 and 1972. These sites—caves and rock shelters, were probably hunting locations along the side of valleys. The density of animal bone and artifacts is just incredible. You cannot imagine it unless you see it.

I applied for a post-doctoral grant and got it. I went to dig a Neanderthal site in Israel in 1962. It was extremely fascinating. I went to Israel feeling I never had been pro or anti-zionist; being Jewish I had a generalized sympathy toward Israel, but when I went there I was absolutely horrified by what I saw. I spent a few weeks on a dig in Spain before I went to Israel. I found Israel more racist and more militaristic than Franco's Spain.

My site was in a valley, a wadi; nine months out of the year it was a dry stream bed which fed into Lake Tiberias (Sea of Galilee). At that time the Golan Heights were still Syrian. There were shellings almost every night. I sat up on the hills and watched the shelling like firework displays. It was incredible.

---

[37]   Lascaux has got to be one of the wonders of the world. In the October 1988 issue of *National Geographic*, probably the most beautiful photographs ever taken of the paintings appear.

I asked my daughter, who was fourteen at the time, if she wanted to come to Israel with me. At that point in her social life she said no, she wanted to stay with her father. He apparently didn't keep very close tabs on her, because she played truant and started hanging out in the back room of a guitar shop with someone who turned her on to dope. I left having a fairly resentful early teen but a still functioning child and came back to find this vastly grown-up young woman who was hanging out with some pretty scuzzy characters—playing truant, which her father apparently didn't even know about until the school called him. Before I came home, he arranged for her to go away to a boarding school in Massachusetts for bright, underachieving kids.

Les enfants terribles

In 1961 or 1962 Lew Binford joined the faculty at Chicago. He was the boy wonder. He is seven years younger than I. He was very handsome, very charming, very bright, very funny. He had been married a couple of times before. When I was writing my thesis our offices were right next to one another. We became good buddies and talked a lot about archaeology. Went to lunch together a lot. He was a heavy drinker and some nights he would leave the bars, come by my house and ring the doorbell at 2 a.m., obviously on the make. I said to him, "I'm sorry, you're very charming, and I really admire your head, but I don't fuck faculty."

When I came back from my dig, Lew was there waiting and the two of us got together then. He was running a dig the summer of 1963 in Southern Illinois and I went with him to work. He was coming up for tenure. Lew was extremely smart, but extremely crazy and aggressive. He had managed to alienate all the senior faculty at Chicago. Hanging out with me, and the two of us going back to Chicago and living together, we knew would be the last straw in terms of his tenure. He said, "Let's get married." I said, "Lew, marriage is not my thing. I've tried it twice and I'm not good at it." "That's because you haven't married the right man." Of course, being a macho dude that was his answer. I said, "I will marry you for the sake of your tenure, but I'll tell you now this is not going to be a permanent deal because I know myself well enough to know that marriage is not my thing."We got married at the end of the summer and went back to Chicago. Susan was away at school.

Lew and I became a professional couple of some note. Our skills were somewhat complimentary. He was New World; I was Old World. He was great on statistics and I knew the Old World data. He was a theory person. I was a data person. We turned out a series of articles and a book, *New Perspectives in Archaeology*, that took the whole field of archaeology and shook it up. [88]

Lew didn't have grad students as much as he had disciples. He was very charismatic and he turned out some real first-rate students in Chicago during the time he was there. He had been a grad student at Michigan, but he had thesis problems and couldn't finish his Ph.D. He couldn't pass his French exam which the University required for him to get his Ph.D. I, in essence, helped him cheat on the French exam which he took in absentia from Michigan. Lew was from a middle-class family from the South. He was an extremely brilliant guy, but couldn't write a sentence that made sense—that had a subject and a predicate. His writing was just unspeakable. My job in the marriage became to translate what Lew wrote into English and to get him his Ph.D.

---

[88] "The articles were mostly on theory and ways of analyzing data that was innovative and unconventional for the time. We questioned a lot of the premises underlying most archaeological interpretations and brought some scientific rigor into the field, in terms of formulating and testing hypotheses, instead of people just looking at data and making up a story.We did the first computer analysis of stone tool assemblages in 1966.That was considered very radical at the time.The program that we used gave us a very powerful tool for examining what variability in stone tools meant and how some factors co-varied with others." For more detailed information see Binford and Binford, "Stone Tools and Human Behavior", Human Ancestors (*Scientific American*, 1969)

And I served another trickier function: one of Lew's fatal flaws is that he's a pathological liar—and most of the time he didn't know he was doing it. He is truly incapable of distinguishing what he wants to believe from what is real. He had a distressing tendency to "improve" data. He would generate a large number of original and intriguing ideas—90% of which bore little or no relationship to reality, but the 10% that were valid were great. I would attempt to steer him away from his more imaginative notions and help him in finding data to support the sounder ones, then help him write them up in comprehensible English.

My role was to be super woman. I could do anything. I could cook, clean house, take his exams for him, translate his thesis into English. I could do all this and still carry on my own career. The first two years we were together we were both turned on intellectually and sexually. It was a very, very high time for us both. Eventually it got to a point where he was claiming all the credit for what we had done and Chicago was going to fire him. I had a teaching job at Northwestern. We lived in the south side of Chicago, 2 miles from where he worked, but 26 miles from where I worked. I drove the 26 miles up and back to Northwestern to teach. Lew, who was a drinker, would smoke dope occasionally, but his real thing was being a workaholic who could work like a fiend five days a week and every weekend get blind, falling down drunk.

Lew did not get tenure at Chicago which surprised no one. In 1965 University of California at Santa Barbara was trying to change its 'surfer school' image into a real school. The University of California has a nepotism law where two people from the same family can't get full-time jobs within the Cal system. Lew got the full-time job and I got a part-time job as a lecturer and we moved to Santa Barbara.

Santa Barbara was a weird experience for me. I had come from a super academic atmosphere in Chicago, out to this essentially 'surfer' campus. I arrived with my hair back in a bun, dressed in my spike heels and knit suits. Little girls were running around in mini skirts and no bras. Everybody was stoned all the time. There were 85 kids in the first class I taught, an introductory course in human evolution. I realized about half way through the course that one of the reasons I was having trouble in teaching those kids is that they were all stoned. Immediately I changed my teaching technique and went into showing movies and slides like show and tell. I was in total culture shock. I think it is true now, but even truer in the Sixties: there is more cultural difference between the East and California than there is say between the East and England or France. Much more. This is really a strange place. They speak the same language and do the same things but, my God, it's a whole other scene.

The chairman of the department and two of the faculty members there, who have since become significant names in the field, made the bargain where this would be the one anthropology department, besides Harvard, where no Jews were hired. Sometime that fall I heard this and made a great point of signing myself Sally Rosen Binford. I also made a point of speaking a few words of Yiddish at the faculty gatherings. The atmosphere got to be extremely tense. The anthropology meetings came up over Christmas that year. The chairman said what we need is someone who is an expert in Southwestern Indians, and someone who is an expert in Africa. We're going to be recruiting. At that point there were many more faculty jobs than there were people to fill them. We were urged to go out and recruit our friends to join the Santa Barbara faculty. There was a guy who had been at the University of Chicago. Alfonse Ortiz, who is a Tewa Indian and extremely bright. Bill Shack, who had been in Chicago with me briefly, went to London to get his Ph.D. because he had been told by the chairman at Chicago that there was no room for blacks in the field of anthropology. I went to the chairman and recommended Alphonse Ortiz for the Southwestern person and Bill Shack for the person in Africa.[89]

---

[89] "Bill Shack is now at the University of California, Berkeley. Alphonse Ortiz is at Princeton."

One of the other faculty members reported that the Chairman's comment was, "Doesn't she know any white people?" When we came back from the meeting, I said to Lew, "I don't want to stay here for another year. I find this atmosphere totally offensive and repressive and it's a rotten department. The library is terrible and the chairman is a fucking racist. Let's contact Joe Birdsell at UCLA (Lew had a three year contract with the UC system) and see if we can get your contract transferred." We went down to UCLA and they were thrilled with the prospect of having us there. So we moved to L.A.

During the early Sixties, when the big boys in Washington decided the Third World was where the action was, a lot of funny grad students started turning up in anthropology. There was a grad student in Chicago, now on the faculty there, a physicist, fluent in Russian, who suddenly developed a passionate interest in the Late Stone Age of the Soviet Union. There was a guy who is also on the faculty of Chicago now who had been in Army Intelligence in Germany. He became fascinated by Spanish prehistory. And people who had been in antiquities trade—the field was really being taken over by intelligence people. What better cover could anybody have, for working in the Third World, than being an anthropologist. It's not just paranoia on my part, believe me. I was becoming disenchanted very rapidly.

Meanwhile Lew and I were publishing like crazy—getting out a lot of great stuff and chairing a symposium at the national meetings where all our students read papers. It was this real dual thing where I was having tremendous professional success and yet becoming more and more disenchanted with the sexism and the racism and the takeover of the field by the CIA and other branches of intelligence.

When a friend of mine who had done field work in East Africa came back, she was debriefed by the CIA about what was happening there. She said nothing was happening in Africa in the last 100,000 years that was of the slightest concern to her, but the CIA debriefed her anyhow. Another friend of mine who had done field work in Iran later on was told to turn over her field notes to State Intelligence, and when she didn't was told that she would just never get any more grant money. There was that kind of pressure.

At UCLA more shit hit the fan, because there was a Southeast Asia program. Suddenly in the Sixties everybody started having Southeast Asian social science programs. A young assistant professor, who was making the same rotten salary as the rest of us, drove a Porsche and had a basement full of French wine and a big house in West L.A. His area was Thailand and it turned out that he was on the payroll. The whole thing got to be really, really hideous.

Once again at UCLA I was extra faculty; I had no permanent post. I was a lecturer and my husband had the ladder position. Everybody was recruiting faculty like mad at that point. We were contacted by the University of New Mexico, where we were both offered full-time positions. It sounded tempting, but at that time the marriage was in very bad shape. I knew in 1967 that the marriage was through, but Lew's and my lives were so connected in the field that it wasn't going to be easy to get out.

In addition to doing the work with Lew, I wanted to follow my own interests and concerns. I applied for a senior postdoctoral grant with the National Science Foundation in 1968 to do further research in the Near East on some Neanderthal sites that were of some interest to me. When I got the grant, Lew essentially said, "If you go I won't be here when you get back." I said, "Now wait a minute here, I've been helping you with your career this whole time." Instead of telling him to get lost and going out and doing it, I folded and agreed to both apply for another grant, which we did—which was a big mistake.

It was probably one of the weirdest and most awful years of my life. I was so furious with him and so resentful. He was drinking and became physically abusive. In 1966 or 1967 at UCLA we were having a fight about something. I said something very sarcastic and he took his hand and just cracked it across my face and sent my glasses flying across the room. He was 6'3" and over 200 pounds. I phoned the cops who were not anxious to help me. One of the cops took him out and put his arm around him and said, "Just love her up a little and it will be okay." I was fit to kill. I had never been struck in my life and I was furious. The cops left and Lew was walking around feeling smug and happy. A few days later I said, "You are so helpless, you can't even boil water. I cook everything you eat and everything you drink. I just want to tell you the next time you lay a finger on me you are going to wonder what the hell is in that cup of coffee, that bowl of soup." "You castrating cunt!" I said, "That's right, you got it, but don't you ever lay a finger on me again!" I had to do something. I was not going to take that kind of crap.

We left Los Angeles and went to France for a hideous year—the year was dreadful, in terms of work, in terms of politics, our relationship. We came back to Albuquerque, which has to be the ass-end of nowhere. I said okay, I signed a contract; I'll teach my classes this year but when this year is over I'm leaving. The more I thought about leaving, the more I withdrew from him, the crazier and more violent he got. He was hospitalized a couple of times because he was hallucinating. He was just mad. He claimed to have a bad heart; they could find nothing wrong with his heart, but he was having seizures. It was just really awful. He went off to Alaska to do field work in the spring of '69 and I finished teaching my classes, put all my stuff in storage, put my dog in the car and split.

I was invited to a UNESCO conference in Paris that summer. I spent some time in France, met some friends and hung around. I stayed with friends in Washington D.C. that year and spent a lot of time commuting between Washington and Cambridge. I was thoroughly disenchanted with anthropology at that time. I was really in a weird position where the subject matter still turned me on. I still follow the journals; I still keep up with what's going on in research, but I thought I cannot sit through one more fucking faculty meeting. I just cannot sit through one more meeting with these bastards. I'm going to stand up and

scream,"You're just a bunch of sexist, racist, right-wing pigs!"
Of course, at this point I had a reputation as a trouble maker in
the field. Being a smart, uppity woman did not win me any
favors. The Nixon administration had come in and research
funds had been cut. I got a couple of job offers—one from
Central Michigan and one from the University of Montana. I
thought I don't want to spin out my sunset years in Missoula,
Montana. I think I'll go back to the West Coast and get a place
on the beach and spend a year just thinking about what I would
do with the rest of my life. At that point I was so involved with
academia. I thought I just can't leave it.

Sex, drugs and FBI

My father died in 1968 so I was left enough money to pay for
room and board and enough clothes to cover my body if I was
careful. I couldn't live a lavish lifestyle, but I could survive
without working, so I had some breathing space. I decided I
would just take a year out and see what happens. I went to L.A.,
lived in Venice. I spent a lot of time walking my dog on the
beach. I smoked a lot of dope, took acid for the first time, took
mescaline, experimented with a lot of psychedelics.[90]

A friend of mine from the East, Ed Brecher,[91] who had
done a lot of sex research, called and said,"There's this

---

[90] "During the sixties a British archaeologist found cannabis in
domestic garbage dumps. It was not just hemp being used for rope;
it was domestically used cannabis. It appeared in Britain from
Neolithic on until Cromwell took over and then suddenly all the
cannabis was gone. The first cannabis appears in Mahanjadaro,
an Indian urban site from about 1500 BC. It is such a widely used
substance. It really goes back a long time."

[91] "He was a pretty well known science writer who, at the age of sixty,
took up research on sex and drugs. He did a book called *The Sex
Researchers*, which is a history of sex research. Then he did one on old
age and sex called *Love, Sex and Aging*. His book entitled *Licit and Illicit
Drugs* is the book on drugs."

fascinating new place I've heard about in L.A. As an anthropologist and as somebody who has had a life-long interest in sex, I thought you might find this interesting. It's a place called Sandstone. Go on up there and see what you think of it and report back." I went up. They had about fifteen acres in the hills above Malibu between Topanga Canyon and the canyon to the North of there, with a beautiful old ranch house. There were seven people living there full-time, in what was essentially a group marriage. They were all middle-class drop-outs who had done a little Fritz Perls,[92] a little psychedelics, and had decided their lives were shit and there must be something a little better than what they were doing. They were experimenting with open sexuality and trying to find ways of forming relationships that were meaningful. The guy who ran the place is brilliant. They decided they could support the place by taking members. The membership were free to come up and use the place during the day for sunbathing or swimming or whatever. There were parties every weekend. It sounded like it would fill a lot of needs and really be fun. It was a fascinating place.

In June 1970 I joined Sandstone and spent the better part of two years up there. I maintained my own place at the beach, but used to go there for weekends and parties. The parties were about 60-70 people; it was a self-selected population. The ground rules were no drugs on the premises, but of course we were all doing drugs, but they were terribly afraid of being busted.

Optional nudity, optional open sex, but the deal was if you approached somebody and they said no, the answer was NO period. No pressure to do anything that you didn't want to do. This huge house had no doors, which meant that everything that happened, happened publicly. Whether you were taking a dump, or fucking your brains out or eating a meal, or playing

---

92 "He was the originator of the 'touchy-feely' New Age kind of encounter that Esalen sponsored for so long. The Esalen Institute, located in the Big Sur area, is noted for it's experimental, creative approach to encounter therapy."

chess, or playing chamber music—whatever you did happened in public, which kept people remarkably honest. The nudity scene was fascinating too, because without the social symbolism of clothes, you had no idea whether the person you were talking to was a stockbroker, a high-steel construction worker or a dope dealer or what. It was really a fascinating place and drew a tremendous number of really interesting people. There were about twelve or fifteen of us that became a really tight-knit group. Some were married and some weren't; some were partnered, some were unpartnered. We had sex together; we did acid together; we howled at the moon together and we became really tight friends. In many ways the friendships I formed there are still the closest friendships I have. I spent a lot of time there in 1970-72. There were nights there when I would put on my anthropologist's hat and just sit back and watch the primates behave. It was fascinating from that standpoint.

In 1970 a former student of mine invited me over for dinner. Another friend of his, Tony Russo, came by who had worked for Rand Corporation. He became totally disenchanted with the Vietnam War and dropped out. He was very active in the antiwar movement. He had this other friend, Dan, who was still working for Rand. The following fall I hung out with Dan and Tony. They used to go off in a corner and have these funny, intense little conversations. I knew they were up to something. When I would ask, they would say, "Don't ask. It's better if you don't know." Every time Dan would open the trunk of his car there would be papers stamped top-secret all over. Tony was being extremely paranoid, saying his phone was being tapped, thinking people were watching him. I thought he's really off his rocker. I took Tony and Dan to Sandstone. In June 1971 the Pentagon papers were published. I was on my way to a party at Sandstone, driving up the Pacific Coast Highway in my car, when the news came on. "We don't know who is responsible for the release of these papers, but it had to be someone who worked for the Department of Defense and Rand." The only person I knew who worked both places was

Dan Ellsberg. Oh, my God, that was what they were up to! Shock! The FBI came up to Sandstone and started asking all kinds of questions. Then a few FBI informants joined Sandstone and the whole thing fell apart very rapidly.

I got a phone call about a week after the papers were published from a lawyer who said he was one of Dan's defense team, but he couldn't talk to me and would I call him from a pay phone. At that point I had been doing enough LSD that I thought maybe I was getting paranoid. This is really bizarre. I called him from a pay phone and he asked did I know a very noisy restaurant where we can have lunch. I took him to this Jewish deli in Santa Monica where the decibel level is incredible. He kept looking over his shoulder. What he had to tell me essentially was that John Mitchell, Henry Kissinger and Nixon were furious and Ellsberg was going to get the book thrown at him. They were going to try to make the release of the Pentagon Papers a vast left-wing conspiracy. Since I had been very active in the antiwar movement and had 'New Left' ties I had to assume my mail is going to be opened, my phone is going to be tapped and I was going to be watched every moment. I thought this guy is crazy! I told him that I had no involvement, and he said knowing Dan and Tony, and your history is such that you are going to be watched. I am warning you. At that point my daughter was living with a young man about a mile from my house and they had a baby about a year before. They were doing a lot of dope and they had all their acid stored in my refrig. I said to this lawyer, what about drugs? He said don't worry about drugs. I said what do you mean, you're telling me I should be uptight about the FBI! He said don't worry if they want to find drugs in the house they'll just plant them there, just don't worry about drugs. It was total paranoia.

I got a call from the FBI saying they wanted to talk to me. I told them my lawyer's name and phone number. You can talk to him, but I'm not talking to the FBI. They said you're being very unco-operative and you can be subpoenaed to testify before the grand jury. I said go ahead and subpoena me. I made all my phone calls from pay phones. The phone company said I was chosen from a random sample and, free of charge, they wanted to install this new phone in my bedroom! I started noticing, when I went out to the grocery store, a car would pull out from the curb with two guys with trench coats and snap brim hats who would follow me to the store and back! It was just crazy, just kooky. This changes your life.

A bunch of us saw Dan off for a trip East at the L.A. airport. People were there taking pictures of us. It was just ridiculous. In September of that year two FBI men showed up at my door with a subpoena to testify before the grand jury. I talked to my lawyer. You can't take a lawyer into the grand jury room, but you can cite the First Amendment and the Fourth Amendment if you don't want to testify. I refused to testify. They had the option of granting me immunity and then if I didn't testify, they could have thrown me in jail for an indeterminate sentence. Thank God, they didn't bother with that. It was really a terrifying time.

That summer herpes hit Sandstone in a big way. I'd been hanging out a lot with Jeremy Slate, an actor and a member of Sandstone, a guy about my age. He was spending a great deal of time at my place. One night we were about to go to bed and he said, "Look at this funny thing I have on my penis." It was a little tiny blister. Within a week we were both just riddled with herpes, which meant we couldn't fuck anybody else. In the meantime Tony Russo had been put in jail, on Terminal Island. Jeremy and I would medicate our herpes and go to visit Tony in jail. It was a crazy time, absolutely crazy time. Dan's trial was scheduled to begin in early '73.

Jeremy and I were both totally disenchanted with herpes and Sandstone. The FBI was bugging just about everyone. My friends were interviewed; my landlord was interviewed. We decided we would go to the Bay Area. Some friends of ours found us a house on Panoramic Highway above Mill Valley. Jeremy was still working in Hollywood part-time, traveling back and forth. Late that spring I got a phone call from Marilyn Burger who was then teaching at Goddard College in Vermont. She said we have an opening here in anthropology and Women's Studies and would I like to come here for a year or two and teach. I thought, oh God, Vermont—wonderful, serene, beautiful Vermont. We packed up all our things and went to Vermont for a year. I had forgotten all about the winters, having lived in California for so long. There was snow on the ground from November through May. It was so cold. After having spent two years as a practicing nudist, having to put on long underwear, mittens, scarves and layers before you could even step out the door! Goddard was a strange school. It was a place where upper middle-class parents, whose kids had done too much drugs and were too underachieving to get into Ivy League schools, wanted a nice, safe place to send them. To put it mildly, it wasn't a very serious academic atmosphere. It was just God awful. Then the Watergate hearing happened, and the Pentagon papers trial happened.[93]

I was glued to the television watching the Watergate hearings and we were all sweating out Dan's trial, because they could have put him away for 115 years, if he had been convicted.

On The Road
"The summer of '73, Jeremy and I left Goddard and bought a motorhome, and decided to mosey on back to the West Coast. We decided we loved living that way. Once again I put everything I owned in storage. It was a marvelous way to live and to travel,

---

[93] The Pentagon Papers were excerpts from a top secret government study of U.S. military involvement in Indochina since the mid 1940's. In 1971 *The New York Times* began publishing articles based on the papers given to them by Ellsberg. After the Justice Department obtained a court order halting publication, the case went to the U.S. Supreme Court which upheld publication. Ellsberg was charged with espionage, theft and conspiracy. Charges were dismissed when it was disclosed that White House officials had created their own special forces unit, "the plumbers", who broke into Ellsberg's psychiatrist's office in order to obtain what they hoped would be damaging information. This was the opening scene of Watergate which would eventually result in the fall of Nixon.

because we always had some of the creature comforts—our own bed and kitchen and a flush toilet with us and at the same time we were mobile. We could stop and see friends all over the country. We spent about two months crossing the country and then lived in the motor home from 1973 to 1976. Went down to Mexico and just travelled. We were road bums. When our money ran out, we would come back to L.A. just long enough for Jeremy to work, to be a guest star on some series to pick up enough money to keep us in gas and food for the rest of the way. We had a great time really. He's a really neat guy and one of my very closest friends to this day.

In '75-'76 we decided to do an RV trip in Hawaii, but we needed a smaller vehicle than we had. We sold our big motorhome and found a place in Stinson Beach to live. We had a custom vehicle made. In July '76 we flew over. There is a four month quarantine for dogs in Hawaii, and our dog was on Oahu in a quarantine station. It was a real nightmare. We stayed on Oahu so we could visit our dog every day. Then we went to Maui and stayed there about eight months and went to the Big Island of Hawaii and stayed there about four months— spent the total of about one and a half years. It's beautiful. I got into snorkeling for the very first time—spent a tremendous amount of my time just flat out looking at fish and eating mushrooms and just going crazy. We came back at the end of '78 and got a place here in the City.

Jeremy's and my relationship takes some explaining. Since we had met at Sandstone it was the assumption of our relationship that it was an open one. He used to see other people, and I used to see other people, but our favorite trip was bringing a friend home to bed and since we were both bisexual it didn't matter whether our friend was male or female. We loved to bring home a friend and play; that was our thing. When we got to San Francisco it became very clear to me here that the most interesting people in this town were gay. I started hanging out with a neat bunch of dykes I knew, and Jeremy started hanging out in the gay baths.

I started to be courted by, and fell head over heals in love with a lesbian who was 20 years younger than I. Jeremy, who could handle a lot of things, just couldn't handle that at all, and so he split. I don't know if it was because it was a lesbian relationship or whether it was because I was in love with her in a way I had not been with him, or the intensity of our connection that he found very, very threatening. Jan moved in with me. We were together for about seven years, which was a fascinating experience. After having viewed the lesbian world from the outside, seeing it from the inside as someone who was partnered, was a totally different experience. I had my anthropologist hat on the whole time thinking—my god, I really should be doing a paper on this whole subculture, but at the same time thinking these were my friends. I just never would do anything to exploit them. I have moral feelings about that.

Then AIDS hit and monogamy seemed to be the wisest option. Every time I get together with my old Sandstone friends we say all we could get was clap or herpes and it didn't kill you— AIDS is deadly.

My relationship with Jan in many way was making a transition from middle age to being old and not doing it easily or well at all. It was just awful and another rite of passage to get through. When our sex lives got to be old, routine and dull, we talked at some lengths about opening things up and getting it on with other people, but it became very clear that we had something totally different in mind. With me there's sex as play, as friendship, as fun, and then there's making love. The two experiences are quite different for me. Jan is the kind of person that always had to be in love to be able to be turned on. She started an affair with a much younger woman, which I found extremely threatening. I was just freaking out and jealous as hell. At the same time just thinking jealousy is politically incorrect, what kind of terrible person am I to feel jealous and being eaten alive by this jealousy. We thrashed that one out and finally she stopped seeing her.

We also thought it might be fun to go back to Maui, so we went back and stayed there about a year. We lived in Haiku near the pineapple fields in a funny little place called "Rice Camp", which was a settlement of Hawaiian and Filipino pineapple workers. We were the only 'haoles' there, certainly the only female couple there. The locals were very suspicious and quite unfriendly. The kids were extremely curious; they would come on the front porch and look in the windows. When we worked in the garden they would ask all kinds of questions, "You guys married, you got kids, what you doing here"— all kinds of things like that. Maui has a fairly large gay contingent, both male and female. There were Hawaii women's conferences which I was active in. The conferences were to get together the women from the five islands to foster support for the ERA. I was one of the organizers on Maui. I ran a workshop on sex and aging.

Things got really, really tense between us over there, mostly over sexual issues. I finally asked her to leave and she came back here. I stayed on over there for six months. When I came back we got back together again, and lived together for a couple more years. Then she started an affair with another woman. It was a very exclusive thing; I was to have no part in it. We finally split up. It was a very difficult experience for both of us. We have finally recovered and are to the point where we are good friends and see each other about once a week or so for dinner and talk."

Anthropology and feminism

In 1979 Sally published an article entitled "Myths & Matriarchies". A small group of very vocal feminists considered Sally's article as treason when she questioned their belief that women, in some remote prehistoric time, ruled, under the guidance of the Mother Goddess.

"I first submitted "Myths & Matriarchies" to MS. when it was a middle of the road, upper middle-class white feminist magazine. Gloria Steinem was then editor. It was rejected.

Dan Ellsberg knew Gloria. I said, "Dan, call her and find out why." The answer was she really didn't care whether or not this matriarchy thing was true; she found it a useful thing for women to believe in. Like the tooth fairy, I guess. I don't know what the hell she was talking about. That struck me as being one of most matronizing, objectionable, stupid things I'd ever heard in my life. I was just stunned.

Oh was I trashed in the feminist press! "She's so male-oriented, no wonder! The male establishment has brain-washed her." That kind of thing that you can't argue against. Charlene Spretnak edited a book, *The Politics of Women's Spirituality: Essays on the Rise of Spiritual Power Within the Feminist Movement.* She included my paper in her book to show she's broad-minded. She and Merlin Stone wrote a response to my article in which they red-bait, which I thought was fascinating. Katha Pollitt wrote a review published in *Mother Jones,* which I cherish. She really trashes the book. I pissed off a lot of the soft-headed feminists. It seems to be so obvious and so stupid—the function of all religion is to rationalize the status-quo. For them to have wasted their time on this instead of equal pay for equal work is trivializing feminism and is a total waste of time. I got hate mail. The article was first published in a magazine called *Human Behavior,* now extinct. The editor said he received more nasty letters from that article than from anything they had published in years.

The focus on the former glories of the Matriarchy drains off a tremendous amount of energy and interest away from current problems, like reproductive rights, equal wages for equal work, medical care and so forth, into this never-never land of what might have been in the past. Angela Carter, in a critique of this whole matriarchy mother goddess thing, said, "Mother goddesses are just as stupid a notion as father gods." I think she's right. The bottom line in equal rights for women is not whether or not there were mother goddesses in 4000 b.c.; it's reproductive rights and getting paid the same amount of money for the same work. Every group invents a mythical past when they were once powerful and strong, like the Ghost Dance among the Plains Indians.

Gray Panthers, on being a grandma, and other involvements

I got involved with the Gray Panthers about 10 years ago, because they struck me as being a bunch of old feisty people and I was coming to terms with getting old and wanted to find some way of combining politics with that. The Gray Panthers seemed to be the answer. I was put on the board and made head of the board and served about a year, before Jan and I went to Maui. Since I've come back I've been active again. I'm now on the Board again and the housing committee.

The point of the Gray Panthers is to build a movement of young and old together. Their slogan is "Youth and Age in Action Together". They work on housing and medical care and other related issues. They are national, but each chapter is autonomous. The Reagan administration cutting 90% of the budget for low-cost housing means that there is going to be no affordable housing in the city. We are trying to organize tenants and tell them what their rights are and what they can do to fight this. We're trying to salvage something from the Section Eight Housing for low-income people. The housing situation in the City is disastrous. During the reign of Dianne Feinstein the stock of affordable housing dropped perilously, and furthermore, she said, "What homeless? I don't see any homeless."

I'm on the board of CUAV, which is Community United Against Violence, which has to do with gay bashing going on in town here. I keep saying I can't go to one more demonstration, but still when political issues come up I find myself out in the street carrying a placard and marching. I keep telling myself it's hopeless, stupid and a real waste of effort. I've been in demonstrations and come very close to getting my head beaten. My efforts have gone into the local level. I wanted to get Dianne Feinstein recalled. I hate that woman so much. She is such a self-seeking and self-aggrandizing human being and so cold. She will be the next governor[94], even though she left the City 180 million dollars in debt. Look what Reagan did and people love him. We have national debt that is out of sight. Once you leave San Francisco her reputation is incredibly good. I worked hard on Harry Britt's campaigns and I worked hard to get Art Agnos elected[95] and trying to get us uninvolved in El Salvador and Nicaragua. Giving money and writing a lot of letters and sending telegrams, and marching in the streets again. Although each time I march in the streets I say this is the last time I do this idiot act, I can't stop. I go on doing it because I get so frustrated I think if all I can do, is what I can do with my body that counts for something, I'll put it out there.

I've been active in politics all my life. I remember when I was 11 or 12 years old going around collecting money for the Lincoln Brigade[96] door to door. My parents had been Left, but as they got money, they became more and more conservative. I grew up during the rise of fascism. Being Jewish gave me a very keen awareness of what was happening. In Chicago I found Ward politics there absolutely fascinating, Byzantine. It really was, just great! I just worked for the local ward-healer, worked on campaigns and canvassed. The first time I remember being photographed by the FBI, I was demonstrating outside the Federal Building in Chicago when

---

[94] Sally made this prediction in 1988, before Feinstein declared she was running, while she was still Mayor of San Francisco. Feinstein was defeated in her bid for governor. In the June 1992 primary, she received the Democratic Party's nomination for U.S. senator.

[95] Art Agnos, who served one term as mayor of San Francisco, was defeated in the November 1991 election in his attempt at a second term by Frank Jordan, former Chief of Police. Harry Britt was appointed to the San Francisco Board of Supervisors when Harvey Milk was assassinated by Dan White in 1978.

[96] See Bill Bailey's story, pages 142-151.

the Rosenbergs[97] were being sentenced in the early Fifties. I was very active during the anti-Vietnam War era. I helped lots of students get out of the country by calling academic connections in Canada and getting them into school there. I told them what organizations were raising money to take care of students who were draft resisters. I was teaching at the time. I said I will not flunk any male student. That was a conflict of interest, but I did it anyway. Academia was so corrupt at that point anyhow.

I have, I'm sure what amounts to very middle-class feelings about nonviolence. How could you not get involved in the civil rights movement of the Sixties? It was happening and I wanted to take part in it. I was on the Selma march in 1965. We marched down the main street of Selma and there was just absolute total silence. The streets were lined with local rednecks. There were thousands of us and all that could be heard were the sound of our footfalls. It was absolutely terrifying. Once we left town—hit the highway, that's when all the cries of "nigger lovers!" could be heard. It was nice during that march to know that the army was on our side. They were lined up protecting the marchers. That was a very rare and wonderful feeling.

When I went to Selma my father said, "Why are you doing this?" I said I could remember them saying to me in the Thirties, why wasn't someone doing something about what was happening in Germany. But to them equating blacks with Jews was so bizarre they couldn't understand it.

I certainly would not like to be a young black person these days, talk about no future—phew! A friend of mine says the whole world is becoming a Third World country. I think that's true—the disparity between rich and poor. What depresses me

---

[97]   Julius and Ethel Rosenberg, members of the Communist Party, were executed in 1953 for conspiring to commit espionage for the Soviet Union. Controversy regarding their guilt or innocence still surrounds their case.

is the real rightist movement in Europe now; it's very, very strong. I was over there last summer for awhile. There's a neo-fascist revival in France and in Germany. If you really want to get scared, it's happening there.

Sally is a volunteer speaker for the San Francisco Sex Information Switchboard. "For the price of a phone call anybody can get information. It is not a therapy or counseling switchboard; it is an informational switchboard. It's for people who want to know what the symptoms of the clap are or where they can find a leather bar on Folsom Street. They run a training program for the switchboard volunteers. I'm their speaker on sex and aging. The gist of it my presentation: use it or lose it. That's the message.

I have a network of friends here, who I am very close to that I really love, from whom I get a lot of support. I'm active in politics, Gray Panthers and groups like that. It seems to be enough right now. Since our initial interview, my sex life is reactivated. I have begun my "Harold and Maude" period. I'm seeing a 38 year old man and a 23 year old dyke. Also occasional group sex parties, safe sex, of course, with old friends.

I am a total food freak. I spend a lot of time cooking food, shopping for food and eating food. It is so funny since when I am by myself I fix dinner. I have friends who come in and the three courses and the glass of wine is there and the table is set. They say"you're doing this for yourself?" It's as if they had caught me masturbating—as though it's indecent to be that good to myself.

My friend asked me had I mentioned the three organizing principles of my life, which in her estimation were politics, food and sex. I said,"Not necessarily in that order."

My daughter has a grown boy and a daughter who will be thirteen. It's great fun. I see them seldom, spoil them and love them and then walk off. Let somebody else take care of them, during teething and being sick and being naughty and all that shit. As my mother put it, her grandchildren were the dividends on her investment.

REFLECTIONS
On anthropology
"I still have an intense interest in anthropology. I have gone over to France the last two summers where a good friend of mine is in charge of a dig. When I got on the FBI list during the Pentagon papers thing it was very clear that any federal funding I had gotten to do research had dried up. I left the field, first, because of burnout, and in the second place, I did not want to associate with people whom I would have to associate with anymore if I wanted to stay in the field. Because anthropology essentially became an arm of the intelligence gathering community. There are some individuals who are free of that and those people with whom I'm very, very close to and I follow their research. I still read the journals and keep up on what's happening in the field because I love it. It fascinates me still.[98]

The research I did in anthropology was significant and of good quality. I am really pleased with that. I am pleased with the fact that I didn't outgrow the principles I started out with."

Advice to women who are considering the field of anthropology:
"Develop a thick skin, a strong stomach and just go for it! It's not easy and research money has dried up amazingly in the last twenty years. In the Sixties if you had a Ph.D. and a reasonable project, you could get funding to do it. Now it's vicious. Nixon cut the National Science Foundation funding for anthropologists about to the bone. The money went to the military where all our resources are going.

The fascinating thing is there have always been a lot of female grad students in the field of anthropology. In the Sixties, when one fourth of the Ph.D.'s in anthropology were given to women, only 10% of the tenured slots at university campuses were held by women. Some place like Chicago never hired

---

[98] "My friends who are still teaching are scandalized by what the kids are doing now—hardly ever asking questions about anything except grades and money."

women and probably never will. It's pretty much the same in academia all over except in the fields of education and nursing."

On special quality of life in the Bay area

"I'm an urban animal; I love cities. San Francisco is one of the last habitable cities left in terms of civility and not being totally trashed. I love the climate, the people, the whole ambience of the City. I love the tolerance it has, plus it is physically beautiful. I love looking down from my window. I love walking the streets.

In 1933 my parents took my sister and me out of school for six months and we took the train out here. I remember the first time I saw San Francisco I promised myself that someday, when I grew up, I would live here. It took me until 1972 to finally make it, but I found it then. We need somebody besides damn yuppies in this town, that's for sure."

On positive and negative changes in the Bay area

"The positive thing I've seen here is the strength of the gay movement, which has been truly effective. Harvey Milk[99] is from my home town, Woodmere, Long Island, by the way. When I met him out here we spent our time trading Woodmere stories. I used to buy camp clothes from his father's store.

I have a view from my front window of downtown so I've seen the skyline look more and more like Manhattan, which I find very depressing. Just the amount of traffic, crowding, cost of housing, the pollution and the number of smoggy days we have—these are all the bad things.[100]

---

[99]   Harvey Milk was the first openly gay person to be elected to the San Francisco Board of Supervisors. He and Mayor George Moscone were murdered in 1978 by Dan White in City Hall. The murder galvanized the gay community in San Francisco literally overnight.

[100]   It's getting worse and it's going to get a lot worse yet. In the Fifties when I first came out to Los Angeles, a friend picked me up at the airport. As we were driving in toward the city my eyes were just burning. She said that's just smog. I said, what's that? Now it's everywhere. Last week it was terrible—that brown air. I couldn't see across the Bay."

Still, it manages to be San Francisco. This neighborhood, I am especially fond of North Beach; for a food freak to be surrounded by Italian and Chinese, you can't go wrong—Italian delis, Chinese fish markets, Korean produce stores.

We need to provide housing that people can afford; get the homeless off the streets; stop building office space downtown; stop making it a little Manhattan.

Naturally I'd love to see a cure for AIDS in my lifetime but I'm not holding my breath for that one. We should have bins of free needles and condoms at every street corner, for God's sake. I have been to a lot of AIDS memorial services in the last several years and I don't want to go to any more. It's rough. I've lost a lot of friends."

On Aging
"You get a hell of a perspective on life. I found that when I was in my twenties, thirties and forties, being a female by myself on the streets, I always found myself being looked at, whistles and all that. Now when I am by myself, in a restaurant or in other public places, I have the same invisibility that a child has so that I can really observe things much more openly. You're freer. A target is gone. All it takes is white hair and wrinkles and to most people you are just invisible. And infinite wisdom, of course. Don't forget that! I am much more aware of patterns in my own behavior, because I have been living with them for so long.

I don't like having my body fall apart and being less strong. I never really thought about my body until I was 55. Everything just worked. I could eat anything; I smoked and drank. I always drank in moderation, because I can't tolerate a lot of alcohol, but it never occurred to me to do something like exercise, because! When I started having disc problems in my back and neck, and went to various orthopedic people, faith healers, acupuncturists and massage people, I was told I should have a spinal fusion. I went to UC Medical Center's library and found there was 40% failure in that and I thought absolutely no way. The woman I was living with at the time said let's join a gym. I said no, I don't do windows and I don't intend to do gyms. She said oh come on, and just through that serendipity of dragging me screaming and kicking to a gym and trying Nautilus machines, after I had gone three times, the backaches I had lived with for three years suddenly stopped. I thought this doesn't make any sense at all, but apparently just building up the muscle tone and keeping the vertebrae from pressing down was enough that now I go three times a week. I come from a long line of peasants, which probably helps.

The feedback in the gym is immediate; when I go I feel great. When I don't go I feel creaky and lethargic and depressed. It really is a wonderful lift. If anyone had told me fifteen years back that I would be a geriatric gym junkie, I would have just laughed."

*J*oe *Sprinz*

"More than other games, baseball gives its players space—both physical and emotional—in which to define themselves."
John Eskow[101]

[101] Kevin Nelson, *Baseball's Greatest Quotes* (New York: Simon and Schuster, 1982), p. 184.

Joe Sprinz, born in poverty in St. Louis, developed his 'God-given' ability to play ball and spent twenty-four years as a catcher in organized baseball, including several years in the Major Leagues. He was number one catcher for the San Francisco Seals from 1938 to 1948 when they won the Minor League World Series.

While sitting at the counter of Original Joe's, a venerable Italian restaurant in the Marina District of San Francisco, I overheard Joe telling one of his 'hit-and-run' stories to a buddy. I was struck by the vividness, the intensity of his telling, as if that particular play had just occurred. When the waiter told me Joe once had played for the Cleveland Indians, that clinched it. I had to hear more.

My family, being from Northern Ohio, were rabid Cleveland Indian fans. My grandmother, who wore a replica of an Indian war bonnet when the games were broadcast on the radio, whooped through the house when the action heated up on the field. My dad drove us to Cleveland to see the Indians play as often as he could. We all played the game—my brother, cousins, uncles, various neighbors and friends—to the very best of our abilities. We understood the "country of baseball" because we came from the region which spawned it. In his marvelous essay, Donald Hall explains that baseball, unlike any other sport, "is a country all to itself with a rich history, a timeless flow of seasons connecting one generation of citizens, both players and fans, to succeeding ones."[102]

Talking with Joe brings back all those hot July afternoons and evenings out at Riverside Park and in my grandparents' backyard where we broke windows with foul balls with great regularity. I have spent many pleasant afternoons with him in his cozy 1930's kitchen listening to him talk about summer days and heroes long past. Joe was at his very best when we talked baseball. I even received a lesson in how to catch a low ball to make it appear to the umpire as if it were actually in the strike zone. For a minute I thought he was grooming me for a try-out. I felt deeply connected to Joe, almost from our first meeting, partly due to our common Midwestern background where the summer religion remains baseball.

Those in the game—the players, coaches, managers, plus the intelligent fans, know how tough it is to be a catcher. Thomas Boswell defines the catcher as "half guru, half beast of burden".[103] It takes a special person to survive in

---

[102]   From Donald Hall's *Fathers Playing Catch with Sons: Essays on Sport* [*Mostly Baseball*], p. 71.

[103]   Thomas Boswell, *Why Time Begins on Opening Day*, Doubleday and Company, 1984, p.159.

that position for any length of time. Joe played as a professional catcher for over two decades!

Ruth photographed him in his Seals cap at Candlestick Park when we took him to a Giants game. Actually he insisted on taking us as he had an old buddy on the gate who let us in free. His nickname as a player (all baseball players with any clout have one) was "Mule", but unlike most mules, he enjoys life. While we were watching the game, he turned to me with his boyish elf-smile, and said, "Gee, that's beautiful, the sun on the grass, isn't it?", as if he had seen it for the first time.

Midwestern spring training

"I was born in St. Louis in 1902. I went to parochial school. The priest could throw a football as good as a quarterback. When spring came we were messing around with baseball. The priest said, "What do you think of the idea of organizing a league among the elementary Catholic schools?" We got four teams and started playing ball. I was playing the outfield and catching.

I never gave it a thought, about being a Big League ballplayer. When I was a pup I'd come out every Saturday and Sunday and play with a group of fellows who liked to play baseball and get a workout. I'd take my glove, walk about two miles and shag fly balls with the big guys. Then finally they let me hit a few. They had a team and they bet. My parents didn't have any money so I couldn't afford it. When I'd strike out with the bags loaded, they run after me and beat the hell out of me.

We used to catch the ball on the first hop, no mask or nothing. This guy swung, let loose of the bat and hit me right between the eyes. I had two black eyes. My parents didn't have any money for a doctor. Later on I found out I had a little sinus trouble. The bone when it healed up, was crooked. Today they would send you to x-ray and several different doctors.[104]

When I was twenty I was working out with some of the Cardinals catching batting practice before I ever played

---

[104] Later, when Joe was playing for Indianapolis, the team doctor operated on his nose after the season was over.

professional ball. The Cardinals would go on the road—some of the team members would be left to work out at Sportsman's Park along with various other Big League ballplayers who were in the area. When I was a kid my dad took me to ballgames to Sportsman's Park to see the Cardinals and the Browns. If a Cardinal player was hurt or in a slump they left him home so he could stay in shape and get extra batting practice.

Somebody had recommended me to Branch Rickey.[105] I got a letter to come out and work out. They said report to the clubhouse and see the clubhouse boy and he'll give you a uniform. They had me catching batting practice to see what I looked like, to show what ability I had. I thought maybe they'd sign me up. One day after I'd been catching for an hour Rickey said, "Get a bat and hit a few." In those days, players never let anybody use their favorite bat. Jim Bottomley, who played first base for the Cardinals, handed me his bat. I could have hugged him. I hit a couple but Rickey didn't sign me then.

I didn't graduate from the eighth grade because a fellow asked if I wanted to go to work for Provident Chemical Company. I told my father it was five dollars a week. He said yes. There were five of us, my mother, father, my two sisters, and myself. He shoveled coal for Anheuser Busch. I saw his callouses. He used to box my ears a little rough. So I went to work. Then I got a job with Simmons Hardware Company and played soccer for them. Then I worked for the railroad, Missouri Pacific and played baseball for them. They had four teams. An engineer, Spav Turner, asked me during the winter of 1924 if I would like to play professional ball. He said, "You want to go to Kansas City?" He was a good friend of Mulebach who owned a brewery and the Kansas City Royals. At that time they were in the American

---

[105]   Branch Rickey, after a brief career as a catcher, served as president of the St. Louis Cardinals, where he was responsible for developing the 'farm system', and later as president of the Brooklyn Dodgers. He brought Jackie Robinson, the first black player to play in the Major Leagues, to the Dodgers in 1947.

Association; they're in the Big Leagues now. He said, "They'll train in Hollywood." I said, "Gee, that'd be terrific. I'll see some movie stars." So I told my father about it and he agreed. They gave me a contract for $300 a month. My mother resented it; she wanted her only son to stay home. I was gone about a month for spring training and then we came back to Kansas City. I was called into the office by the general manager. He said, "We have no room for another catcher; we only carry two." They asked me if I would be willing to go out if they got me a job on one of the Minor League teams. I said yes.

That night I said a few prayers at the hotel. I couldn't call my father. We didn't have a phone because we couldn't afford it. The next day they sent me down to Enid, Oklahoma on the train with about twenty other fellows. We unloaded and came into a dormitory; we all had cots and that was it. We went out to the field and starting working out. The manager was one of the catchers, and there was some competition from another catcher, but I signed up with the Enid, Oklahoma team in the Southwestern League for 150 bucks a month. That was a Class "D" team—that's as low as you can go in baseball.

They only had sixteen players. Once in a while someone would get hurt so I told them I could play the outfield and the infield. Spav Turner, who signed me up, said, "Play as many games as you can. There's a 130 games scheduled and if you can play about 100-110, you get a record. If they're looking for a catcher or an outfielder, they'll say, this guy played. He had a pretty good record." So I made the first year. I hit about .290.

Then I went with Shawnee, Oklahoma. Centerfield was about five hundred feet! Right and left fields were about four hundred.[106] That was like nine country miles! That was the biggest ballpark I ever played in. I don't think Babe Ruth could have hit one out.

---

[106]   For comparison, SBC Park, home of the San Francisco Giants, has the following dimensions: center field—399 feet; right and left field lines—309 and 330 feet.

They had two pitchers. One was an Indian about 6'4", over 200 pounds. So I got him for a roommate. I was in bed already and he come in with a quart of whiskey. It scared me for a minute. I heard about the Indian—when they're drinking, be careful; they go on the warpath, raise a lot of hell. He said, "Don't worry, Joe. The stories you hear about us is not true." I had a good night's sleep. I got along with those fellows.

While I was playing for Shawnee, one of the [opposing team's players] slid into our catcher at home plate. I guess he gave him a leg like Ty Cobb used to do. He'd slide on his side and then with the other leg knock the ball out of your hand. There's tricks to all that stuff. I was playing the outfield. The Indian pitcher picked up this guy. I thought he was going to throw him over the fence. He was so big that the guy who was sliding didn't want to take him on. When the guy looked up at a fellow who was 6'4" and an Indian—Indians in those days would fight you to the last draw.

We were playing poker in the hotel room on a Sunday. I was dealing and the sheriff busted right in—we didn't know who the hell it was at the time. I grabbed the money and he grabbed the cards. He took us all down to court and wanted $500 bail for all seven or eight of us who was playing. A local businessman, a Mason, put up the bail for us. I never had that kind of money—five hundred dollars. I passed up the jail. I went to court next morning; it cost me eight dollars. After it was all said and done the judge said, "We have churches here; you go to church." I was going to pop off but I thought I might get fined some more. After we got back to the hotel I went up to the clerk and told him off. "Here we're guests of the hotel; I think you're in cahoots with the sheriff." I guess he thought I was going to pop him in the jaw. That was stinko. He was in cahoots. The door wasn't even locked. We never gave a thought to something like that. It was pouring down raining so they called the game off. You just play poker or else read books.

I got some experience and then I was traded to Arkansas City in 1925. Then I was sold to Des Moines which was in the Western League, a Class "A" team. I got $300 a month. Shano Collins was the manager. He was playing with the Chicago White Sox when they had that scandal, the "No Hits", in 1919[107] He wasn't involved in the gambling but he was on the team. When he was finished in the Big Leagues he came down to manage Des Moines. I never asked him about the scandal; it was none of my business.

The year I was with Des Moines I played poker and was busted. But after I'd seen all these fancy toilets in the hotels, I borrowed $300 off a jeweler who took a liking to me because I was born in St. Louis and so was he. I gave him an IOU and sent the money to my father for the toilet and bath. It was the best $300 I invested. Before that, we had to go to the back yard.

My father saw me play while I was playing with Des Moines. We went over to Terra Haute and played to make some extra money—like a little world series—the Western League and the Three I League. Pug Griffin, our left fielder, was a big guy. He slid into the third baseman and knocked the ball out of his hand; they started fighting. My father was there and so were my friends. They come out on the field to help us out. Everybody come out on the field—the police and everyone else. That ended the series. There was no more baseball. And the players didn't get paid.

We won the pennant in the Western League in 1926. I continued to play with Des Moines in 1927. During the next winter I was sold to the San Francisco Seals for $15,000 and three ballplayers. I caught 156 games here. We played at the stadium at 14th and Valencia which they called the "Booze

---

[107] Eight players on the Chicago White Sox team were accused of accepting bribes to throw the World Series in 1919. Although they were acquitted in the courts, they were permanently banned from playing in organized baseball. *Eight Men Out: The Black Sox and the 1919 World Series* (New York: Henry Holt and Company, 1963), Eliot Asinof's excellent book on the scandal, was made into a movie.

Cage". When you'd buy a ticket they'd give you shot of whiskey and a sand-wich. All the big stevedores used to sit in the "Booze Cage", between third and home. They were wolves. If you made an error, strike out, they'd get on you, tell you about it. I can still hear them hollering. But as far as having any trouble—fighting or having spectators call you names, I got by pretty good. I guess I mind my own business.

In the off-season I used to work out with the teamsters to stay in shape. I said, "Do we satisfy you in the playing?" They said, "Yes, Joe, as long as you hustle. We want our money's worth." I went by that. When I left St. Louis, Father Dreher said,"Joe, God give you ability; give your best at all times" And that means, a working-class of people, they pay a dollar or two dollars, they want their two dollars worth.

We only had twenty players and we played 190 games. It was quite an experience. A young lady wrote me a letter. She'd gone to the ballgame with her sister and then she read in the paper where I was from St. Louis. I called her up and she and her sister invited me to dinner. I liked what I saw and I thought,"If I ever get married, I think I'll marry her."When I had a good dinner that almost settled it. When you're playing ball and you're not at home and you get a home-cooked meal, it's like a million bucks.[108]I found out later that it was her sister who did the cooking. (*Laughs*)

I went home to St. Louis after the season was over. I was holding out. I was making $500 a month. The Seals had offered me the same money for the next season. I was being compared with Johnny Bassler; he was with Detroit, in the Big Leagues. He was making 6-7 thousand and I was making about $3,500, so I thought I'd go for that. Walter Holke, former first baseman with Philadelphia who represented the Indianapolis ball club, came to my house and said, "Indianapolis bought you. You can name your own ticket cause they need a catcher." I got $700.

---

[108]   When I asked him,"What if she (or her sister) had been a lousy cook?", Joe replied,"I'd have got waivers on her."

So I had a pretty good year, hit pretty close to .300. I found a league I could hit in. I was with them in 1929 and part of '30, then they sold me to Cleveland in the Big Leagues."

The Big Show

"Although I didn't sleep so good I caught the ball game [*his first in the Major Leagues*] after I got off the train. I caught a left-hander. I could have caught him bare-handed. YOU could have caught him! He didn't have much stuff.

I hit against Alvin Crowder who was pitching for Washington, and by golly, all I did was pop'em up in the air. He had a good fast ball. Earl Averill, the centerfielder who was out here in San Francisco and was sold to Cleveland the year before, said, "Mule,[109] you'd better start swinging. You can't take strikes up here, you gotta start swinging right off the reel." I didn't catch for awhile. Once in a while I'd catch. I caught Wesley Ferrell a couple of times and Mel Harder; they were both good pitchers. Wesley's brother was named to the Hall of Fame but they never did mention Wesley and he had a great record.

We were playing against the Yankees. It was one of my thrills in baseball. Between home plate and the backstop, maybe 100-150 feet, you got a place to roam, as we call it, for a foul ball. I went back and caught it and turned around. Lou Gehrig was tagging up from first and I threw a perfect strike to the second baseman who tagged him out. When we came back the next year I got a little raise. I was making $6,500. Today they make millions.

In the Big Leagues the homebrew was better, and the coffee. (*Laughs*) You play with the best ballplayers,You see the best ballplayers that are playing in the American League.

---

[109] When I asked why they called him "Mule", Joe said,"The only thing I can think of was I played soccer back in St. Louis, besides baseball. I used to play in the mud, in the snow when it would melt. Did you ever plow through mud? Or try to run or walk through it? I guess I looked like a mule plowing through there. Maybe he was steady and slow, but he still got the job done."

When I was in the Minor Leagues I was a first-string catcher. I caught every day. I was a bigshot. I could do as I pleased. I could go out and get drunk and come out the next day and sweat it out and still play. You get away with a lot of things you wouldn't in the Big Leagues. They watch you more. For example, McGraw, the manager of the New York Giants, would have Cozy Dolan, his 'stool pigeon', sitting in the lobby checking anybody coming in after twelve o'clock. He'd report to McGraw then they'd take you out on the field and make you run till your tongue hung out or fine you. You had more freedom in the Minor Leagues than you did in the Big Leagues.

I was with the Cleveland Indians in '30 and '31. One Sunday I was catching and Fay Thomas was pitching. He throws a fork ball. I said, "Nice going." He said, "Yeah, but the other catcher, the experienced Luke Sewell, never calls for that pitch." It's a little difficult to catch but as long as he could get 'em out, I'd call for anything, even spitters.[110]

The next day I saw in the paper I was sold to Columbus, in the American Association, a Double A club. I was cut to $4,000. The management and I had a talk and couldn't get together so they suspended me. They didn't tell me the reason I was cut from the Big Leagues. I drove back to St. Louis. I was suspended for about a month.

Then I got a letter from Branch Rickey, the general manager of the Cardinals. We didn't have a phone because my folks couldn't afford it. I came up to his office and sat there waiting while he shuffled papers, wondering what the hell he wants with me. Instead of saying "Mr." Rickey, what have you on your mind, I mentioned his first name. I guess he was going to fix me up and put me back in the Minor Leagues again because

---

[110] The pitcher throws a fork ball by holding the ball between his first two fingers which causes the ball to break down when it reaches the plate. Spitters, which are now illegal, were created by the pitcher putting something on the ball, namely slippery elm or tobacco juice.

I didn't call him Mr. He asked me if I would go down to Houston—that was a Class "A", but it was a terrific league. He said,"They'll take care of you."That meant they'd give me a good salary. I think I got about $600-700 a month.

Later, when I was with St. Louis in '33, I caught a few games. Bill Walker, who was with the Cardinals, and I had built a cabin in the Ozarks. I asked him, "What do the pitchers and other catchers think of me?" He said,"All the pitchers like your catching." It was the owner who didn't like me. I wasn't a lap dog trying to butter him up. I wasn't no butter guy. Maybe that's the mistake I made.

I was outspoken. In all the years if I'd think there was something wrong, I'd talk to the players. Like in Arkansas City, in 1925 or '26, when I found out we weren't going to get paid, I held a meeting. I wanted somebody to be a witness, to come with me, when we talked to the owner. I promised the owner, "We won't go on the road. If we don't get paid, we won't play." Next day we got paid off in silver money—dollars and half dollars—seventy-five bucks worth.

So I reported to Shreveport, Louisiana. I caught three innings. It was hot as hell. They played all day ball; there was no night ball then. I told the manager,"I don't think I can make it." He said,"Hit." I hit into a double play and went over in the shade and sat down. I almost passed out. I was wobbling, not catching. The next day I started running and one of the old timers said, "Joe, you gotta be careful down here. You run too much and you'll get down to a nub." I took his advice. The next Sunday I played in Wichita Falls, Texas and that was hot as hell too. I staggered through that. I caught Tex Carlton, who was a pitcher with the Cardinals later on. From then on I was all right. But, I couldn't hit you ! The next trip we made around to Shreveport I got five for five. I started hitting then.

A lesson in concentration

"They had a split season. In 1932 when we were playing Beaumont in the Texas League we won the first half of the pennant. We beat 'em two games. The team which won three games would be declared winner of the first half. We were two to one. I was catching the fourth game. The coach of the Beaumont team was hollering at Tex Carlton, our pitcher. I told him, "Don't pay any attention. You got rabbit ears. He's trying to get your goat. The batters won't hit you with a tennis racket!" Carlton was still listening to the Beamont coach. I wanted him to just keep on going like he was pitching, but he was paying too much attention and it bothered him. I told him two or three times so finally I got mad and threw the ball hard and broke his finger. He was finished for the year.[111]

Carlton threw side-armed. I would go a step from home plate to catch it, and they would swing at it! I caught on right away that the coach, a former catcher in his day, knew they couldn't hit that side-arm pitching. You watch hitters—that's my job, to watch hitters, to see how they move their feet. Well these fellows when they'd swing at the ball, they were swinging at his motion and not at the ball. They weren't following the ball. When I have to shift my feet from homeplate, to go out of position to catch it, you know damned good and well the hitter isn't following the ball.

We were battling to beat those guys. We were ahead by a few runs. I got a base hit. The fellow who followed me bunted. I slid into second base and broke up the double play.[112] The

---

[111]   "Out at Seals Stadium in the old days they used to holler and get bottles and make noise and disturb some of the players. They could throw a firecracker and it never bothered me. One of the guys asked me if I got up to hit with three men on base was I nervous? I said no, I guess I was numb all the time. I just went up there and you either do or you don't. You give your best shot. If I got nervous or excited, I'd never make it."

[112]   "I'm on first base and the ball is hit to the shortstop. He throws to the second baseman and I slide into the second baseman and knock him down by tripping him. He falls down and can't complete the double play. He can't throw the runner out at first. That's what they call breaking up the double play."

second baseman fell on top of me. I tried to get up; I picked him up and was about ready to hit him with my fist when I turned around and there were two police officers behind me with their guns in their hands. I thought I'd better not start any fight here. A few innings later, Carey Selph, our second baseman, stepped on their first baseman's foot. He threw the ball at Selph and hit him in the back. Selph resented the first baseman hitting him with the ball so he came back and they started a fight. The police came out again with their guns in their hands. After we won the game I picked up the heaviest bat I could find. I walked out and didn't know what the hell to expect. It was the first time I'd ever been in Beaumont. In other cities I played in the police never did come out on the field. They just let the fellows fight it out. But here, they must be trigger happy.

I finished the season in the Texas League. The next year I was still with Rickey. I belonged to him. I was out on option—that's what they called it in those days. I was signed up with Columbus where I was with Paul Dean, Dizzy's brother, and Bill Lee, who went to the Cubs later. We had some guys who could really throw hard. I made the club and stayed with them for about a month, then I went up to St. Louis with the Cardinals where I roomed with Dizzy Dean.

They used to say Dizzy popped off. He could pop off, but he could back it up. Pepper Martin and he and I used to go have a couple of beers after the ballgame. We were playing in Brooklyn. We went to one of those speakeasies. Some of the customers were agitating Dizzy. "Are you as good as you say you are? Are you as good as Grover Alexander?" Alexander was one of those old-time pitchers. He was quite a drinker—strong too. He won 373 games and lost 205. Dizzy said,"Yeah, maybe you'll come out tomorrow and watch me pitch." They had those "B" girls who put the lug on. They'll see a guy come in and they'll warm up to him and hustle him for drinks. Dizzy was with Martin, buying their dinner and the bartender said he owed so much—maybe $30. Dizzy said,"What are you talking about? I only had a couple of beers." So they got in a beef. I told Martin, "You want to borrow some money?" He says, "Hell, no. Not to pay for somebody else's drinks." He had a whole wad of money. Pepper Martin was our third baseman. He was from Oklahoma—a wild horse of the whole state. He was built strong. I wouldn't want to fight him because he'd probably beat the hell out of you. He was pretty good with his dukes. So we got out of that place all right. The next day, the first inning they got five runs, but Dizzy beat Brooklyn,"the Bums", ten to five.

It was quite an experience to go around with those guys. We did a lot of things that I wouldn't put in print. We had fun, relaxed, let's put it that way.

After I got back to St. Louis Rickey sent me over to Baltimore—that's the International League, Double "A". Buzz Arlett was an outfielder who had a lot of ability. He was a big guy, 6'4", who could have stayed in the Big Leagues. I told him one day, "If you'd just play like this every day—" He said, "What the hell". He used to buy alcohol five gallons at a time. His attitude seemed like maybe he didn't want to play in the Big Leagues. He was a big shot in the Minor Leagues—like I was a catcher. I could play every day and drink and have fun. Some of those guys, like down in the Texas League, they'd rather play down there than go to the Big Leagues. They had more fun. I roomed with Arlett one road trip. I never slept at all. His girl would call up about three o'clock in the morning and ask where he was.

I was considered a pretty good two-fisted drinker but at least I went out and played. Several times I felt lousy but I went through it. And I didn't go through the motions; I gave my best shot.

Southworth, the manager with Columbus, would check on us at twelve o'clock at night. We were playing in Kansas City one time. It gets as hot as hell there. I told the bellhop to send us a case of beer up. I was sweatin' it out. Southworth came in and checked me and the rest of the guys in. The bellhop, who was about a half an hour late, apologized. I said,"You did us a favor. If he had caught us drinking beer in the room it would have cost us fifty bucks a piece." Southworth was a pretty good drinker too. Practice what you preach.

When I played with Des Moines I got acquainted with a big family. They made good home brew. The mother invited us to dinner so I asked the manager, Shano Collins, and a few more players. She played the piano and could sing. We had a hell of a time, and since Shano went along with us, the next day he can't say anything. O'Doul, the Seals manager, never bothered you either.

The next year I was sold back to Indianapolis. All this time I was still corresponding with Winifred Hartman. She was a hat designer. She and her sister had a millinery shop right on Powell Street. She stopped by Indianapolis to see me on her way to New York. We'd see each other for a few days, then she'd continue on with her business. Once in a while I would make a date with other women, but not to go steady. She appealed to me. I said, "Well, I'll get married." But she had a fur coat, and I said to myself, "She's going to be expensive." So that scared me away a little bit. That was the Depression. My father worked hard. I watched him down at the brewery shovel coal and pull ashes. That was hard work—hard on his back. He was laid off for a year and a half. I was playing ball and I'd send money home every payday. I got thinkin', if I get married to Winifred and have children, could I make it? So we kept on communicating. I had to think twice.

She wrote to me, "Why don't you ask to get traded and come back out in the Coast League?" [*They had been corresponding and seeing one another intermittently for eight years!*] That winter I was traded to the San Francisco Missions. I played with them in '36 and '37. The manager came up to me after Winnie and I got married and said, "I'm going to move the Missions to Hollywood. Do you want to go down there or stay here? The Seals want to try to make a deal for you to stay here." So they did, and I stayed here with the Seals from '38 to '46. We won the pennant in '46. That was my last year of active playing.

Winnie was a wonderful woman. There were certain places in cities where you heard about different women who were hot for ballplayers. But the only one who was really sincere was Winifred. When I was single I used to gamble and play the horses and shoot craps and I'd have my drinks. I took her to the horse races when we got married. She liked horseback riding but she didn't want gambling or drinking. She saw me make an ass out of myself a couple of times. I got in a beef and got hit in the head with a chair. That was my last one. I quit from then on. That was in St. Louis before we were married.

When I was away on the road I would write to Winnie every day—once in a while maybe call her up. Several times I took her and our son down to Los Angeles and we stayed in nice hotels. We'd go to some of the shows, get passes to the studios. But the other times, she never squawked; she kept busy.

In 1939 they held the World's Fair on Treasure Island. There was a celebration of one hundred years of baseball. Another catcher, Larry Woodall, and myself caught five balls in a row which O'Doul dropped from the Tower of the Sun which was only about 425 feet. But then when I tried to catch a ball dropped out of a blimp from 800 feet I strained my eyes so I could see the ball—I saw it too good! It hit me right in the mouth. My lips were lacerated; I had eleven cracks in my jaw, and I later lost five teeth. A lot of times I meet a guy for the first time, he says, "Are you the guy who tried to catch the ball out of the blimp?" That's me. I guess I was stupid but nobody told me the danger. The publicity man for the Seals got the idea of getting a blimp. My wife went crazy trying to feed me for several months on just juices.

The worst part, next year I caught batting practice every day—guys hitting fly balls. I did a lot of praying that I wouldn't lose my guts, be ball-shy. That's why I say God was good to me. I caught for seven more years. The trainer used to put sticks in my nose to relieve the pain.

Gas House Gang II

"People talked about the St. Louis Cardinals being the 'Gas House Gang'. When I was with them years ago we were playing Brooklyn. Frederick, a good hitter with Brooklyn, comes up to bat and one of the Cardinal players said why don't they knock him down—that means throw at his head. I was waiting for somebody to do it, but nobody did. When we played them again back in St. Louis I happened to be catching Dizzy Dean. I flipped my thumb—that means knock-'em down. So he knocked Frederick down. I come up to hit and I went down twice. With the stuff the pitcher had, if he had hit me it wouldn't have hurt me. We never had any helmets in those days either.

The Cardinals didn't show me they were the 'Gas House Gang, except for Dizzy. In my way of thinking, when I was with the Seals, Harley Boss, the first baseman, and Lefty O'Doul, the manager, showed me more about 'Gas House' when we used to play down in San Diego. We were guaranteed a fight with those fellows cause they pitched out of the sign (the scoreboard behind the pitcher was white which made it difficult for the batters to see the ball coming out of that white background); it was a little tough to follow. They used to dust us off. The pitcher would throw at the batter's head to intimidate. During one game Brooks Holder slid into second base and got in an argument with their second baseman. O'Doul come out and said, "What's the matter?" O'Doul came out to help Holder but he popped off to O'Doul so O'Doul gave him a left and that was it. We were fighting amongst each other, what the hell, so nobody got thrown out of the game. Then Frankie Hawkins went out after the pitcher with the bat. Then Sam Gibson, one of our pitchers, who heard a lot about Mulligan, a coach with San Diego, being a good fighter, got him in one of those 'waterfront' bear hugs and started squeezing him. Everybody got in it. I'd call ourselves, the Seals, 'Gas House Gang II.' That's 'the Gas House'—tit for tat.

Bob Johnson, our trainer, said, "Pick out a spot and hit him and if he don't go down, run." I said, "What if you can't run or hit?" He said, "That's too bad, then you be a lover instead of a fighter."

Tough, and centered like a zen archer in a hurricane

"A pitcher gets in a jam—like down in Los Angeles during the playoffs Seals v. Angels, 1940, we had them three and two and we had to win one more. Ray Haril had a good fast ball—he had one, but he didn't have it for about six or seven innings. We were throwing sliders and junk pitches, so about the seventh inning he started getting his fast ball. In the ninth inning they had three men on base. Johnny Moore came up to hit. He was in the Big Leagues and was a good fast ball hitter. A couple of guys got to talking on the mound. I said, "Let's go; let's get the hell out of here!"[113]

Before Johnny come up the pitcher struck out a guy with fastball. So we threw a fast ball to Moore and he fouled it off. The next pitch I didn't call for a curve because his best pitch was his fast ball. I said to myself, it's getting dark, the lights had just come on, and you're used to hitting in the daytime and the pitcher has his fast ball. You're going to get his fast ball! I think he might have been guessing curve ball. He swung and popped it up to right field and the game was over."

Lefty O'Doul, Manager, Gas House Gang II

San Francisco has honored him by naming the drawbridge over Islais Creek on Third Street after him.

"He was a good manager. You could talk to him. He'd want you to bunt—the players would come charging in, anticipating the bunt. I'd say, "How about swinging?" He'd say, "Okay". He'd let me do it because I can get a piece of the ball. My experience is, if you're running in and I'm swinging, you're afraid I'm going to hit the ball back at you or the bat might come out of

---

[113] I wondered what the catcher and pitcher said to one another when the catcher went out to the mound. Joe said, "Once in a while I'd go out and say, 'Dizzy, besides your Pall Mall your best friend is your dollar bill.' He'd relax and laugh. Or you'd say,'What's cookin'? I'll give you ten to one they don't think much of you.' Get his mind off of what's he's doing. I always said something to relax 'em. Players got to be relaxed."

my hand. O'Doul played good solid baseball, nothing out of the ordinary.

Sometimes some of the fellows would go out and have a bad night, he never said a word. The only time I heard him bawl out a guy—he was in a beer joint and told them who he was—"I play with the Seals." He had a few drinks and O'Doul found out about it. O'Doul said, "If you're going to have a drink, go by yourself someplace. Don't let anybody know who the hell you are." He never got mean. I never heard him fine anybody. If you put out for him and hustled every day, he'd go along with you no matter what you did. He was a good man to work for. We understood one another. If you wanted to take a chance, like hit and run,[114] he'd go along with you. He knew you were trying something—you were trying to win.

Integration
"In the old days they had a lot of Negro ball teams. Jackie Robinson[115] was a good athlete all the way around. What people would tell me, they'd knock him down and spike him. Like Branch Rickey told him, "They're going to give you hell." They gave it to him. They really did.

---

[114] 'Hit and run': There's a man on first and the batter is instructed to protect the runner, i.e., he has to swing at the ball regardless of where it is thrown—in or out of the strike zone. The purpose is to advance the runner.

[115] Jackie Robinson was the first black player to enter the Major Leagues in 1946. Jules Tygiel's *Baseball's Great Experiment: Jackie Robinson and His Legacy* (New York: Vintage Books, 1983), is a thorough and stirring account of the integration of baseball. Robinson emerges as quite human as well as an extraordinary hero. According to Tygiel, "From 1945 to 1959 Jackie Robinson and the blacks who followed him into baseball appealed to the 'heart of America.' In the process they contributed to the transformation of the national consciousness and helped too usher in a new, if still troubled, age of race relations in the United States." p.9.

Satchel Paige[116] pitched out here against the Seals in an exhibition game in 1941. He was quite a character. He started dusting us off. So I told one of the pitchers, "Don't knock him down—hit him". He hit him in the ribs. We beat him. Paige, like Dizzy Dean, had a rising fast ball. He threw the ball by 'em. The ball is going away from a right-handed batter so you try to pull it and you pop it up. I had a big heavy bat, I could pop it into right field. (*Laughs*) When Paige was throwing at us I come almost out after him. The umpire, Marty Drury, said, "Good thing you didn't go after him. You'd have got killed, all the colored people up in the stands." They were gambling. I had a bat in my hand; I wasn't going to hit him with the bat, but I was going to take a punch at him. One of the colored fellows on the team, who had six children, and I were talking at the plate. We agreed that there was no need for it because we were all trying to make a few bucks. Paige had half a heat on. The umpire said they were drinking on the bench. The next day he was supposed to pitch over in Oakland. He didn't show up. McDaniel pitched; we beat him one to nothing. He went with Los Angeles. He was a good pitcher and a good fellow too. But Paige, I don't know,—maybe he got too much money and started drinking or something.

Bob Thurman, who eventually played for Cincinnati in the Majors, was the first black player on the San Francisco Seals team. He could run like a son-of-a-gun. He had good power, a good hitter. He wouldn't talk. He was one of those quiet sort of guys.

When a left-handed hitter is hitting against left-hand pitchers, instead of getting their rear into the ball (that's what

---

[116] Satchel Paige, who was signed by the Cleveland Indians in 1948, had been pitching in the Minors for years—in fact he was in his mid-forties at that point! He was not only an incredible pitcher way past the point when most pitchers are rocking on their front porches down on the farm, but one of the funniest players in baseball. One of his quips apropos to this study: "Age is a question of mind over matter. If you don't mind, it doesn't matter."

you do to get your power), they have their bazzaza out. Like in golf, you get your hips, your whole body, into the ball. You don't have to swing hard. I told him, "When you hit against a lefthander, you have your rear out." He said, "Let me know." So he was hitting down in San Diego and he had it out so I hollered, "Get your big black 'so and so' into it!" After the game we were in the shower together and he said, "Yeah, I heard you". I was a little leery about it; he could have knocked the hell out of me, but he didn't say anything.

When he come up with yellow jaundice I went to the hospital. I thought, "I want to find out what makes this guy tick." I talked to him and he told me he was a sergeant in the Army. I says, "Bob, we're for you". I tried to encourage him because he was the only black ball player on the team; maybe he was a little self-conscious of it. I just told him what I thought. He and I got to be great friends. Nobody made a complaint. He was one of those guys who mind his own business and never popped off.

He was with the Commission of Baseball here a few years ago. He was out at the park and first thing you know, "Hi, Joe, how are you?" I like to fell over. He hollered at me; most of the time they wouldn't pay any attention to you."

San Francisco Seals Win '46 Pennant!

"We were happy it was all over with because we were battling Oakland. They were only a game or two behind us. To go through 160 ball games to win the pennant and beat Oakland—it's an accomplishment. After the game was over and we won it, I ran down into the dugout and straight up in the clubhouse. I don't want anybody to jump on my back and I'm not going to jump on anybody else's. You see those fellows, they jump on your neck; somebody could get hurt. I just went home and was elated with my wife. I never even had a highball. I stopped my drinking a long time ago. I just had my dinner and was happy. I always used to pray that nobody got hurt—that we had nine healthy fellows, we give our best shot and win."

The Adjustment

"Fagan took over the Seals in 1944. He put in a lot of money.
He put all the signs in on the fences and put in a first-class
ball park. We traveled first-class and the food and hotels were
better. I was a scout and coach for Fagan [*after he retired from
active playing in 1946*] and he paid me $900 a month. Then
Fagan got out of baseball and the Little Corporation took
over. Danny Miller, the former secretary for Fagan, organized
the Little Corporation. He was selling preferred stock. He
had some of the girls—stenographers, and one of the fellas
who ran the concessions, to invest maybe 500 or 1000 dollars.
Miller doubled his own salary. The stockbroker said, "Joe, if
you think it's good management buy it, if not, forget it." I
forgot it because Miller was a finagler.

The team drew good that year. Then I was fired. I had
about three and a half months pay coming so they gave me a
check—a week's pay. They mailed it to me, instead of taking me
in the office and saying,"Joe, we can't use you anymore. You're
making too much money";be fair about it, or call me an SB. It
turned out that I just got that money. The appellate judge,
Raymond Sullivan, took my case. He wrote to the
Commissioner of Minor League Baseball, but I told him I
didn't have a contract. Mr. Fagan didn't believe in contracts.
That was his policy. I trusted him. But see these other guys
were on a wing and a prayer. According to one of the
maintenance men, Miller would help himself to paint and
lumber for his house. Everybody had keys to the place. Mr.
Sullivan said he would take it to court. He was doing this for
nothing. When he found out there was no contract, he dropped
the case.

I guess my trouble was I'd pop off. Heath, the manager for
Little Corporation, was talking about Mr. Fagan not buying
any ballplayers. I said, "What the hell are you moaning about?
He got you on the payroll; what are you worried about? Take
what you got and do the best you can." So that wasn't a very
good remark to make to the manager. I was supposed to be his

coach, you know. A lot of times coaches are always sitting on the manager's lap. That's something I couldn't do. When I was catching, O'Doul would be over here, I'd be over there. I'd always stay away from the manager. If they had anything to say, if they were going to criticize me, well, come over and talk to me.

These guys cut me off short. You wonder what you're going to do when you didn't go to college or anything like that. Jack Kavanaugh, head of the probation department, who had put me to work on the off-season as a probation officer, got me a job with the District Attorney's office as an investigator for the welfare department after I finished baseball.

I was still trying to get a job scouting for Philadelphia. The general manager wanted me to commit myself as to how much money I wanted. I didn't say anything; I wanted him to tell me. My wife said, "Don't you think you've had enough of traveling? Why don't you stay home once in a while?" I caught on. It hit me right between the horns. I thought maybe I'd better stay home with my wife and son and let them see me. I'd been traveling for thirty years. Then I simmered down. I worked out playing badminton and tennis. I had a little dose of scouting—you're all by yourself. You go in a little town and you don't know anybody. I used to either take a walk or if anything was interesting in the town, I would go see it. But a lot of these guys go in bars, drinking. I had no problem getting adjusted after my wife told me that.

We only had one child, a son. As I said, I'd be playing the outfield as a kid and I'd strike out and they'd start beating the hell out of me. Well, I caught on and as soon as I struck out, I was almost home. Then I smartened up a little bit. Another guy and I used to wrestle; then we couldn't beat one another so we got boxing gloves and started fighting. I hit him with my left and knocked him down. I thought, "Well, Jeez, I can use my dukes." From then on I wasn't on the receiving end. I decided I didn't want my son to go through what I did so I got him over to the Olympic Club. Spider Oakes was a good boxer in his day and I wanted him to show him how to take care of himself. He told me before he could do that he would have to do some swimming. He started swimming and that's when he come up with that polio. He was eight years old.

He lost the use of his left arm, but he had guts and never looked for sympathy. We used to play back here (*indicating his backyard*) with the badminton bird and a small bat. When he was in the sixth grade his baseball team won the championship in their league. They played the finals in Seals Stadium. He played first base and the outfield too. He caught and hit one-handed. He'd drop his glove and then throw. I was sitting by first base and some of the guys said, "Look at that one-armed guy—what the hell is he doing out there?" These are the things you have to swallow. I didn't say anything. They kept on watching him catch it, drop the glove and then throw the ball. I think the guardian angel helped me. I could have got in a fight. They watched him awhile and said, "He's doing alright!"

We'd play handball and I'd use one arm. He said use both of them. Don't feel sorry for me—he didn't say that, but I caught on. He played trumpet and he could swim with one arm. Later he played golf too. It was terrific the way he could. He didn't give up. That's why I admired him. To this day I've never heard him complain."

In the 1940's Joe volunteered to teach in the baseball school sponsored by The San Francisco Examiner. He served as a coach for three years. Joe also served as president of Little League in San Francisco for several years.

"We would go around to the playgrounds here in the City and teach the fundamentals. I had the honor of showing kids how to hit. Later some of the fellows would come up and say, "Remember me?" I'd helped them with catching or made some suggestion to them. They never went to the Big Leagues, but they enjoyed themselves wherever they played baseball. It was gratifying; I had a lot of fun. I used to always tell the youngsters when I taught baseball to pick up sports. Take up golf, tennis; you have contact with people and you can get to talking and you're not bashful."

My wife and I both had an interest in sports. We played tennis—mixed doubles and golf. We also went horseback riding. If I'd catch Tuesday, I wouldn't catch till maybe Sunday. Between catching assignments I would be out in Golden Gate Park playing tennis to stay in shape. We worked together. That's what you got to do when you're married—fifty/fifty.

I started piano lessons about ten years ago. My wife and I liked music. I used to take lessons before I went to work. I enjoyed it. I liked those old timers, like *Alice Blue Gown*. I like some classical, but not too deep.

My wife had cancer. She took so many medications it made me sick. We were married fifty years. We celebrated fifty years on September 8th, then on November 8th she died, in 1986. So we had fifty years together.

I belong to a group of retired ballplayers—Old Timers' Baseball Association of San Francisco. Some of the old Seals, some Big League ballplayers, and the rest are semi-pros who played around here. We got politicians, judges, all kinds of people. We meet once a month for dinner. There's a lot of line drives and nobody gets hurt. At my age I can't run. I had a plastic hip put in my left hip and then there's arthritis in the right one. Still I belong to the Jewish Center and work out over there two or three times a week. I swim but I don't swim very good. That's one sport—I picked it up dog-fashion in the Mississippi River. I went swimming one Sunday and all the other guys jumped and I dove. I stuck in the mud; some guy pulled me out. After that I got a little scared of water. I do exercises that relieve the pain. I use the pull-up bars and do some stretching and strengthening exercises. Then I either go in the pool or take a jacuzzi. I get loosened up a little bit. I gotta keep moving. I'm grateful to the Lord he gave me eighty-six years of life and I can still move around."

He also took tickets at the local Catholic high school football and basketball games on Saturdays during the school year until he had a stroke.

REFLECTIONS
On Baseball

Baseball has changed since the mid-1940's, to the detriment of America's Pastime, in some people's estimation, certainly in Joe's.

"Today they got a pitching coach, a catching coach, an infield coach, an outfield coach—coaches all around. When I played the only coach you had was the manager. He'd sit on the bench. Maybe one of the outfielders would go to third base and tell you to come on or stay there. You didn't have any coach to tell you how to play. When you played in Class "D" and you wanted to go up, you paid attention. You had to think.

I remember during my second year with Enid, Oklahoma, there were three men on base. They put in a pinch hitter for the first baseman. I forgot about him having a bad ankle—that's why he wasn't playing. So I called for a change of pace[117] and he hit it down in the next county! That guy with that bum leg— you could slow up by him when he had a good leg, but when he had a bad leg he was a little careful. That was a pitch he could hit; if it had been a fastball he wouldn't have got around on it. He just hit flatfooted between the outfielders and it kept on rolling. The manager, Ben Diamond, called me one SB after another while I was still catching. I sat on the bench and he called me some more. He was a catcher in his day. I never made that mistake again. I said to myself, "Joe, you're going to have to either smarten up or learn how to fight; you can't be taking that." So I got smartened up.

If you're thinking you don't have to have anybody telling you what you are doing wrong. If you're in the Big Leagues you're supposed to be a Big League ballplayer. What does it

---

[117] "Change of pace is when they slow up on the fast ball. The pitcher will give you a big windup. It looks like he's going to cut loose and he just eases up on the pitch. It's timing. It's a deceiving pitch. They also call it 'pull the string'."

take? You have to have brains; you have to think; you have to have a good arm; you can run—so forth.

The current catchers all catch one-handed. I was told to catch with two hands. When I was catching with Des Moines I caught one-handed and Forest Cady, the umpire, who was a catcher with Boston in the old days—1914, said, "Catch with two hands." If the ball is low, out of the strike zone, today's catchers come down with it; they should come up with the ball. That's what Cady was telling me. You get a strike for your pitcher that way. Now I caught a lot of guys, not to be bragging about myself, and I asked, "Why do you want me to catch?" They said, "You get strikes for me." I caught on to what Forest Cady told me. You see that guy who is with St. Louis—he's down like a snake sitting on his butt. He drops his hand and loses the strike.

Today, you'll see the catcher go up ahead of the plate and he's looking for trouble. Just stay at home plate and let him slide into the plate. A lot of times they'll give you this stuff when you're standing up and hit you in the mouth—that's football—football players do that.

Wesley Farrell, a pitcher with Cleveland, had good control, a good fast ball, and change of pace. I caught him when we were playing Washington. There was a man on second and third and one out. I called for the curve ball and he struck the guy out. I threw the guy out at third. They were hitting and running. The pitcher had confidence in me. We worked together—both minds work the same. Like if a pitcher has a fast ball, then he loses it, then a couple days later he comes back and gets it again—the catcher knows this. Like with Roger Craig [*former manager of the San Francisco Giants*], he called for a lot of pitchouts and everything else. I can't see it. If I'm one of the Big League catchers, and I know my pitcher, I should know what his best pitch is. Craig tried to be a manager plus a player. He's tried to do the thinkin' for 'em. He just over-managed.

When I played with Cleveland I caught Walter Miller when we were playing Washington. Joe Judge, the first baseman with Washington, was on first base. Sam Rice, the right fielder, was up to bat. He tapped the plate and tugged his cap so I pitched out. I guessed right, see, and I threw him out. You gotta think. When the manager gives the batter the sign to hit and run, then the batter does something unusual, like tap the plate or tip his cap, to tell the man on base to be ready to go on the next pitch.

Pitchers today—they can't go nine innings. In the old days they went nine innings and they could drink and still pitch good ball. They have too many changes. Now you have a starter, an in-betweener, and a finisher. In the old days a guy started and pitched nine innings. He was in better shape too. You can't tell me they're in good shape—all these Giant pitchers come up with pulled muscles in August. They must be drinkin the wrong stuff! (*Laughs*)

I kept in shape. I played professional soccer in St. Louis in the wintertime and on Tuesday and Friday I would run ten miles. I also belonged to the Concordia Club, a German Society. The instructor gave you some of the damndest exercises. I did this to keep in shape.

Today you got ballplayers wearing batting gloves. You ask a guy why do you wear gloves. He can't give you a definite answer. In the old days they used rosin and tobacco juice and they hit .300 barehanded. Now they're wearing gloves and they hit 250-260. When it was cold weather back East you could probably wear gloves. It would keep the stinging out of the bat. But when it's hot, like 100 degrees, why would you want to wear gloves? You hold the bat, you got a feel of it. I don't think you got a feel of it with gloves.

Astroturf is not good at all. In time you get muscle burn. I guess they don't think of the safety end of it. I like Mother Earth—even when I played soccer, even though it was muddy. There's a give to the earth; with astroturf there's no give at all. It'll stove your legs in.

Where I think it's changing is the delay of the game. The players take up too much time to get settled to hitting. I don't think they have confidence in themselves with hitting. They fix their gloves and adjust their wrist bands while they're standing there, then they go up to hit and take a strike, then walk toward third base and start messing around with their glove again. Why are they taking so much time? Years ago they'd play the game, nine innings, in two hours. Now they take two and a half to three hours. It might be due to commercials. They got to get their commercials in, but besides that, the players take so much time. It's slowing up the game, now that baseball is televised. TV saved baseball and so did Babe Ruth. He hit all those home runs and was a colorful ballplayer. They say he drank a lot of beer and ate a lot of hot dogs, but he still went out there and performed.

Today a player can put himself up for bid. Maybe the Yankees or some other club will want you. Sometimes it protects the ballplayers. Then again sometimes they go too far. But just like betting on the horses, it's my money. I can do what I want. Here they're paying an attorney or an agent twenty or thirty percent! To pay somebody to talk for you, I can't see it. Let's put it this way, I go to the racetrack with ten dollars. I'm going to bet my own horses. When I lose it I'm going to lose it. Why should I pay some guy twenty or thirty percent when the Lord gave me the ability?

In my day I'm like an animal. They do whatever they want— if they want to sell me—like when I was with the Seals in 1928 and couldn't come to terms, they sold me to Indianapolis. They wouldn't even give me a raise. Today they have an agent who goes to bat for you."

What happened to all those colorful minor league teams around the country such as the San Francisco Seals, the Oakland Oaks?

"The Big Leagues broke it up. People who live in the country, they can stay home and watch tv and see the Big League games. Today, like Enid, Oklahoma, or any of those small towns, they don't have anyone to take it on the lam to promote baseball. Years ago, when I was a young fellow, there were eighty minor league teams! Just think of all the kids they could sign up and play in the summertime.

I talked to one of the scouts with the Dodgers and asked why don't they have more minor league teams. He said, "It costs too much money." I said, "How the hell does it cost too much money when you sign up a pitcher for two or three million dollars and he comes up the second year with a bad arm?" My point is this: pool the players—say in California you got eight teams and you find that out of those eight teams you got about twenty ballplayers you can develop. Then whoever needs ballplayers, like Philadelphia—they haven't got a good club, or San Diego, say they needed a pitcher, they could pick him out of the pool and pay whoever helped develop him. That way they wouldn't be losing so much.

Also you'd curtail a lot of this dope. You'd have kids playing, being on their own—give them a taste of life. I got a taste of life; it was an education [*when he was first in the Minor Leagues*]. I had to wash my own clothes. My pants I put underneath the mattress to press them. If some of the fans invite you for dinner—you always look for fans you can get acquainted with and have a homecooked meal. See, that's an education. In other words, you know how to take care of yourself. Many of the young Major League players could really have benefited from more Minor League experience.

The players today, if you want an autograph, they charge you. It really gets my goat. Now they charge $10 for an autographed picture. Kids would write to me and they'd give you a card to sign. Sometimes they'd ask for pictures. My wife said, "Why don't you charge them?" I couldn't. When I was with Cleveland I used to go down to the bull pen and warm up the pitchers. I'd sit down and if Babe Ruth didn't come up to hit, he'd come over and shoot the breeze. The kids would come around for his autograph; he'd never refuse 'em."

And in some ways maybe the Game hasn't changed so much.

"Baseball is just like politics: you got to kiss their rear once in a while. If you go out and buy newspapermen a few drinks— like when the Seals made a road trip to Sacramento, after the game was over we had a few drinks in the beer joints and some of the newspapermen were there too. I said,"When the hell are you going to buy a drink?" I just tell them the truth. The other guys wouldn't say anything. That was my big problem: I popped off. I'd tell 'em what I think. A lot of those newspapermen, they got expenses from the ball club and their meals along the road. One fellow, who was selling programs out at Seals Stadium, said,"They've got fishhooks in their pockets"—that means they don't pull out any money to buy a scorecard. That was a good expression.

A lot of newspapermen used to hang out at Breen's, a saloon at Third and Market. People talk freely when they've had a few drinks. That's one of the things you've got to be careful of, when you talk to a newspaperman. When I was here in '28, I got talking to one of the newspapers, on the bench, before the game started and next day they misquoted me. They added something to it. It's like I was saying about Dizzy Dean and Pepper Martin, when I was with them, things they were doing, I would never tell anybody about it. It's their own business, is the way I look at it. That's personal.

One of the players come in and started raising hell,"I'm going to beat the hell out of this newspaperman!" I said,"'Bones', when you're going good, read the paper; when you're doing lousy, don't even look at it." He got the hint."

On accomplishments

"In my baseball career God was good to me. He gave me ability to play ball and instead of going to school I helped my father, went to work. He gave me courage when I got hit in the mouth with the ball—that I wasn't ball-shy. I was an active player, as a catcher, for 3,000 ball games from 1924 to 1946. I got some bumps, a couple of broken fingers, but not bad for a catcher with that many games. I had a few injuries like getting spiked, but they healed up pretty good. I guess that was due to the food my mother and my wife gave me to purify the blood. And to know guys like Babe Ruth—he was a great in baseball, and

O'Doul, the manager of the San Francisco Seals, and Shano Collins, the manager for Des Moines in the "A" League—they were nice fellows to play for. Players like Rogers Hornsby and Jim Bottomley[118]—you met those fellows and they were great people.

I made a living. I didn't have to work with a pick and shovel, although I did all those kinds of work in the off-season to keep in shape. I met a lot of nice people including some movie stars like Francis Robinson, George Raft, Victor Borge, Jackie Cooper. Out of fifty states I've been in forty. I didn't make much money, but I had a lot of fun. When I started out in Class D ball I made $150 per month; today they make millions. But I have no regrets. I enjoyed it and made a lot of nice friends all over the United States."

On special quality of life in the Bay area

"You've got trees, the ocean—you can go fishing, you can play golf. You got the waterfront. Years ago the ferries were very interesting. When we would go to Sacramento we'd go on the ferry and then take the train; fans would talk to you and be friendly.

You got so many different people; it's entertaining, just to talk to them. You got a lot of stories, a lot of laughs out of them. That's like baseball—you talk about it and get a lot of laughs out of it. That's all life is anyway—if you don't get a laugh once in a while, you're not human."

On positive and negative changes in the Bay area

Joe was concerned about the density of population in the Bay region. He remembered a time when the Bay area was easy to negotiate by automobile, when two-lane roads connected one community in the area to another with open farmland between.

---

[118] "Sunny Jim" Bottomley played first base with the St. Louis Cardinals; Rogers Hornsby played second base—both were extraordinary hitters in their day.

"In the 1930's I used to take the street car from where I was living in the Mission to Winnie's hat shop on Powell Street. All the women were dressed so nice with hats, and the men with spats and canes. They really dressed. You could rent a room for ten dollars a month. Living was reasonable."

Joe's baseball career spanned 24 years! Anyone who has played even sandlot baseball knows that being a catcher for that length of time is a remarkable feat.

The following is a list of the clubs for which Joe played

Enid, Oklahoma, 1924
Arkansas City, 1925
Des Moines, Iowa, 1926-27
San Francisco Seals, 1928
Indianapolis, 1929
Cleveland Indians, 1930-31
Indianapolis, 1932
Houston, Texas, 1932
Columbus, Ohio, 1933
St. Louis Cardinals, 1933
Baltimore Orioles, 1934
Indianapolis, 1934-36
San Francisco Missions, 1936-37
San Francisco Seals, 1938-48

Thelma Kavanagh

Joan: "My sword shall conquer yet: the sword that never struck a blow."
from *St. Joan*, George Bernard Shaw

Thelma Kavanagh, who experienced rural poverty as a child growing up in northern Minnesota, overcame a physical handicap to become a teacher who volunteered to teach the "dumb" kids. After retirement she moved to San Francisco's Tenderloin district where she fights for the rights of the elderly and the poor.

Thelma bears resemblance to a medieval prioress. It is something about the planes of her face—like twelfth century cathedral arches—long, spare, curvilinear lines. Like a prioress, she is not afraid to be in charge, in fact, she rather likes it. As 'housemother' at 350 Ellis, the subsidized apartment building she essentially manages without pay, she watches carefully over her flock and keeps the Housing Authority on their toes in that process. The people who reside there, many of whom are old and frail in body, look to her to solve their day to day problems ranging from getting checks cashed to finding a suitable place for guests to stay in the Tenderloin. Like a priest or doctor, she is on call.

The first time I visited with her, I thought how depressing to live in this neighborhood surrounded by poverty and potential violence on the streets every day. She quickly let me know that this was her chosen turf. She thrives in the Tenderloin, like a tender but hardy weed shoot pushing through the cracks of the sidewalk. It is all a matter of perspective. Ruth and I roamed the streets with her one day as Ruth wanted to capture Thelma's image on film against the tattered backdrop of 'the Loin'. A young man tried verbally to stop us from continuing our westward movement up the street, claiming it was dangerous to walk those blocks ahead even though it was noontime. He may have spotted Ruth's expensive cameras, one of which was hanging around her vulnerable neck. I was a bit apprehensive about the visibility of that equipment as well, but Thelma soon put us somewhat at ease with her confident stride and her greetings to various folk moving along the sidewalks. She obviously is known on the streets. Her appearance is so unassuming and yet she appears almost regal in her bearing. She buys her clothes from the neighborhood thrift shops. She patronizes the local Asian restaurants. She wants to fit into her chosen environment, not stand out as some Lady Bountiful.

Thelma, for the life of her, cannot understand why we were interested in her lifestory. She certainly does not believe that anyone would want to read about such a quiet, backwater existence, but the reader will see how she is quite capable of emerging to twist a few arms at City Hall when necessary. She reminds me of a shepherd—calm, stoic, direct, pragmatic, but mystical in general outlook, and always concerned about the well-being of her flock.

Cold North Childhood

"I was born in Waupaka, Wisconsin in 1914 and then we lived in different places in Wisconsin. My memories from Abbotsford, Wisconsin, which is a little German farming community: all around us were German people. We lived near the dentist who had a housekeeper from Germany. After the War she was packing a box for the German children. She was telling how the German children were just like us—they needed a doll, they needed colors. I got a feeling for other people that way. Then I loved a series of books in the library—it wasn't a very good library—*My Little Japanese Cousin, My Little Chinese Cousin, My Little German*—all that series. I was so bored with my own childhood. I didn't have any sisters or brothers. Then I read about these interesting little people who blew their noses with paper handkerchiefs. They did wonderful things that I could tell about at school.

Hard times hit. My dad had failed in the hardware store. His partner did the bookkeeping which might account for it. My father had very little education and very poor eyesight, but was a very bright man. That's a tragedy in life. He was the youngest of fourteen children so he didn't get glasses. We went up to a lumbercamp town. My dad said, "We're just going to camp out until I get something better to do, so don't let this bother you." There was one little neighbor girl who wanted me to play. I said,"Where do all the kids in the school come from?" She said, "They're Finlanders. You wouldn't want to play with Finlanders, would you?" So living there I found out how wonderful the Finnish people were. They were just the nicest people—plain and kind and honest. I made friends there.

My mother and dad made friends with a couple and we were invited to their house. They had a boy who was staying there and he was nice. I was only about eleven but I know a nice boy when I see him. I heard all this awful talk about the Finns. "I'm not walking with a Finlander."Then I found out that Milo was a Finlander! Milo was so good to me; we were friends for two years. One time we were out picking berries and Mother said, "Thelma, I don't think you're doing any picking at all. Come over here and let me see what you've got."With that I tripped and fell and lost the few I had. Milo, quick as a flash, stuffed half his berries into my pail. I went around and she said, "Well, that's a lot better than I thought."

I have lived among poor farmers. You think city people are poor—poverty in rural areas is terrific. I know something about that. People are so proud. The subject of food just keeps coming up all the time because there was always a kind of starvation for green vegetables. There was no fruit, no vegetables to speak of. One time one of our teachers taught us how to make soup. She made it right there and gave it out. That was a great event, I'm telling you! It was like a party. We all had a cup of soup.

I was always a good student so I was one of the good kids who were allowed to serve milk to the kids who were underweight. I can remember a huge can of milk. I would serve this milk but I wanted some myself. We were told exactly how to do it—just a cup measure and pour it. These children came by at recess time and got the milk. I wasn't enough underweight to get it.

We had some of the most wonderful teachers up there because they were people who probably other schools didn't want. One of them lisped—imagine a second grade teacher who lisps! She was the most wonderful woman. Another one was divorced—terrible! A divorced teacher couldn't get a job anywhere. Another one was not a citizen. She came from Canada. So we got all these 'terrible' people and they were just wonderful. That was the last place anyone would look for a job. Who wants to go into a little mill town that has a population of fifty. Actually it was a tri-county school and the farmers brought their kids in covered wagons. It was amazing.

I think that year and a half up there in the middle of the forest with all that poverty helped me always to identify with the poor.

We went on to Edgerton, Wisconsin where my dad became a well driller. He did well. Things were pretty good for us. But I was a funny looking kid. I came from the North—in long underwear. The other kids, down in the southern part of Wisconsin, who by this time did not have to wear long underwear, were in three quarter socks. Although I changed quickly I was surely a freak to walk in like this in long underwear, a big coat, and heavy woolen clothing. These kids had a clean blouse every morning. I wore a different outfit every week. It was altogether different. I was really freakish. I went into an eighth grade class, but there were two too many kids for the classroom so the principal promoted two of us to high school. That was quite a social adjustment. I did fine in high school, but I was a strange kid. I hated all my high school years, but I did very well academically. I was younger and I was a country kid. Edgerton was one of the most prosperous cities in the country. My folks had a nice home there, that wasn't the point. I hear all the time about teenagers who think nobody likes them. I felt that way. I was an honor student, but that doesn't make you popular either.

My folks were very, very strict with me. The boys weren't exactly chasing me all over the place, but I could have gone out to different things, but my parents wouldn't let me. I wasn't allowed to dance. I was just miserable. I think my dad was afraid something would happen to me, because I was so naive. And my mother—her family were Baptist and Methodist and of course everything was sinful to them. She said, "I don't object to playing cards; your dad and I play cards, but don't play when Grandma's around."

We took care of the grandmothers, winters. They lived in very cold country and so they came down to our house and lived for the winter. It was my mother's mother and her grandmother. There were the four generations of us in one house. It was a little hard on me. For one thing they were Baptist; I wasn't supposed to play cards, dance, and all kinds of don'ts. Mother just said, "You know I don't care for this, but the grandmas would feel bad." My mother was 5'2" and her mother was about 5' tall and the grandma was a couple of inches shorter. It was all these little women. My other grandmother

had died before my mother was married. She was a big
Pennsylvania Dutch woman. None of us ever saw her. My
heritage was unknown to my mother. As I just grew to my
normal proportions, she thought I was a monstrosity. She didn't
say that but her shock—"Oh my God, what's going on here?
She can't need shoes that big!" I saw a book in the library called
The Lummox and I actually associated with that. I thought I was a
lummox. Later, when we moved to a city that had large
Norwegian, Polish and German populations, I realized I wasn't
big. I was just like the rest of them.

My daughter is considerably taller. But because I had such a
bad self-image, I thought I was so horrible. My daughter
thought she looked like me. With my bad attitude toward my
own looks, she thought that reflected on her. So she suffered
terribly from that. I notice that is true in other families too.
Just because the mother, during her teenage years, particularly,
when she wants to be absolutely, perfectly beautiful, and she
finds some flaws in herself, passes this on to the daughter.

One time a boy in school who was talking about the senior
banquet said, "I know you're not going."Tears came to my
eyes and he said, "Oh, hey, I'd take you myself—there's nothing
wrong with you. Everyone's scared of your dad." My dad worked
at the golf course at the time and he was around these young
men who'd talk about girls, I suppose. He'd say, "Well, anybody
who fools around with my daughter . . . !"They liked my dad.
He'd been a boxer. My mother made him get out of boxing;
she didn't want him to get hurt too bad or have his looks
spoiled. He was quite a guy.

Big City
"I moved to Milwaukee and lived with my brother and his family
when I was seventeen. I got a year of education at Milwaukee
State Teachers' College. I didn't like the school; it was just
some more high school. I expected college to be something I
could sink my teeth into. I wanted to go to the University of
Wisconsin. I would have had to work. There was a teacher who

said I could come to their house in Madison. I could have gone if my mother had let me. She wouldn't even discuss it. I went to the school doctor and asked her to write me a letter saying that I couldn't be in school because of my skin. They weren't allowing me in the swimming pool because I had acne. The doctor said, "Why do you need a note if you're going to go home and stay?" I said, "Because of the gossip in a small town." She read everything that came from high school about me and my family. She said, "You need the city and the city needs you. You stay right here and finish out the year. There are lots of jobs in the city. Even being a mother's helper wouldn't be so bad because you move into somebody else's home, see how other people live. Do anything, but don't go home. If you do, you're going to marry some farmer's son. Don't ever stay more than two weeks when you go home." I followed her advice. I respected her very much.

I had ten jobs in one year. It was Depression time. I bottled vanilla in a basement and then the man came down in his shorts to help me—his wife was gone. I decided I didn't want to work there anymore. The day before Prohibition ended I worked in a bakery making pretzels. I did do a mother's helper job and I learned a lot.

I got married when I was twenty-one. I married an older man. I was twenty-one and he was forty-two. When I met him I had a Depression type job, a waitress job before I went to school. The chef said, "When I get my paycheck I'm going to take you out." Before his check came he said, "Look, you're a nice girl. I want to tell you something. I'm married and I should send this check home to my wife, but I want to go out with you. What should I do?" I said, "Send your check home." He said, "I know somebody that would really like to meet you and I'm going to introduce you." I said, "I don't want to meet him." There were guys all over the place—always somebody wanting to take you home. I knew what that was all about. He said, "No, this is a man who will appreciate you." He introduced me to my husband. We weren't terribly smitten with each other at first.

But the chef was right; we were a very good combination. We weren't very financially able and he had a heart ailment, but I'm glad I met him. It was really great for me. I'd marry him again if I saw him coming down the street.

My husband always sympathized with me about my complexion problem. One day I was looking in the mirror and just feeling terrible. The twin boys were playing in the front room, and he said, "Boys! Do you think your mother is pretty?" And in one voice they said, "Oh, yes !"

In school the Dean had told me, "That dreadful rash! It's no use, you can never be a teacher." I went home broken-hearted. I took a business course. Then my husband sent me back to school and I got my education. He put me through the University of Wisconsin. He said, "I can't get insurance because of this heart ailment but you can go to school." So that was my insurance. He died at sixty-three, leaving me with three kids. The boys were sixteen then.

My kids were probably the first of the latchkey children in that area. One of my boys, Tom, said, "I hate to ask you again but I was late again. Will you write another excuse?" So I wrote, "There is no excuse, but I'll give you a reason. My boys get up in the morning and there's no one in the house. They have to get their own breakfast, find the clothes they're going to wear and maybe have to iron something for themselves." I never had to write another excuse for school. There weren't any other children in that area who had to do that, as far as I know.

When I had to choose a subject to teach I wanted a science— biology. My advisor said, "I thought you said you had a family to support. The only thing I can promise you that a woman can get a job in is English." That was in 1950. So disgustedly, I took English. The first year I taught in high school, however, I taught biology. The moral to me was, "Do what you want to do, because that's the thing to do."

I wasn't so much bored myself as I figure I was boring the kids—the same boring grammar year after year. I protested, and other people apparently were protesting about the same time, and they began confining grammar to the first year of high school. So when I got into teaching senior high I wasn't inflicted with that monotonous grammar.

I graduated from the University when I was thirty-five. I worked for three years for Milwaukee County in institutions. First, for the Milwaukee County mental hospital. I was a psychiatric aide. I did such a good job because I liked it so much. The pay was low so they promoted me to the juvenile detention home where I got a hundred dollars a month more. I was a childcare supervisor which was pretty low on the totem pole. I had to take the girls out for recreation. We played mostly volleyball and basketball. The 'nicest', most 'acceptable' girls, the easiest to take care of, were on the first floor. Upstairs they put the ones who might cause trouble. It turned out that they were often the minority kids. I helped a girl fix her hair in the hall one night. We got so we were setting hair at night in the hall. I had been told never to touch any girl because they would say that you had abused them afterward. Malarkey! This was somewhere around the civil rights movement and people were very sensitive about race. I would just put my arm around one of the girls on the way upstairs or give her a push, saying, "Do you need some help getting upstairs?" just to make a little contact.

I'd been warned, "Don't go in their rooms. You are subject to be beat up." I went in the room of this black girl and sat down with her. I said, "I can't take you outside anymore. I'm sorry, you're going to have to stay in while we go out today. You want to know why?" She said, "Yes, I want to know why!" I said, "Because you're a leader. You're a real leader, a natural leader. I'm not a natural leader. I'm a leader because I'm getting paid to be a leader. When we got out there I say, 'Okay, girls, we'll do this', and you say, 'Okay, girls, we'll do this'. And they like you better than they like me, so I can't work that way. You've got two leaders out there and I have to admit to you that I'm beat when you're out there because you're more popular and more of a natural leader than I am so I have to leave you inside. It's a tricky thing to do but I'm the one who is in charge." She thought that over and said, "Gee, I want to play. Oh, I'm not going to do that." I said, "Do you think I should give you another try? It's not that you're so wrong. You have leadership qualities which you'll be using out in the world when you get out of here and get your education, but I can't compete with you. Well, let's go out again and see." That was the end of that. She was just fine.

A social worker came to see me. She said, "I wanted to see what was going on." One of her girls had tried to get in from outside. She was actively trying to do something so she could get back in the detention center. She wanted to be in there with us because we were having a nice homey situation in there."

A unique entry into civil rights

"Four years after my husband died I was teaching full-time, but I had no social life at all. I was just staying at home, reading, gardening. One morning I awoke and saw his ghost, his spirit. Although I couldn't understand what he said to me, I got the message, which was: "Start living, girl. Don't do this anymore. Don't grieve." They say that nothing happens by accident. Just before that, the close of the school year, I heard two students talking about some work they did in an inner city church. He told me the street intersection. It was in a black ghetto area. I dismissed it from my mind. But very soon after I had this experience I wrote a letter to the pastor of this Presbyterian church offering to volunteer my services. When I went down there he told me the things I could do and was very happy to have me. He said, "What I really need is people who will come and join the church and be here on Sunday." In a very short time I was made an elder so I was in a decision-making body.

By that time I had gotten involved in the Urban League. They were quite active in the beginnings of the civil rights movement. When we needed an assistant pastor, I said, "It's time we get a black assistant minister for this church. In this neighborhood, that's what we need." Somebody said, "Oh, no!"

I couldn't believe it. It was a doctor, a very fine young physician. The minister said, "Why not?" He said, "Black ministers are not properly trained yet. If we get a poor one in here, it will set our movement backward." We finally compromised. At least we would interview a black man who had applied. When he was interviewed, he was hired. As far as I know, he is still there. A very fine minister.

A twelve year old boy wanted to join the church and his parents weren't involved. I stood up with him when he joined the church. He called me his godmother. He came to our house all the time. He was insulted out in my neighborhood. People would say, "Where are you going out here? Who do you know? What are you doing out here?" I was so angry. Even people would say to my children, "What's that black kid doing out here?" They said, "He's a friend of ours." I decided to move. Leonard said, "Where are you going to move?" I said, "I don't know, but it's going to be someplace where you won't have to be insulted when you come visit me. I bought a very nice house in an area that was in between a black and white neighborhood— it was getting integrated. I was happy to leave my lily-white neighborhood. Leonard came there often with lots of his friends.

I got involved in a number of things. We met with the police about their treatment of black women in the area. At that time black women objected to being called by their first name when the police didn't do that to anybody else. I was Mrs. Kavanagh, but they'd pick up a black woman and she was "Henrietta" or whatever. We told them we wanted consistency. They decided to call everybody by Mrs. or whatever their title was."

1963 March on Washington

"I called my friend in the Urban League, who was the social worker in the church, "I'm thinking of going on the march to Washington. Are you going?" She said, "No, because we didn't plan it." I didn't realize that the NAACP was really the one who was getting this trip together. But she said, "I think it's great. I encourage you to go. I think it will be a great experience. There are probably not many white people going." I said, "It won't bother me any." So I went and it was true. I think in the back of the bus there was either a white reporter or a white minister cause I would see him when the buses stopped. It was great. I really didn't know much about Dr. King at that time, but I heard part of that great speech that he made. It was a great experience.

I got some reverse racism. I was almost not allowed to go into a black church to sleep. The minister, when he saw me, he stiffened up—it was just not right I was going to come into that church. The others told him I was with them and I was part of the movement. I slept on one of the pews. Different times during the night, the young man I had been riding with, would come and see that I was okay. He didn't say anything, but I was half awake most of the time.

The whole thing took about three days. It was great. I wouldn't have missed it for anything. I'm just so happy I went. One experience we had was looking for people from Mississippi cause that was the worst state, we thought. People said Mississippi isn't showing up. Then we saw a bus with Mississippi. Everyone who got out of that bus had new blue bib overalls on. We stood there and the tears ran down our faces. It was very moving.

At the church in Milwaukee we weren't just some nice white ladies taking care of the children. One lady got worried because her daughter and I were running games in the gym on a Sunday night. She said, "I'm worried about you two, these big boys coming in here. I'm going out to Wabatosa (a suburb in Milwaukee—very nice homes) to get a couple of men to be over here with you." I said, "No, don't you do that." She was just so upset. She said, "There have to be men." I said, "Okay, then we'll find some black men whom these kids can look up to, not some nice, white men out from the suburbs." The minister found them—a doctor and a man who was director at the YMCA. We started to get black men in there to lead the Boy Scouts and other things. Next thing we knew, some of the parents of the children started coming to church. It was very nice.

I started volunteering there in the summertime. I didn't know whether I was accepted or not. At the Christmas program the black parents came and our church was pretty well filled up with black people. One little boy, whom I had been working with a lot, climbed over all these people and sat next to me. He put his foot up on my lap and said,"Tie my shoe." I tied his shoe and sent him on his way again. I thought, I've been accepted. I knew I fit. It was a great experience.

We had a race riot. The neighborhood was a place where there were very nice homes. Successful black people were buying homes in there at this time. I didn't know there was going to be a race riot. But apparently the word was around among the black people. My little godson, Leonard, called me and said, "I can't go with you tomorrow night. Don't go. My mother doesn't want you to." I said,"What are you talking about?" He said,"Did my mother ever ask any favor of you before?" I said, "No." "Well, she asks you now, don't go tonight, hear?" I said,"All right." I thought somebody is going crazy. Then I got a telephone call from a woman who worked at the church. She said, "Can I come over and see your new house?" After she looked at the house. She said, "Let's go outside and talk. It's so nice." I thought it was kind of funny. We went out on the sidewalk and visited. People passed by and saw us together. That night it happened. They sent in the National Guard. I stood in my window and cried to see the National Guard come in for such a situation. I was out on my front porch upstairs and so was another woman across the street. The Guard said to her, "Go inside! There's a sniper loose. You'll be killed!" I went inside and looked out the window and my black neighbors waved at me and I waved at them. God, it was awful. There was quite a bit of destruction, but they told me afterward that it was planned. A certain white-owned store, for example, paid one of my godson's friends to stand on the counter and watch everybody that came into the store to see if anybody was stealing anything. It was so insulting to the people who came in there. His store was pretty badly treated. I was told afterward, that things didn't happen by accident; some people got what was coming to them.

The 'we don't need you' movement was on. I asked a young man, who was active in the NAACP and with whom I had been on the march to Washington, "I want you to tell me the truth now. Do they want white members or don't they?" He said,"I'll tell you the truth. No, they don't because they feel they have to do it themselves now. I hate to say that." So I didn't go into the NAACP. I just tended to my knitting at the church and that was fine. We got some VISTA workers who helped there and widened the children's opportunities. We took them out and integrated a few beaches where no blacks had ever been and some of the restaurants. We just had people look at us funny. That was my last exciting experience in Milwaukee."

The 'dumb teacher'

"I was trained for high school, but I took elementary school jobs because the 'baby boom' children had not reached high school age. I would get jobs in August—the leftovers. I had three years of that kind of teaching. I said,"I'm not going to kid myself. I'm going into high school or I'm going to quit." I had very good grades, the best of everything. I went into the Milwaukee school system, which is not noted for being good, and said "I want a straight answer from you. I don't want to waste any more time coming here. Would you ever hire me as a teacher in your school system?" He said,"No."They wanted good looks and my face was badly scarred from acne.

I read a magazine article about this new dermoplaning operation. I thought, "Let them experiment on me. I don't care. I'm going to find out." I called the Medical Association and they sent me to the man who was head of plastic surgery for the whole area. He charged me only $300 for the operation which made a difference in my life. I was no longer a recluse.

At a teachers' meeting in my suburban high school, the principal said they were seriously considering separating the classes—separating the poor readers—the slow kids. We had poor readers and bad actors because compulsory education, of course, causes that. He said, "Who will take one of those classes?" I raised my hand. I wasn't a very popular teacher either. I said, "I will. I'll take more than one, but don't load me up with it so that I am called the 'dumb teacher'. You can give me a good proportion of those classes and I'll handle them." So he did. That was really my forte. I was really good at that.

The classes were reduced in number, never more than twenty students, quite often seventeen or eighteen. We talked it over. They said, "Yeah, we're the dumb kids." They were really hit with that idea. I said, "No you're not. If you weren't up to normal intelligence you wouldn't be here, but you are poor in basics. I suggest taking one day reading, one day writing, one day speaking, one day listening, and the fifth day we'll do a combination of things." When I submitted a plan for it, I called it "English Workshop". When they walked into my class I said, "If you don't have a pencil I don't want to hear about it, Just come up and take one off the desk." The kids took nothing home with them; there was no homework. Remember, these were kids who hated school, who had jobs. They were in school because they weren't eighteen yet. We changed it into a communications class. I taught them things like how to write checks. I often called them mister. I told them they were ready to go on a job and shouldn't act like clowns. I showed them how they would use the language arts in their jobs.[119]

---

[119] "I was very close to Alice-Chalmers and rode on the buses with Alice-Chalmers workers with whom I visited. I found out that when they selected a foreman from a group of workers they chose someone usually on his language ability—his ability to come to the foremen's meeting, take notes. He had to call in his men who were working under him and explain to them what he had heard at the foremen's meeting. He had to be able to listen, speak and write. A person who could do that could be a foreman and get much better pay."

When I felt that they needed a little uplifting I used the union meeting. The people who sit there like potatoes and let everybody else run it don't count, in contrast to the person who says what he thinks and makes himself understood. That's how I taught and it was very successful. I think there are creative ways of teaching. You have to see where the kids are and where you want to take them.

One class had a bright boy with a wonderful personality in it. I had told the kids, "I don't normally check IQs; I don't listen to your teachers from last year. I say, 'Please don't tell me that, I want him to come in with a clean slate.' But I did check something that was bothering me. One boy in this class has the same IQ as one of the honor ten. Afterward a boy came to me and said, "Mrs. Kavanagh, is that me?" He later went to Marquette Dental School. I know it was because he found out he really had what it took.

Sometimes I would go home and ask my own teenage boys, "What should I do in such and such a situation?" They'd tell me. "There's a kid passing notes. I took the note and then what should I have done?" One of my sons said, "What did you do?" "Probably the wrong thing. I dropped it into the wastebasket." He said, "No, that was the right thing. If you read one of those notes you might never like the kid again."

I knew that I was about having all I wanted of teaching English. I had accelerated writing classes and nobody could write. It was so boring—all the piles of paper! I'd acquired a nice home and everything and I didn't realize how full up I was with it. I thought, "When I'm sixty-five and can take my Social Security, I'm out—I'm going to quit." When I was sixty I went home one night and on my dining room table someone had put a paper with the headline, "Widow's Pension". At sixty you could get a widow's pension from your husband's Social Security. I burst into tears. I didn't know that meant so much to me. When time for contracts came, I wrote, "This will be my last contract. They were stepping on old teachers anyway. They like to get rid of you because your salary has gone way up and they can get two new teachers for not much more than one old teacher gets. That's how I got out happily when I was sixty.

When I got out of teaching I thought, "Ah, now I've got time to write. I dashed off an article about the diphtheria epidemic in the 1800's. Seven of the children in one of our families were dead. It's very cold up there and they couldn't bury them so they put them in a bedroom in the back until warmer weather came. It was such a tragedy. I saw their graves this summer when I was back. I had been prepared for all kinds of failures but when I took it down to the *Milwaukee Journal* they published it immediately—a big article on the editorial page. That was nice to see my name there, even if it was misspelled. The article was timely, in the sense that, here we've got another epidemic; get your kids immunized. There was a moral to it. I also had a couple of little articles appear in a teachers' magazine— small payment, but nice.

I got interested in ESP. One time I was going on vacation and I didn't know where I'd go. I'd been to Civil War sites, to the West, to Washington, D.C.; suddenly I got the idea of going to Boston. It was one of those things that just come to you. I couldn't justify it until I found out that Salem was very close to Boston and I am descended from the Salem witches. When I got to Boston a woman came up to me in the hotel and said, "Are you going on the Salem trip?" I said, "Yes." She said, "Could I be with you?" I said, "Why, yes." Little by little she told me she was a professor at a college in New York and she was an alcoholic on one of her binges. She was drinking and she knew it would get worse before it got better. She asked me to stay with her on this trip.

I had a room in the same hotel, but I never slept in my room. I went to her room and stayed with her. We telephoned her mother. I told her I was bringing her daughter home. We went to New York. Her mother said, "I knew this was coming on, and I began praying, long ago." I said, "Maybe that's how prayer works, so maybe it reached me, I don't know." I don't know where I got the idea to go to Boston. I never did go over to Salem except for the usual places—a lobster dinner and the House of Seven Gables. It was very interesting. I made a nice friend. She wrote to me afterwards.

My kids know I like experiences like that. They try to get my religious ideas. I said, "All I know is there's life after death. I'm not sure who God is or what he looks like or anything about it. Maybe he's a black woman, I don't know. Maybe there is no God, in the sense that we know. But, I know there's life after death, that I know. I think there's some very strange things that happen to us, that can't be explained in science yet. I've been reading a book lately on time. There is no past, present, future—that's just something we've made up for our convenience. My kids accept me the way I am. I'm sure they think I'm a little wacky—well, not wacky, but a little different.

I'm glad I had my mother in her last year and I was close to my folks in their last years. We lived in Milwaukee and they lived in a little town about seventy miles away. I was over there once a month or so until my father died and then every weekend. Then she came to Milwaukee and lived with me."

'Think East, Go West'

"When I quit teaching I decided to go East. I thought, "That family history is interesting. I'll go there and look up my grandfather—where he was born and raised. I may go to England and Ireland and Scotland and Germany." I had a grandmother, who was Pennsylvania Dutch, which is Old American German. Then I thought, I've got to see my daughter first. She's in Portland, Oregon. While I was up there I was very tired out somehow, from just breaking up a big house. I had a suitcase, that's all I had left. I was just going to visit a week, but I was there about seven weeks. She encouraged me to stay. I just rested and slept and slept. I got to listening to KGO night programs. I said, "Lee, San Francisco must be interesting; I'm going to go that way and then go back the southern route to the East." Well, here I am.

I almost believe in angels. I was sick when I came here. I felt myself getting sick at my daughter's. I hid the fact that I had bronchitis and said it was just a little cold. I came down here and asked Travelers' Aid for the nearest YWCA or YMCA. I went over there and went to bed. I ran into an old gentleman on the street who carried my suitcase. I've never had anything like that happen since. He stopped at North of Market Senior Center and said, "Now you come over here and eat. There are other people our age." I went over there because I didn't know where else to go eat. I was pretty sick yet. I never saw him after that. I used to go over there at noon and eat and go right back to bed. I did that for a couple of weeks.

The woman who was president of the North of Market Senior Center had just quit. They were having a meeting and one man got up and said, "There isn't anybody here qualified to be president of this organization." I went back the next day and was sitting there again, disinterestedly, and the man got up and said, "I have an apology to make. I've found there is someone here who is qualified to be our president, and that's Thelma Kavanagh." I don't know where he got his information. I was sixty-two at the time. So I said, all right, there's no big problem. That was a very active organization, the North of Market Senior Service Center. We were quite active in the International Hotel controversy and we took part in the protests.[120]

---

[120] The International Hotel, home to mainly elderly Filipinos and Chinese, became one of the focal points of the San Francisco housing movement in the 1970's. The I Hotel, as it was affectionately known by those who fought to save it, unfortunately was located between Chinatown and the Financial District. As San Francisco's traditional blue-collar began turning white, Hong Kong investors bought the property in 1973 with an eye to the inevitable downtown expansion. The Four Seas Development Corporation sought to evict the tenants over a four year period during which large rallies and demonstrations to save the I Hotel occurred. The sheriff, Richard Hongisto, spent five days in jail for

Then a woman, who was very active in this house, said to me, after I'd been there maybe a year, "You know I can't keep up what I'm doing at the house [*referring to the Housing Authority building Thelma lived in*]. I wish you'd come over there and live and be president and run things." I said, "I can't, I'm sorry, I have a teacher's pension and my income is too big."When I went to Housing and told what I had, it was well within the range to be here. So I came here and I've been president for years. It isn't much, but this morning, three times while I was doing things, I had calls. I had to make three calls about a man who wanted to apply to live at Dorothy Day House. A woman telephoned about getting her check cashed because someone else had been doing it and can't do it anymore; I'll arrange that. And a man came to me who needed a big pot from the kitchen because he's going to have company and the pot is very important; he doesn't have anything like that.

We make money here because I don't mind running garage sales and such. We've got over $1,500 in the treasury. They never had anything like that before. We bought a piano. The other day thirteen of our people went to the zoo and I saw that each of them had five dollars in an envelope. When they got

---

refusing to evict the tenants. Finally, in 1977 the eviction proceeding took place "in a midnight scene of high drama, with 2000 I-Hotel defenders surrounding the building and 400 police and sheriff's deputies, led this time by a somewhat metamorphosed, ax-swinging Sheriff Hongisto, battering their way through to empty the building of its few dozen remaining tenants." *Chester Hartman, The Transformation of San Francisco* (Totowa, New Jersey: Rowman & Allanheld, Publishers, 1984), p. 234. The International Hotel became a rallying point for those caught in the housing crunch, which always manages to effect the poor and elderly first, caused by the rapid expansion of the downtown office-based economy. Hartman's book gives a detailed historical blow-by-blow description of the struggle between the powerful downtown corporate forces and the neighborhood groups who formed to save their communities.

there with the Senior Escort Program person they didn't have to pay any admission, so they had five dollars to buy food.

This building has no name, except its address—350 Ellis Street. There are twelve floors and ninety-six apartments. Capacity would be 120 people. It's a Housing Authority building. A lot of them have gone to very sad circumstances; you read about them in the paper how they've gone to dope. We've been fortunate, although this is a bad neighborhood. The Housing Authority is very strict here. If someone doesn't behave, he gets out. We do try to maintain a nice building and I think we do. We have a very mixed population, which is representative of the neighborhood—heavily Chinese and other Asian nationalities. We have a few people who are not seniors, but they're disabled to some extent. We have a black population and a minority of Caucasians. It's a nice mix and we get along well together. I think that's the best part of it—we get along well together.

The social work has been cut down to a real minimum and will be done with entirely, because the philosophy of the Housing Authority is that they are not to furnish social work; they're to furnish housing. There's a lot of need for anybody, like me, who's willing to do some things. We have a monthly birthday party, except in certain months where we have a big Thanksgiving, Christmas or Chinese New Year dinner. It's easy for me to run these things and to make money. I don't see any sense in just having money in the bank—it's to use for people. Unfortunately, people keep dying or going away to live with their children for their last days, so I say let's use that money. We bought various things here, like a barbecue and big barbecue burners, a big Bingo set. Now we're talking about a VCR.

Nobody likes to take leadership. The Housing Authority tells you to have elections and all the rules you're supposed to follow. There isn't anybody else that wants to be president here. I got out once, figuring nature hates a vacuum—if I get out somebody will go in there and be leader. But nothing happened, so I just went back in. That's how I do with the church—things that nobody wants to do, I do, because I don't have any special talent that I know of. I saw a cement truck the other day, which had a sign on it: When you see a need, fill it. To me, I'm always doing something that no one else wants to do. When I first came to San Francisco I had bronchitis and went to the doctor. He asked me why I was settling here. I surprised myself. I said, "I'm looking for a reason for being."Then I found out I was needed; I was needed right here.

The main thing I've done through the years is the Senior Escort Program. Mark Forrester had a small escort program which somehow got phased out. He made a point of getting acquainted with me. He was working for the Health Department and had in mind starting another escort program. People were saying they couldn't come to the North of Market Senior Center to eat because it wasn't safe to walk through the Tenderloin.[121]

There was quite a clamor to have an escort program. He got me to get some seniors together to be an advisory group. We were funded, very reluctantly, by the Commission on Aging. He became the director. I headed the Senior Advisory Council; we always had to fight to get money for the program. I was always appearing before the Supervisors, before the Commission on Aging, to get money. We were always fighting with the Commission on Aging to keep the escort program funded. I remember one day Mark said, "Can you get about thirty people and we'll march down to City Hall". I knew a Filipino family; they could produce ten people easy. I went to the hotels and rapped on a few doors. I sat in the lobby of the 'K Marlton Hotel and talked to people. Mark didn't believe it; they were all coming in. One day when we had a lot of people from Chinatown, one of the men on the Commission on Aging said,"We've got the Chinese hordes here."

---

[121] The Tenderloin is a jumble of small, down-at-heel hotels which are home to elders on fixed incomes, immigrants, mainly from Southeast Asia, and others living on the gnawing edge of poverty.

There was a Senior Escort office in each neighborhood with a supervisor and several escorts. Mark and I had our headquarters in the North of Market office. A very important segment of the program was the senior component. We had a city-wide council which met once a month. Each neighborhood had an active senior group. In Visitation Valley, the ladies used to bake cakes and things so the escorts and the people who dropped in the office always had food. It was very pleasant. Someone brought a refrigerator in. It just made it very homey. In our office we had senior volunteers who would help in any number of ways. There were no vans at the time. They did their escorts on foot, as much as possible, and on Muni and by taxicabs. We heard about these buses which were on sale at a very reasonable price so we bought them. I had a campaign to raise money. My aim was to make six thousand dollars. We made around six thousand, four hundred and with that we bought whatever we needed for the buses—for example, hubcaps and safety devices for elderly riders. It was a remarkably good program. It gave a lot of seniors something to do that was worthwhile. We had this city-wide meeting every month for years.

Finally, they put the funding under the police department instead of having us beg from the Commission on Aging. Then there was a scandal related to Mark's house. He was cleared in court but, as he was technically an employee of the police department he was fired from his position. The program deteriorated after Mark was removed.

I wrote a paper on Mark's behalf and mailed it out to Supervisors, to everybody. Then Mark started his *Forrester Papers*[122]

---

[122] Mark Forrester, with the aid of the excellent editing abilities of Thelma Kavanagh, puts out a searing, muckraking paper several times a month. He writes about his experiences in the mean streets of San Francisco, focusing on the plight of the urban underclass. He attacks the bureaucratic inhumane systems, such as the Department of Social Services, which perpetuate the problems they are designed to solve. Mark and Thelma send the paper to everyone who is anyone in the local power structure as well as those who contribute to the paper's subsistence.

again, which I agreed to finance. The immediate value to me was a chance to let Mark have a voice, to say anything he wanted to say because I felt he was ready for explosion. I didn't know whether I could do it on my little income so I got a Vista job over at Old St. Mary's Housing Committee. I worked over there for a year. Mark and I understand each other pretty well. He's a very bright guy, but he uses too many adjectives. He uses such big words and I have to check the spelling of them. In the last paper there were some words he had made up! I said, "If you make them up, how do you expect people to understand—that isn't communication." He said, "Yes, it is, and they'll get the joke; you don't have as much humor as some people do." We have that kind of argument. Every Saturday night Mark comes over here and takes my rough draft of his paper and goes through it again, and then I do the final draft. The next week I put the paper out. That keeps me busy.

I do a lot of work at St. Boniface Church. I went to the Bible class at St. Boniface and just decided to get involved in the community down there. I had never been Catholic before, but it doesn't matter to me what religion a person is really—or what nationality or race. They just make use of me every way. I go on Tuesday morning and we count the money. I got on the church council which has been dissolved because a new priest is coming. I'm on the operating board of St. Anthony's Foundation[123] which

---

[123] "It involves going to monthly meetings. I'm on the executive committee because I'm the secretary. No one wants to be secretary so the new member got that. As a result, I have the pleasure and privilege of meeting with Brother Kelly Cullin, who is the vice-chairman, and Jose Medina, who is on the police commission and our chairman. The three of us have to meet once a month and I enjoy that. Board members have to be liaison person with one of the activities that the Foundation carries on including the dining room (which provides lunch and dinner for hundreds of homeless people each week), the thrift shop, the ABA (Adult Benevolent Association) which includes the free milk program. Almost everybody in my building, including myself, receives three quarts

I'm proud of. I'm the sacristan at St. Anthony's—now that's an important job. I wash and iron the linens—the altar cloths. It's just one of those things that nobody wants to do.[124] In the Bible didn't they have the old woman who worked at the temple? For two years I've helped with the teaching of the children on Saturday mornings. I go to the Cadillac Hotel[125] three times a week; a new program is being started up there to employ young people to clean up the area. I'm the financial secretary. I have to keep track of the payroll. All these things keep me busy. I won't get rich or famous, but I'm doing all the things I like to do.

I'm on a committee, United Tenderloin Community Fund, which meets only every other month. I am one of five people who decide how the money, which is gathered from new hotels in this particular area, should be spent. The hotels pay the money to the San Francisco Foundation and then we send out recommendations every two months to the Foundation. Up to now at least, they have just paid them every time. Of course we do give good recommendations. There are all kinds of ethnic programs. We helped the Sizzler get started down here. Leroy Looper, who owns and operates the franchise, was on the committee, but we all decided at the beginning that people

---

of milk each week. They do visiting in all the hotels where seniors live. They give birthday and Christmas presents. It's just remarkable all the good things they do. Then there is our program, the direct services. There are two sisters and a counselor and the woman at the desk whom I relieve at noon. I'm the liaison person for the Madonna Residence which is for low-income women who need more care. They furnish two meals a day there."

[124]   Since this interview she had quit her sacristan duties to devote Wednesdays to her own writing.

[125]   Thelma's friends, Leroy and Kathy Looper, bought and restored the decaying Cadillac Hotel with the aid of grants and loans. The dealers and junkies had to relocate as the Loopers run a clean and comfortable hotel for seniors, setting an example for what can be done to make the Tenderloin a liveable neighborhood.

should not be penalized for being on that committee, but should abstain because of conflict of interest when we voted.

Lately I got very excited when I heard that buildings like this [*indicating 350 Ellis Street where she is living*], specifically the HUD buildings, were in a precarious position because their contracts were about up. When that happens they could be sold to private parties. There's a new senior organization called Housing Alliance for Seniors, which I'm vice-president of, unfortunately. [*Laughs*] It got started because of this understanding that senior housing was threatened. A lot of people would love to have this building so I said I'm going to be here and fight. I read recently where it had been decided that HUD cannot sell those houses. I'm having a little trouble finding out just what the situation is with the Housing Authority. I think that we are protected by the decision on HUD, but I don't want to rely too much on that either. I want to be sure to fight for senior buildings. I don't have to worry about myself. I don't have to live here. I could live a number of places, but I like living here.

I'm representing the tenants, with another woman, in helping to choose a new director for the Housing Authority. There's the Housing Commission and then the tenant representatives. It's been a very interesting experience. The Housing Commission actually chooses, but they will confer with the mayor before they make the final choice.

Another thing I do is work at the admission desk at the St. Anthony's Foundation. The have a number of different projects, I found out since I'm on the Board. One of them is direct services to people who walk in off the street. They ask for anything, from a toothbrush on up. They ask for diapers, bags of food, counseling, help to get a hotel room, help to let them go home—some things I would think other agencies would be doing. I do have free information sheets there—"Free Eats" and a long list where they can get showers, haircuts, counseling. Sometimes we have a sheet for employment. I was in there one time at noon hour and there was no one there to help. People were just desperate and the place was closed. I said, there should be someone here, so I went to work there.

My experience as a teacher is a wonderful background for what I do here. I have close feelings for people who are poor or who are looked upon as odd or handicapped in any way. Ethnicity I love.

Every night, almost without fail, I make a little list for the next day, where I'm going to be and what hours."

Changes in the Tenderloin

"I know how I've seen it change in the last twelve years. One time a few years ago, people find this hard to believe, there were no children. There are thousands of children in the Tenderloin now. When there were none, somebody came along with a baby, and you know how when you see something very beautiful, how the tears come? That's what happened to me. I was so moved to see that baby. I just wanted to hold it. There are kids all over the place now. That's how it's changed. There are now whole families living in places really suitable for one person. The influx of the Vietnamese and other Asian people is another factor. There are more black people in evidence here than there were, although I don't know whether they live here or not. A lot more agencies have developed, for teaching English to the various nationalities, for example. I know that through my contacts with the Tenderloin committee. I think the children are the most obvious change. It bothers me that they're living in places that aren't family-sized places to live. We need more playgrounds for children. They opened Boedekker Park. That's fine, but who's playing basketball? It's grown men. We have to have more places for children.

There are all kinds of things that need to be done here. Everything is so expensive. Hotels are so expensive and we really don't have places where you can ask people to come in and stay. One of the ladies here, who is on a very low income, her brother called and said,"Is there anything cheap around there? I'm booked at $90 a night." Just recently I found out that what used to be the YWCA on Sutter Street has rooms available for $35 so I can tell that to people here now. If they're going to have guests, that's the place to go. Someplace where people could put their handmade things to sell would be nice for seniors. Childcare is needed so people can go to work.

It's a neighborhood that has a lot of elderly people in it. There's a lot of senior housing within a few blocks of here and South of Market has a whole cluster of senior housing just a few blocks down there. Some people say, "The poor seniors, they can't go anywhere else; they have to live in the terrible Tenderloin. The fact is that people live here because they like to. It's close to things, like the library. I don't go there any more because I don't have time, but that was one of the big attractions to me. Theaters and churches are close by. Seniors do like it here. I don't see that changing. There is improvement going on in the Tenderloin all the time, like this new project where they're going to have people sweeping the streets. Some of the things that have happened here have really got me interested, like the influx of Asians. I don't know what's going to happen. I'm interested. If anyone needs anything and I can help with it, I will."

A Tenderloin elder is a tough elder

"I just live like the neighborhood, which makes me acceptable in the neighborhood. St. Anthony's Thrift Shop brings clothes over here. I bought six pairs of slacks for a dollar apiece; that's what I wear. I was talking to a black man one day about something that happened to somebody on the street and how scary it is sometimes. He said to me, "You don't have to be worried on the street." I said, "I'm not scared particularly, but I know the dangers out there." He said, "If anybody touched you, there'd be people running to help you." I'm not so sure.

I ran into a man who used to work at Glide[126] down on Sixth Street[127] one day. He was sitting on a car. He looked very disturbed; he came over and took hold of my arms and visited with me. He was making conversation all the way down the street. He said, "Thelma, it's good to see you." He gave me a hug. I realized he was saying to people, "This is a friend of mine, leave her alone." I didn't say anything to him about it; I just talked to him. As I came to the end of the block I turned and crossed the street because there was something going on down that street that he was protecting me from. I don't know what it was. I used to go out more evenings that I do now. A man stopped me one night and asked for money. I looked him in the eyes and said, "You don't really think that I, living in this neighborhood, would carry money with me, do you?" He said, "No, I guess I wouldn't if I lived here." You never know what will happen around here.

I put out a little paper for a while called *The Tattler*; then I changed it to the *Kavanagh Papers* and discussed various subjects relating to seniors. I have things I like to write, but there is a very definite generation gap. I have decided to go back and allow some time for writing. I'm up early in the morning doing lots of reading. One piece I want to work on, which I haven't started yet, is about my dad and Father Harlan. My dad was such an old Protestant. He had lots of Catholic friends, but he

---

[126] Glide Church, which is just down the street from the apartment building where Thelma lives, has maintained a progressive reputation since the 1960's. The congregation, which is led by the Reverend Cecil Williams, is a polyglot mix of races, cultures, ages and lifestyles.

[127] Those blocks of Sixth Street adjacent to Market Street, the main downtown thoroughfare, form the heart of the downtown ghetto. Firetrap hotels, porno bookstores, small-time drug dealers, down and outers of all types fill this scene. A frequent area for homicide and robbery, it is not a nice neighborhood for a stroll even in the daytime.

didn't like priests, for some reason. Then we got in a hard way
of life and he took on a salesman's job. Somebody said, "Go to
the priest, He'll buy something." Dad reluctantly went to the
priest's house and they became good friends. Everything he
sold, old Father Harlan would buy. Then the priest got him a
job at the golf course. It was such a strange, unlikely friendship.
So I want to try it in my mind, at least, and maybe in writing,
two ways: one is fiction and the other is just the outright story.
It's pretty well in the past so all the principals are dead and
gone. I'll work on that.

REFLECTIONS
On accomplishments
"I'm proud of my children; they're all so great. It troubled me
that they wouldn't get an education and they've all got it. I'm
proud I got a good father for them. But right here and now I
just am really very pleased with my life—what goes on here in
the house, and I go from here now to work at St. Anthony's.
I'll meet with the executive committee of the St. Anthony's
Foundation. I enjoy that very much. I like to know what goes
on; I want to be at the center of where things are happening. I
like being on the executive committee of the St. Anthony
Foundation; I like counting the money at church; I like
knowing what the problems are. I like to be right there. I like
decision making. I'm good at it. I can make decisions quickly.
I'd rather make a decision and be wrong, and then right it,
than to just drift. I can't stand that.

On advice to young
"I can't think of any great words of wisdom, but so many look
for a way to develop their own career. If they'll just try to be
helpful, really helpful. There's always an opportunity for that.
My son-in-law went into the Forestry Department and the
next thing I knew he was re-writing some of their material.
You know how the government writes things. Their writing is

terrible. If people look for where they can really do something that somebody else can't do—I think that's important.

I'm not good at giving advice. I was telling my daughter, who is a counselor, that I've given advice and it's come out very badly so I don't do it any more. For example, a young man came to me and said, "Thelma, I've got a chance for two jobs and I don't know which one to take. One is a warehouse job and one is in a bank."We talked a little about it, and I said, "Now think of it this way, the warehouse job probably pays more, because banks are notorious for bad pay, so if you want money right now, quick, I'd take the warehouse job. But if you're looking for a career, and a career in banking would interest you, then it's worthwhile to take that." Now aren't those nice words of wisdom to hear from an older person? So he took the banking job and combined it with the idea of quick money. He took some free samples and, as I understand it, went to jail. So don't ask me to give advice. I have enough trouble living my own life with all its complexities."

On positive and negative changes in the Bay area

"The rents. So many businesses are closing because the rents are too high. There are more and more Asian people of course. This house used to be a lot of white people; now I'm the only Caucasian on this floor, which I don't mind at all. I love the mixture of nationalities and races. I love it that a lot of the people here are Buddhist. Children and families in the Tenderloin, more poverty and people are getting meaner.

I had someone snatch my wallet at the front door the other night. I went to the outside door, foolishly. My friend and I had been to a class down at the church. We were just going to get on the elevator and somebody banged, banged, banged on the door. We have a card key, and if you forget it, you just have to rely on catching somebody to let you in. I went over and opened the door just a little bit. This strange young man and I looked each other in the eye. I said,"You don't live here." I had the card key and my wallet in my hand; he just reached over and took it out of my hand. I saw the card key drop so I put my foot on it and kept my leg in the door so he couldn't have done anything without hurting me. I talked him into giving me my wallet back. I said, "You've got the money out of it now. There are things in there that I can use that will be no good to you. Give me my wallet back." He gave it to me. I banged the door shut then. I said to my friend, "Look, now he's got my card key!" He was picking it up. I opened the door and he handed it to me. I figure that maybe he recognized me."

On special quality of life in the Bay area
"One of my sons, a teacher, was just enamoured by the street entertainers, for example. We never had anything like that in Wisconsin. Those kinds of things are fun. I enjoy the nonsense[128] down at the cable car turn-around at Powell and Market Streets, but of course it has got too bad what with the homeless. In all the years I was involved in things in Milwaukee, I was in city hall only once. I feel perfectly at home in city hall in San Francisco. I've talked with the mayor and the supervisors. Government is so close, that's one thing I love. I've testified in city hall many, many times. I love the racial diversity. It seems like there's more creativity here, more freedom. I was glad there was a refuge for gays here because I've always been aware of having teachers, people in the church and other who were gay, who lived miserable, tortured lives. There's lots of things for the elderly to do besides sit around."

On Aging
"When you get old you finally are who you are. I've thought about that a lot. For the first time in my life I am who I am. I

---

[128] The "nonsense" includes street musicians, evangelists, poets, beggars, political haranguers, pickpockets, soothsayers, bag ladies, tourists, and other assorted folk, who seem to gravitate to the cablecar-heart of downtown SF for fun, trouble, and/or profit.

had to find out here really who I was, because at home I was my mother's daughter, my father's daughter, I was the Nourse girl, I was my husband's wife. Even in my sixties I heard myself referred to as "Lee's mother" when I visited my daughter—always somebody's something. Here, I've really been just me. It's very enjoyable."

fterward

"Thus men of character are the conscience
of the society to which they belong."
Ralph Waldo Emerson

We are in crisis as a community, as a
nation, as a species. We are proving to be too smart and greedy
for our own good. Americans do not want to face the mistakes
of the past; in fact we ignore its existence and shove those who
could enlighten us about it into death camps known as nursing
homes. We put old people away from us as if by their absence
we can deny death as well as the past. Instead, we lose one of
our most valuable resources. The irony is that never have we
needed the wisdom and experience of our elders more than in
this time of accelerated change.

We chose these six elders as examples of models for aging.
They tell us important things we need to know about overcoming
difficult obstacles, about the benefits of constructive rebellion,
about taking risks, about courage and honor, about pioneering
spirit, about living fully in the moment.

They tell us how a supportive, strong family of origin creates
a new generation who then can serve as role models for the next.
Currently, when 60% of American children spend at least part
of their childhood in single parent homes and therefore,
according to Louis Sullivan, the former secretary of Health and
Human Services, "are five times more likely to be poor and twice
as likely to drop out of school",[129] we need to understand this
American tragedy and look for realistic solutions. Knowing what

---

[129] Fatherless families called U.S. tragedy, *San Francisco Examiner*, January,
1991.

constitutes an affirming family is just as critical as defining the family which is unable, for whatever reason, to be committed to the well being and growth of its members.

Dorsey Redland's family represented the best of the pioneer spirit: self-reliant, tough but generous to all within their boundaries. The mother, from old New England stock, descendant of the founders of Harvard University, and the father, Norwegian immigrant, eager to wrest out a place in the West, created a legacy for their children which encompassed far more than land and cattle. Heritage is not handed down on paper; character is carefully taught and nurtured. Dorsey's parents consciously and thoughtfully empowered their children to become not merely functioning adults but thinking, independent, confident, creative people who could thrive under difficult circumstances. Dorsey advocates intelligent risk taking because her family encouraged her to do so. Her story is so reinforcing regarding children's need for strong role models, for cohesive family life, for rooted connections. These factors fostered the unfolding of a creative and brave spirit.

After her husband died, Dorsey replicated the large family she had known as a child by becoming a foster mother. She used her parents' guiding principles and techniques, connecting both her natural son and the foster children to her own childhood in the process. She experimented with 'participatory democracy' within the private realm by establishing family meetings where all members felt they had a voice and purpose. She rightly is proud that they are all doing well today.

Ida Jackson's family of origin was so extraordinary, so irrepressible, particularly considering the setting and time. She experienced life long support from her family, enabling her to act out the family's goals and dreams, created many years before in that danger zone, feudal Mississippi. Ida is living testimony to what is possible when one has the backing of a strong family, committed to social change for themselves and others. The odds are doubtful whether she would have made it out of Mississippi and into the University of California on her own without the aid of her family. The strength of such a family is more than the sum of its parts; from them she received an exponential rate of nerve and determination to succeed. As a very young woman Ida knew her destiny.

Every family was scarred by the Great Depression. No one was left untouched by it, but those at the bottom suddenly found themselves falling into a blue hole. When Joe's father was laid off from his low-paying, hard-labor job, Joe was starting to make a name for himself in the minor leagues so naturally he helped his family financially even though he was in love with Winifred Hartman and wanted to begin his own family. He delayed his marriage for eight years because he knew he could not support two families. I was told as a kid that 'the country of baseball' encourages character development. Joe's story substantiates this midwestern belief.

Sometimes it is almost enough to have one strong person on your side. One wonders what separates those children who grow up in poverty, who witness wide-ranging, human-fueled horrors at home and on the streets, and yet manage to become productive citizens, from those who either perish as children or who become so stunted by their early experiences that they never reach a fraction of their potential. What is the key? What factors make the difference? I suspect in Bill's case two elements both shielded him from the natural self-destruction which permeated the streets of Hell's Kitchen and gave him the courage to break away from his father's and step-father's path, as well as endure future hardships.

His mother, born in poverty in Ireland, illiterate, unskilled, prone to marry drunkards, nonetheless came through for Bill by not being intimidated by authority, not even by the hegemony of the Catholic Church. She left Bill's father when he knocked her around even though she knew how difficult survival would become for her and her children. In those days there were no battered women's shelters and most women workers were paid starvation wages, but she took her children by the hand and moved away from him in spite of that grim reality. When the nuns at school criticized Bill's lack of shoes and physical appearance, she attacked them for being callous, un-Christian hypocrites. Although Bill was embarrassed at the moment, he never forgot his mother's stand. Most mothers in her position would have accepted the blame and shame which the nuns tried to heap upon her. Acts of courage are all relative to the particular situation. An acquaintance told me of uncovering a nest of mice in a shed. The mother, with babies hanging on her teats, rose on her hind legs in a position of defiance, combat ready to defend her young. Her courage was awesome in the face of the odds. Bill's mother, like the mouse, helped her children survive in a most brutal world. Bill often would call upon her strength of character in the years that followed.

Bill, like many bright children, developed an enormous curiosity about the world beyond the confines of his own habitat. He was drawn to the waterfront, partly by economic necessity, but also by a craving for adventure, for a different perspective. One needs luck to survive deprivation. Bill had his mother and his curiosity to aid him in escaping the gravitational pull of Hell's Kitchen.

Especially for Dorsey, Ida, Joe, and even Bill, although his experience with family life had its dark side, their families of origin gave them a solid foundation on which to build their lives.

Our models overcame various obstacles including those which halt many people's progress: racism, sexism, poverty. Joe and Bill, particularly, were forced to deal with the issue of poverty very early in their lives. They learned to fight to protect themselves on and off the field and the waterfront. If you wanted to survive on the streets of St. Louis or New York City you had to be tough; that is how males are socialized in working-class neighborhoods and ghettoes. Joe used that toughness, combined with his athletic ability, to compete in professional sports, helping his family of origin survive. Bill took his street-fighting prowess to the waterfront where he proved himself to be a man of conviction as well as courage.

Bill abhors violence and yet curiously his life has been filled with it: his childhood in Hell's Kitchen, the waterfront, the Spanish Civil War, World War II. Possibly this is the case with great-hearted warriors. Through the experience they come to despair over violence as a method to solve problems. I believe that Bill was always a peacemaker by nature, but being powerful physically and committed to socialist principles, he could not escape the essential battles of his time.

Bill's story is hardly that of Horatio Alger. He did not rise from poverty to riches or even to the blessed middle class. Staying true to his early principles, he did not overcome childhood poverty to become what he calls a 'privileged character', but a leader whom working men and women could trust and respect.

Thelma, who overcame poverty and physical disability to become a teacher, refused to retire to the middle class suburbs even though her children probably would have been relieved if she would have done so. Many people in her position profess the bootstrap theory, rejecting any notion that an unjust economic system is responsible for the widespread poverty which exists in the richest nation on earth. She fought for the Tenderloin residents because she understood their struggle to survive in a cold world.

Ida and her family did not live in the dire poverty which most African American families faced in the early 1900's, but they were close to that line despite their heroic efforts. They did have to confront a most debilitating, demonic monster: American racism in its most virulent habitat, Mississippi. Remembering the suffering she saw as a child, she returned during the Depression to help those in desperate need.

Ida achieved her education goals, not just for herself or even just for her family, although certainly her family's encouragement and financial support contributed to her success, but "for the race". She felt an obligation to use her talents and intelligence to further the black cause as it was defined in that era. She was entrusted with a mission, as were other young black scholars, to achieve in realms which previously had excluded all non-whites. When she began her studies at the University of California, Berkeley, in 1918, she was one of eight black students. **Eight!** Although the administration and the student body did not welcome blacks with open arms, she and her family had seen much worse than not having their picture published in the *Blue&Gold*. They had faced death to help change the manner in which blacks were treated in the South. When whites tried to steal her father's land at the turn of the century— not incidentally when it was commonplace for blacks to be burned alive for much slighter reasons—her father defied the status quo by taking his case to court. The Jacksons were a brave family who fought for their rights as citizens, even though eventually they were forced to leave Mississippi in order to pursue their dream.

California symbolized a new freedom to Ida's mother and father, but she was the one destined to experience it most fully. Ida could face the racism at CAL and within the Oakland public school system because her heritage provided her with the strength to prevail in extreme adversity. She was prepared for the struggle. Ida loves CAL even though the administration has not always been as gracious and appreciative as it was when she received the Berkeley Citation, the highest honor bestowed on graduates. Although she had completed her course work for a Ph.D., she was unable to find a professor to sponsor her for her doctoral thesis. This was her chief disappointment as a scholar, and certainly a discredit to the University of California. To be denied the honor of a Ph.D. due solely to racism was a much deeper blow to Ida than any social ostracism. She believed in the power of education to destroy racial bias. She believed the world of academia existed above the petty and mundane prejudices of the 'real' world. Ida's parents convinced her that the key to ending racial discrimination and oppression was education. But in spite of this bitter awakening, she remained loyal to CAL for giving her the opportunity of acquiring a first-class education at a time when it almost was unheard of for blacks.

The new racism, including the resurgence of bigotry on college campuses, disturbed Ida, but she was still aware that things have changed for the better since her student days. The pioneering days, when only eight black students attended CAL, are over. Likewise, in the public school system in the Bay area, black teachers are no longer rare. The battle for quality education opportunity for minorities certainly has not been won, and with the acceleration of poverty and the consequent increase of drug use within the black community, the future looks bleak for many black children. Ida, who served as a model of hope and perseverance for so many years, despaired over the lack of strong role models for these young people.

In their migration to California in 1918, Ida and her family were a part of the first wave of the great internal migration of blacks out of the South.[130]

The fragile, emerging black middle-class was intent, not only on survival, but change. Ida's mother and father knew that if their children were to have the opportunities which

---

[130] Several books chronicle the waves of migration out of the South: Neil Fligstein, *Going North: Migration of Blacks and Whites from the South, 1900-1950* (New York: Academic Press, 1981); James R. Grossman, *Land of Hope: Chicago, Black Southerners, and the Great Migration* (Chicago: University of Chicago Press, 1989); Daniel M. Johnson and Rex R. Campbell, *Black Migration in America: A Social Demographic History* (Durham, North Carolina: Duke University Press, 1981). Nicholas Lemann's *The Promised Land: The Great Black Migration and How It Changed America* (New York: Vintage Books, 1991) is a critical account of the second wave of migration beginning in the early 1940's. Lemann calls for extensive federal intervention to deal with the overwhelming situation which many urban blacks face. "The ghettos bear the accumulated weight of all the bad in our country's racial history, and they are now among the worst places to live in the world." When Ida first came to Oakland in 1918 the dream of a better life was a real possibility with the support of the small but tight-knit black community. Today she is deeply disturbed about the future of her community.

guarantee first-class citizenship that they must leave the South. For enterprising young black men such as Ida's brother, the railroad[13] provided a means of escape. By working as a waiter on the trains heading West, he was able to make enough money to move his mother and sister to California and fulfill his father's dream. Ida, who was her father's beloved child, did not hesitate to take full advantage of the chance to use her exceptional intellectual abilities. Black families, like Ida's, were moving North and West, not only to escape a feudalistic social and economic order, but to find a place to be, to expand their wings, to experience another country.

Many of us who have moved to California in the last several decades did so out of choice, not necessity. It is important to understand the significance of the black migration to the cities of the North and to the West coast. Ida's parents realized that their children could not survive in the South with the attitude which they acquired from their parents. They were carefully taught to question authority and to assume their equal status with others regardless of race. For blacks, needless to say, this was a dangerous position in the South prior to the civil rights revolution in the

---

[13]   Black men who worked on the trains as waiters, cooks, and sleeping car porters became the vanguard of the black organized working class. The first successful black union, the Brotherhood of Sleeping Car Porters, later helped to finance the early stages of the civil rights movement in the 1950's. King's Montgomery bus boycott could not have taken place without the financial support of the Brotherhood. The railroads waged a bloody battle with those who tried to organize the Brotherhood. Thanks in large part to C.L. Dellums, uncle of former Congressman Ron Dellums, the West coast chapter of the Brotherhood of Sleeping Car Porters was established. When I was doing graduate work in the 1970's I interviewed C.L. Dellums regarding his experiences in organizing the Brotherhood on the West coast. It was my original intention to include him in this book. Unfortunately, he was too ill to be interviewed when we began this project.

1950's and 60's. After they were settled, Ida and her family helped other black families who were making the transition. The family took in other black students, not because they needed the extra $20 per month room and board, but to help others acquire the necessary education which they viewed as the door to opportunity and equality. Change would surely accelerate in a positive manner as more and more young blacks earned college degrees from outstanding institutions such as the University of California. Ida's family implicitly understood the necessity to support others to achieve a better life for blacks. The commitment to family extended to the black community for pioneers such as Ida and her family. In the process of building a new community, predicated on seizing opportunity and not merely surviving the status quo, Ida, and others of her generation and circumstance, overcame enormous obstacles by focusing on the ultimate goal: the advancement of blacks in the less hostile environment of the San Francisco Bay area.

Ida concentrated on the prize with an intensity which may be difficult to understand in the self-gratification/destruction ethos of the late twentieth/early twenty-first century. When she first entered the University, her mother told her that she had the backing of the family to take her education goals as high as possible, but "boys and books don't mix". The sacrifice was one she was willing to make. It's hard to imagine a present-day teenager giving up that critical aspect of life voluntarily in order to pursue a college degree. In our modern campus setting, with coed dorms and general permissive atmosphere, students would laugh at the idea. Ida, surrounded by family and friends and a supportive community which admired her quest, did not live a solitary existence. Judging by her personality, one would wager that she was always well-liked as she has a wonderfully sly sense of humor, but she never did marry and create a family of her own. She focused all of her considerable energies on pursuing her education in order to set a standard of excellence for others to emulate and to enable her to be of service to those whom she felt needed her most—young students of color.

On a different front Dorsey and Sally fought separate battles for gender equality during the time when the 'feminine mystique' supposedly enthralled all white middle-class women. In 1950, when Dorsey was studying law, only 4.1% of lawyers and judges in the U.S. were women. This was not territory for the timid. To be an aggressive, ambitious professional woman in the 1950's was looked on by men, and many women as well, with open hostility.[132] But she had a father who took her to the courthouse to observe a trial "where you get paid for arguing" and a mother who told her, "We have to strike our own paths." No wonder she relished the opportunity to go to the 'cow counties' to try cases. She knew her audience as she was raised among country folk. She enjoyed breaking through the stereotype then as she enjoys dissolving the one surrounding older women now. These are opportunities for her to 'stretch out', to lob in her best stuff while her opponents are slightly off-center. She gives no quarter and expects no breaks, but she does demand a fair fight as the San Francisco Police Department found out when she confronted the often twin issues of police brutality and racism in court.

---

[132] The post War climate regarding the place of women, now that the men were back: Rosie the Riveter get back in the kitchen and rattle those pots and pans! Two-thirds of all college women in the 1950's acquiesced to the new 'feminine mystique' by failing to receive their BAs. Bette Davis was out; Debbie Reynolds was in and the very thought of women's equality was an un-American aberration which was likely communist inspired. A woman who aspired to a career was considered a deviant at best. For younger readers who do not know what life was like before the resurgence of the women's movement in the late 1960's, and for those of us who have blocked that climate from our memory, I recommend reading Rochelle Gatlin's *American Women Since 1945* (Jackson, Mississippi: University Press of Mississippi, 1987). She presents a thorough examination of the climate vis a vis women's issues just after World War II and how the contemporary women's movement evolved out of women's involvement in other post-War social struggles in the 1960's.

She made the courtroom her domain partially by connecting with the people who worked in that milieu—the clerks, the bailiffs, the people who in Dorsey's words, were "putting in their time to make the system of justice work". Immediately she established herself, her reason for being there—not to win a beauty contest, but to defend her clients to the utmost of her ability which they soon found out was considerable. Here was one Wyoming cowgirl who caused more than one D.A. in Northern California to shake his head and wonder aloud, "Where the hell did that broad come from?"

Sally's early confrontation with racism helped her to develop the feisty spirit needed at a later date to confront the sexism which pervades academia. Growing up in the 1930's in an upper middle-class Jewish family, Sally did not find it difficult to make the connection that all forms of racism are abhorrent and dangerous, despite her parents' views. Early on she was a rebel with a cause and she has never deviated from the stand she took as a little girl in the second grade, in essence, a stand against her parents and teacher.[133] During her growing up years she confronted her family with their own racism, risking their censure and displeasure. Many years later, at her high school class reunion, the president of the class, referring to her as "the troublemaker", further identified her as "the rebel", the one who saw it from a different perspective. In a very real sense, she was an outsider.

If Sally had remained within bounds she would have had it made, at least in the material sense. But she hated Vassar—the snobbish atmosphere, the elitism devoid of intellectual content, and the general banality of the upper middle-class lifestyle. She

---

[133] In this work we are not suggesting that one should automatically honor and obey all elders without question. According to the historian, Forrest McDonald, the early presidents, Washington and Jefferson sought out those who were wise and just for counsel and guidance. This is something our current leaders might do from time to time. This action not only connects generations, but enables us to take a step, hopefully, toward enlightenment.

gravitated toward a professional field dominated by a clique of white, Anglo males, eventually creating her own niche within it, enabling her to criticize that good old boy network. Her struggle against this rigid, entrenched, antediluvian, misogynist, racist enclave became her impetus toward personal, as well as professional, freedom."If ever my feminist conscience was formed it was during the experience of being a grad student in the anthropology department at the University of Chicago."As in her personal life, she led a somewhat stormy and adventurous professional life. Barely tolerated as a graduate student, she did not let that deter her from her goal. Women, especially aggressive women who also happened to be attractive and Jewish, did not fit into this WASP male scene. While working on a dig in France, Sally was treated like a servant by the Harvard professor in charge. She refused to either play that role or quit, demanding, instead, to be treated as a fellow professional.

Her article, "The Politics of American Anthropology", published in the Fellow's Newsletter of the American Anthropology Association in 1973, remains a blistering attack, not only on the racism within the field—expressed by the blatant exploitation of the subjects, the Native Americans being the best example, but also the growing trend at the time toward using and planting those who were engaged in field work around the world in covert 'research' for the CIA. Sally obviously was not afraid of taking on Big Time Authority, after all she already had done so as a child. As a consequence of this published moral indictment of the anthropology community, she would never again secure research funding.

The bohemian viewpoint unwittingly provides a safety valve for mainstream, middle-of-the-road America. Someone said America's survival is due in part to our ability to absorb dissent. Without vigorous dissent we would soon lapse into neo-fascism, which we came very close to doing during the McCarthy era. To the horror and titillation of 'regular' folk, one of the cornerstones of bohemian lifestyle always has been sexual freedom—moving as far away as possible from the bourgeois all-American apple pie nuclear family norm. Sally's participation in the Sandstone 'experiment' allowed her the freedom of intimate expression without the constrictions of 'bourgeois' marriage and family obligations. One would suspect that her experiences within her own family as a child led her to these 'radical' departures in human configurations and relationships which were evolving at Sandstone and other unconventional settings during the 1960's.

From her earliest rebel days when she 'hung out' in New York jazz clubs, to the present, as she continues to fight for the rights of elders, gays, women, and anyone else who needs a genuine hand, she demonstrates her commitment to the creation of a more equitable and open society. Experiencing the privileges and amenities of life among the upper middle-class, Sally easily could have opted for life as a Junior League matron. Wealth can be a two-edged sword. Probably that early economic security allowed her to open the creative side of her nature to the sun at a very young age. She remains a curious being, never content with the party line, regardless of the host.

Whether criticizing the anthropology establishment's practices and motives or, much more difficult, questioning the methodology of feminists, who, despite the lack of solid evidence, zealously cling to the belief that women, at some dim point in prehistory, benignly ruled, Sally demonstrates her commitment to the principles of good scholarship. She did not permit her own subjective want-to-be's to cloud her objective investigation. Although a feminist herself, her stance on the issue of the past glories of The Matriarchy make her persona non grata in some circles. Thankfully, she is more interested in the truth than in popularity. One can count on her to call us on our own errors of wishful thinking, particularly when it lies within her field.

Anyone who takes on such sacred cows as Louis and Richard Leakey, as well as a vocal wing of the feminist community, shows real chutzpa. We need people like her who are not afraid to speak their minds, who are rigorous, disciplined scholars, who deeply care about the outcome of the on-going struggle between those who would destroy their own mother earth in the sad pursuit of profit and those who would walk lightly in order to let future generations have a chance to flourish.

Like many persons who move to a different beat, Sally remains curious and alert to contemporary issues and twists in the plot. She has experienced life from the Other side. The gypsy would come to rest in San Francisco, still the most natural haven in America for those who seek to explore all corners of the dream.

When I asked Sally what she would choose as an epitaph, she said, "It was a hell of a ride!"

Rebellion takes many shapes. One wonders if it is an inherited tendency. On Thelma's father's side her family traces back to Rebecca Nurse, one of twenty-seven people who were convicted of witchcraft during the Salem 'Outbreak' in the solemn, sinister late 1600's in the Massachusetts Bay Colony. If Thelma had lived in the same milieu as her famous ancestor, she would have preceded Rebecca to the gallows.

In a current feminist interpretation of the New England witch hunts Carol Karlsen draws an interesting profile of the women who were accused. They expressed "dissatisfaction, however indirectly, with the power arrangements of their society and in doing so they raised the specter of witchcraft, of female rebellion against God and man."[134] Rebecca Nurse became a victim, unconscious of her own role in the uprising against patriarchal rule which is still playing out. As that venerable patriarchal New England leader, Cotton Mather, put it "Rebellion is as the sin of witchcraft."

Thelma, being a twentieth century woman, is conscious of her own rebellion against the status quo. Women have had plenty of time to learn about the tilting at windmills and the slaying of dragons—as well as the hanging of witches. Thelma

---

[134]   Carol F. Karlsen, *The Devil in the Shape of A Woman: Witchcraft in Colonial New England* (New York: Vintage Books, 1987), p. 152.

certainly has. She understands how power operates, at least in the City of St. Francis. She became a voice, for seniors and others who are dis-enfranchised—the homeless, the Asian immigrants, anyone who genuinely needs help. She is not a charismatic soap-box rabble-rouser, but rather a behind-the-scenes mover. By being directly involved in the life of the community as a resident, rather than merely being an outsider who is sympathetic to its problems, Thelma truly represents those whom she wishes to serve. All of her fine efforts, as editor of *The Forrester Papers*, as secretary of St. Anthony's Board of Directors, as head of tenants of 350 Ellis Street, as co-founder of the Senior Escort Service, and all of her other community activities, focus on the well-being of the neighborhood. She gives the Tenderloin residents hope by being there, by being vocal and visible and accessible. If you love your community you want someone like Thelma to live within its boundaries.

Thelma is quick to anger when it comes to injustice, whether it be against a friend, such as Mark Forrester or against any group of people who are penalized by our society for being old and in the way, poor—worse still, sick and poor, or different in visible ways—color, culture, handicapped. Her love and concern for "different" goes back to her childhood—the Finlanders, the poor farming folk, the hated Germans. At an early age Thelma developed an empathy for those who were on the edge of American society. Being both sensitive and bright, and in her own words, "odd", she too was "different" and could identify with the stranger at the gate. Because she has no fear of the dreaded 'Other', she has been able to cross lines and reach out directly to people who do not live in the mainstream.

As a young woman she was treated by some as a leper due to severe acne. The most touching moment in our conversation came when she talked about her husband's reaction to her despair as she was looking at her scarred face in the mirror. Instinctively, because he knew the beauty of her being, he posed the question to the children, "Do you think your mother is pretty?" As she was telling me this story her eyes filled with tears—in fact there wasn't a dry eye in the house. By having a disfiguring skin condition she lived through such deep anguish, which all of us can recall by conjuring those mostly invisible self-inflicted wounds of our teenage years. Thelma learned to come to terms with those marks. She excelled academically which, as she says, did not endear her to others either. Due, in part, to her physical handicap, she pursued purpose. I would bet she is far happier than any of the 'popular' girls who attended high school with her. She subdued that enemy within, that deep, secret pain which so easily could have defeated her by forcing her to become a permanent recluse. Instead, she walks every day as if through a garden as she travels through the mostly bleak reality of her chosen place—the Tenderloin.

Our elders struggled with issues of class, race, gender, and disability, often fighting lonely battles in the process. It is little wonder that they all ended up living in the San Francisco Bay area whose citizens have a history of tolerating differences and championing causes. Since the Gold Rush days this region has attracted adventurous spirits from around the world.

They dispel the popular myths that the elderly grow more conservative, withdraw from life, and have little to contribute to society. They lead us to question pat notions about our history and give us hope that we can be creative and productive and rebellious toward the status quo—until we bite the dust. In her pioneering research, Dr. Marian Diamond, Professor of Physiology and Anatomy at University of California, San Francisco, contends that the brain continues to develop until the end of life. Our elders' testimony supports her thesis.

Fortunately, they heeded Saroyan's exhortation, "In the time of your life, live . . .". Bill's story reads like an adventure movie script. It would have been surprising if Bill had not gone to Spain to fight—as unlikely as Hemingway staying home. But before he went off to fight the bloody fascists, he took part in the war at home, on the docks and on the ships where men were brutalized trying to make a living in the maritime industry. Working conditions were appalling.

Unfortunately this was true for workers in most other industries in the 1930's. What separated the maritime workers from the coal or steel workers was the opportunity to perceive their lot from a larger perspective, an international viewpoint.[135] Bill, before he left his teens, already had traveled more than most of his contemporaries would do in a lifetime. On his first time out to sea he encountered revolutionary ideas when an IWW organizer gave him a copy of their paper, *The Industrial Worker.* Bill's curiosity propelled him to ask questions and to keep his eyes and ears open wherever he went. When he discovered the Marine Workers Industrial Union, formed by the Communist Party to be the organizational vanguard in the maritime industry, he found a new family and a renewal of purpose. As a union organizer he was subject to jail, beatings, and the continual threat of death.[136] Maritime workers were

---

[135] There are several reasons for "the seaman's long-standing reputation for openness to revolutionary ideas" according to Bruce Nelson. In his fine work, *Workers on the Waterfront: Seamen, Longshoremen, and Unionism in the 1930's,* he states that seamen "were among the most exploited and oppressed groups of workers in the United States. They knew well the meaning of deprivation and were keenly aware of the enormous distance between the lives of the rich and poor. Secondly, and of even greater importance, they lived on the fringes of society and had little or no recourse to family, church, ethnic, and other institutions that served the purpose of reconciling working people to the hegemony of the employing class or of creating a stable subculture that reinforced an alternative value system."p.25

[136] For those of us who were born after The Great Depression it is hard to fully understand how vicious life was for a large number of Americans who were struggling to survive. It was a time of massive and bloody strikes and a time of quiet desperation for many too proud to beg for food to feed their families. Studs Terkel presents a personal, close-up view of the Depression by talking with those who experienced it in *Hard Times.* I consider it the best quick course on the Depression for those too young to remember.

outside the mainstream as much as artists or cowboys, and like them, were both admired and scorned by 'polite society'. Like Bill, many of them were young and strong and unincumbered with on-shore responsibilities. They were not afraid of German officers on board the *S.S. Bremen* or the waterfront cops and thugs in Baltimore. These were brave men who welcomed the struggle.

Bill, I believe, went a step further, by dedicating his life to the cause of working people receiving their just share of the bounty created, in part, by their labor. Those early days in the MWIU and the Communist Party built his confidence as an organizer when he began to realize that his fellow workers trusted him, listened to him. His family of origin, fragmented and troubled by poverty and alcohol, could not fulfill his need to belong to an exemplary family, one which was seeking to be of service to the entire human community. Bill was home in the MWIU and in the CP of the 1930's.

The fellowship of adversity is a galvanizing agent, a powerful force which allows a small group of dedicated people to accomplish gargantuan tasks.[137] The successful 'Baltimore Soviet' was a beacon light reaching way beyond the port of Baltimore. It was shut down precisely because of its success; the shipowners understood that if this kind of energy was left unchecked, i.e., if Bill and his cohorts spread their good works to other ports, then the shipowners iron rule would be broken on the waterfront and on board ship. The great maritime strikes of

---

[137]   My experience with this phenomenon came as a result of volunteering as a field worker with the Congress of Racial Equality (CORE) in the mid 1960's in the South. We were a small band of people dedicated to social change, and due to our age, impervious to the threat of death. When Bill and I spoke of his early organizing years I could identify with that almost religious feeling of belonging to a "family" whose purpose was embedded in the democratic dream of a square deal for all because this feeling was reborn thirty years later during the Civil Rights era.

'34, '36, and '37 could not have taken place without rank and
file leaders such as Bill. Bill and his "comrades" were part of an
army of workers who fought "a fierce and protracted struggle
for control of the work-place"[138], during the Depression.

You have to be tough to be a professional athlete. You must
conquer the twin fears of pain and defeat every day. Fans called
Joe, "Mule", back in St. Louis, because he was rock-steady. He
knew how to keep on keepin' on. If your father shoveled coal at
the brewery then you could either follow him, developing the
same calloused hands and pain-wrenched back, or, if "God gave
you ability", then you play ball—always to the best of that ability.

Joe played hardball. As he tells us, he was not adverse to
calling for the spitter or defending himself and his turf—
homeplate, in a most vigorous fashion. He was "no butter guy"
with management either. He spoke his mind when he felt it was
necessary, like the time in Arkansas City when rumor had it that
the players were not going to be paid. Although he didn't agitate
for the integration of baseball—few, if any, white players did—
when the San Francisco Seals hired their first black player, Bob
Thurman, in the 1940's, Joe watched him carefully and when he
saw that Thurman played full-throttle and minded his own
business, he went to visit him in the hospital and told him, "We're
for you, Bob." Joe was a respected, seasoned player with a lot of
experience behind what he said and did. His acceptance and
respect for Thurman was an influence which I'm sure made
Thurman's progress to the Majors easier. The integration of
baseball served as a signal, a signpost for what was yet to come
during the great civil rights struggle which surfaced in the 1950's.
Baseball, being such a visible and vital part of American life,
gave integration a dramatic and irrevocable start—before Little
Rock, before Atlanta, before Montgomery, before Birmingham.
Bob Thurman played in the Majors, for the Cincinnati Reds,
from 1955 to 1960. Making a name for yourself coming up
through the minors was no easy job. The "Gas House Gang"

---

[138] Bruce Nelson, *Workers on the Waterfront*, p. 7.

image prevailed. The catcher traditionally has functioned as the brains of the team, but also like the goalie in ice hockey, he is the last defendant of homeplate. It takes a special person to crouch behind home-plate—savvy, tough and intuitive.[140] Joe learned early from his mistakes. He realized he had to either "smarten up or learn how to fight". Actually he did both.

Baseball makes visual what is so compelling in the American experiment. Baseball, alone of all American sports, has a rich history and mythology. Some of the past greats, who are now part of American folklore—the 'Babe', Lou Gehrig, Dizzy Dean, Rogers Hornsby, touched Joe Sprinz' life directly. Baseball represents teamwork, as well as individual displays of talent, and most critical in counter to our slash-and-burn mentality, continuity from one generation to the next. Baseball is about playing hard but fair. It is about endless summer and green fields. Unfortunately now it is also about super-stars and mega-deals, but somehow the crystal essence of this nineteenth century game survives. Baseball is our unique contribution to sport and those who play it will continue to be our heroes for it is an heroic game. There is no hiding place on the playing field. Joe, being a work horse minor league catcher during most of his career, gave the Pacific Coast League fans a chance to observe a professional athlete in motion, "playing for his life", year after year. Seals fans remember Joe fondly because he was always in the game. As Thomas Boswell so aptly states, "[T]he guiding principle that most often keeps people oriented through all their passages and changes is a governing passion

---

[140] Asinof comments: "There is something unique about the position of a catcher that intensifies the emotion of a ballgame. He, alone, sees the entire action in front of him, feels the presence of the umpire behind him, urges his will on every pitch, on every ball-strike decision. He squats behind the hitter, hollering through an iron-leather mask, working a pitcher, harassing the batters, getting meaning out of every pitch." Eliot Asinof, *Eight Men Out; The Black Sox and the 1919 World Series* (New York: Holt, Rinehart and Winston, 1963) p. 69.

for excellence. In baseball that's what you discover at the heart of the order."[141] If the San Francisco Bay region possessed arms, Joe would portray the throwing one—over the Golden Gate and out to the Farallones in the West country of baseball. A Man for All Seasons.

Courage takes many forms. Bill faced the goons on the waterfront, the fascists in Spain, and the HUAC interrogators. Joe stood his ground behind home plate and came back to the game after the near fatal attempted stunt catch at the World's Fair. Dorsey confronted the San Francisco Police Department. Ida and her little band of dedicated teachers braved the potential violence of racist rural Mississippi. Sally attacked the sexist academia establishment and the CIA. Thelma fought City Hall while living in one of the most dangerous neighborhoods in San Francisco.

In the telling of their stories our elders swipe the dust off the history books. Discovering how Ida, Dorsey, Thelma and Sally confronted the given gender limitations of earlier eras gives us real knowledge about the nature of sexism and its historical evolution. Ida, who was forced to fight on two fronts simultaneously, tells us how sexism and racism traditionally intertwine, making it even more difficult for black and other women of color to succeed. All of the participants give us a sense that history is a live, palpable drama, capable of influencing the future provided we become aware of its processes and continuities. Ida's struggle to bring health care and education to blacks living in rural poverty was part of a practice begun by black clubwomen at the beginning of the twentieth century.[142]

---

[141]   Thomas Boswell, *The Heart of the Order* (New York:Viking Penguin, 1989), p xix

[142]   See Paula Giddings' *When and Where I Enter: The Impact of Black Women on Race and Sex in America* (New York:William Morrow and Company, Inc., 1984) for a detailed account of the critical social work undertaken by black club women, beginning in the early 1900's, around the issue of lynching.

Sally's challenge to the academic sexist status quo, Bill's fight against home-grown fascism when he confronted HUAC, Thelma's participation in the civil rights movement of the 1960's, are all important acts. Significant events such as these had particular outcomes precisely because committed people were involved.

It is an American tradition to love and admire the lone warrior doing battle against impossible odds, although many times the applause may be delayed a decade or two, often after the 'hero' is dead. Bill's stance against American fascism is a good example. During McCarthy's reign of power all left of center artists, writers and labor union folks were suspect. Innocent until proven guilty was suspended during the McCarthy period. One of the few public critics, the journalist, I.F. Stone, attacked McCarthy where he was most vulnerable, i.e., in his zeal for security he imitated the tactics of Stalin, violating a number of our Constitutionally guaranteed rights, including the right to a fair trial.[143] Bill was one of hundreds of people who were summoned before HUAC, publicly humiliated, accused of being a Red, and then hounded out of their jobs. At last the shipowners and others who benefited from controlling the maritime

---

[143] I.F. Stone wrote the following at a time, 1955, when folks were nearly lynched for far less. "Few will dare to say it now, but the time is coming when the truth will be recognized, a truth which the Framers of our Constitution wove into the fabric of American government. They saw that there could not be freedom without risk, that no stable society could be built except on a foundation of trust, and that when trust was violated—and only then—a man could be punished. They did not think it was the province of government to police men's minds, or that it had a right to punish them unless they committed some wrongful act. They would have been horrified at our growing system of thought police, of guessing-game "law" about prospective crime, and indeed most of all by our obsession with 'security'." I.F. Stone, *The Haunted Fifties* (New York: Vintage Books, 1963), p. 75-6.

industry, with the aid of the FBI, and in the name of patriotism, were able to bring these upstart unions to heel. McCarthy harangued about the dangers of destruction by implosion, i.e., the infiltrating of American institutions by the 'reds'. Now it is so obvious who was practicing this shameful game. Bill is a survivor, not only of the streets of Hell's Kitchen, the Spanish Civil War, the waterfront, WWII, but of the most dread attack of them all: McCarthy's witch-hunt. He tells us that it can happen here given the right conditions if we are not mindful. After listening to his story one knows something about, not only the events of his life, but of his character. By telling his story, he adds another piece to the historical puzzle, helping us, in the process, to face the truth about our collective past.

"To finish the moment, to find the journey's end in every step of the road, to live the greatest number of good hours, is wisdom." Ralph Waldo Emerson.

In the process of putting this book together Ruth and I became involved in the lives of our subjects. Like with old friends, we learned something about both their triumphs and their follies. We realized that our attraction to them was not merely due to their past deeds, but rather to the steadfast and resolute nature of their characters as revealed both in their life stories and their interactions with us. While working on the photographs Ruth observed, "It takes a genius to be happy. Inner peace is not easy to find. These people have achieved that. It's more than what they have accomplished. They possess an inner resolution which enabled them to push themselves beyond their own limitations." We believe something of the interior being of each of our subjects is revealed in the telling of her/his story. We learn about the essentials—about truth, beauty, courage, honor and love from those who precede us.

For those of us who are in the Middle Ages, we need to face what is inevitable about the aging process and how others have dealt with it. For the young, many of whom no longer have access to elders in their everyday life, just to become sensitized to the problems and concerns of their elders is a start.

If one is reaching the high end of life—late 80's and up, often most of one's friends, associates and family are dead. It is difficult, if not impossible to find good caretakers, even with money. Physical disabilities, susceptibility to life-threatening illnesses, such as influenza, loom larger. One's world begins to shrink. An elder is less mobile while the outside world becomes more hostile and less familiar. One becomes a stranger in a strange land as the reference points disappear.

I am convinced that the positive side of growing older holds little comfort for those who have lived lives of "quiet desperation", for life's two-edged prize remains knowledge and wisdom as the result of experience and a lifetime of 'study'. Two-edged because enlightenment in old age also can lead to, "If I only knew then what I know now" which can spark a new round of regret and sorrow.

For those who have lived fully and creatively, there seems to be a need to leave a defined trail, to somehow present one's life as a complete and bound work. Although all of us exercise editorial rights over our own past, selective memory does not preclude us from understanding an individual life and how that life is part of the larger historical experience framed within a particular time and place. History lives when we listen to a respected elder tell us about what life was like in the 'olden days'. The whole truth of any era or person or people or place will never be known, but if we carefully listen to the stories of our elders we may develop a sense of the ambience of a lost time. As Emerson expressed it, "Civil history, natural history, the history of art and the history of literature,—all must be explained from individual history, or must remain words.[144]

---

[144] Ralph Waldo Emerson, *Emerson's Essays* (New York: Thomas Y. Crowell Company, 1926), p. 12. I have used the words of Emerson throughout this work to highlight the stories of the elders as I believe Emerson, and his friend, Thoreau, served as the conscience of their own difficult time.

Our elders, whose stories you have read here, are six very different, very complex beings who have all lived through difficult times and circumstances. Reaching out to them, crossing that deep generational gap, helps connect us to our collective past.

In the end what really matters is character. Do people live up to their own ideals? Can they transcend their own limitations and prejudices to rise to the occasion? Do they contribute to the well-being of the community in which they reside? Do they seek out meaningful life work which allows them to give their very best? As one of Studs Terkel's subjects in *Working* so astutely stated it, "I think most of us are looking for a calling, not a job. Most of us, like the assembly line worker, have jobs that are too small for our spirit."[145] Ruth and I are lucky to have made new friends over the course of this project. Sometimes when I am listening to one of them talking about a moment long past, I can see her or his face as it once was—full of hope and promise, with new worlds to explore.[146] It is hard to leave that time when it was all before one like some golden city ready for the conquest, but I believe these elders would all agree with Casey Stengel's old chestnut, "It ain't over till it's over". The struggle for wisdom and autonomy goes on.

It takes courage to not despair. We can take heart from their on-going struggle. Let us hear the stories of our elders and help them through the inevitable exigencies of old age whenever possible. In turn they can help us out of the maze if we take time to listen. If they have not lost heart, how can we?

---

[145] Studs Terkel, *Working: People Talk About What They Do All Day and How They Feel About What They Do* (New York: Ballantine Books, 1972), p. xxix.

[146] I am sure that every person, as they grow older, has experienced the opposite, expressed so succinctly by a Japanese poet, Kakinomoto No Hitomaro, living in the eighth century A.D. "A strange old man Stops me, Looking out of my deep mirror" Kenneth Rexroth, *One Hundred Poems from the Japanese* (New York: New Directions Books, 1964), p. 24. When she was quite elderly, my mother said that she was shocked when she looked in the mirror because in her mind's eye she still saw herself as she looked when she was sixteen.

UPDATE

Ida kept her sense of humor honed to combat the inevitable limitations of old age. She was quite proud that the University of California at Berkeley published her life story as part of a series on the first black graduates. She remained active by visiting friends, attending sorority conventions and working on projects such as establishing a memorial library in rural Mississippi in honor of Dr. Arenia Malory, the founder of the school where Ida launched her education and health projects in the 1930's. Ida died in 2000.

Dorsey fought to make a comeback from a very serious accident. In October of 1989 she was hit by a car, resulting in multiple fractures and head injuries. She spent eight months in a wheelchair, battling the entire time to recover. She devised a rigorous therapy program which eventually included swimming. Even while still confined to the wheelchair, she continued to practice law. She died in 2000. She and Joe were two of the toughest critters I ever met. They didn't know how to quit.

Although Bill was forced to move out of his 1906 earthquake "shack" and suffered from asthma, especially during the winter months, he flourished in his new digs in a comfortable senior housing complex near his beloved waterfront. Bill can be proud that Proposition H, which would have allowed the developers to ran wild up and down the waterfront constructing condos and hotels, was defeated in the 1990 fall election, thanks in part to his efforts. He lobbied, spoke, petitioned, appeared on local television, and would have laid down in front of the bulldozers if necessary. He was part of a pilot film project to raise money to finance a movie about the merchant seamen during World War II and the BBC interviewed him for a documentary film on the McCarthy era. He was able to finish his autobiography, *The Kid from Hoboken,* before his death in 1995. He needed another eighty years to finish all of his projects.

Sally loved her rich North Beach terrain where a Bohemian coffeehouse, a Chinese laundry and an Italian restaurant can co-exist on the same block. She continued to donate her time to the Grey Panthers and the San Francisco Sex Information Switchboard. Sally died in 1994.

Joe, who suffered a stroke in the fall of 1989, which left his throwing arm and one leg paralyzed, fought to make a comeback. He pushed himself in his regular physical therapy sessions just as he did on the playing field. For his 88th birthday, Ruth and I took Joe to see the Giants play. I called their public relations office to see if we could get good seats with wheelchair access and also if they could flash his name and a happy birthday on the scoreboard. When Al Rosen, the General Manager of the Giants,[147] found out I was calling about Joe Sprinz, he sent me a dozen tickets for one of the luxury 'sky boxes' so Joe could watch the game in style and comfort with his old buddies. Joe died in 1994.

Thelma fought on in the beleaguered Tenderloin. She stopped going out at night as the streets became a war zone. She edited the explosive *Forrester Papers* which continued to take direct shots at the local powerbrokers and sacred cows. She was an active member of the Senior Action Network, formed to improve security in all of the senior housing units. She fought for the survival of those at the bottom—the elderly poor, the street folks, and all of the many displaced people who end up in the Tenderloin. She refused to play it safe. Thelma died in 2002.

---

[147] Al Rosen played third base for the Cleveland Indians from 1947 to 1956.

Bill Bailey was reinstated in the Marine Fireman's Union and his seaman's papers returned at Longshoremen's Hall, San Francisco on July 5th, 1989, the 55th anniversary of 'Bloody Thursday' during the 1934 strike on the Waterfront.

(Dorsey Redland, the author and Bill Bailey, from left to right)

layout and design by Claudia Müller printed at the CCSF
Graphic Communications Mission Campus by Smiley Curtis
and Johanna Rudolph

Printed in the United States
60091LVS00002B/271

9 781413 481532